GREAT, GRAND & FAMOUS
CHEFS
AND THEIR SIGNATURE DISHES

TEXT BY DAVID GLYNN

Presented by Fritz Gubler

2009 Great, Grand & Famous Pty Ltd
© Great, Grand & Famous Pty Ltd

Great, Grand & Famous Pty Ltd
45 Hume St, Crows Nest NSW 2065, Australia
Telephone: +61 2 9437 0438
Facsimile: +61 2 9437 0288
Email: admin@greatgrandfamous.com

Managing Director: Fritz Gubler
Publisher: Carolen Barripp
Managing Editor: Raewyn Glynn
Communications Manager: Helen Cameron
Sales & Marketing Manager: Leonie Hale

Book Design: Louise McGeachie and Raewyn Glynn
Photo Research: Tracey Gibson

Text by David Glynn
Author's dedication: For Louise

Picture credits
Michael Small: p. 6; Fritz Gubler: pp. 7, 151,185; Joaquín Aldeguer: p. 15;
La Pyramide / Thierry Vallier: pp. 14, 16; The Art Archive / Château de
Thoiry / Gianni Dagli Orti: p. 24; The Art Archive: p. 202; LeGavroche:
pp. 67, 68, 166; Mosimann's: pp. 98, 99, 103, 104; Michel Guerard/Tim
Clinch: pp. 40, 43, 44; Le Manoir aux Quat'Saisons: pp. 112, 115 (below);
Pierre Gagnaire/Jacques Gavard : pp. 121, 122; Pierre Gagnaire/Peter
Lipmann p. 125; Joël Robuchon: pp. 1, 132–134, 137, 138, cover image; The
French Laundry/Deborah Jones: pp. 156, 157, 161, 162; Daniel Boulud/ T.
Schauer: pp. 173 (above right, below), 174; Newspix / Jason Busch: p. 180;
Tetsuya's/Seung Rok Baek: p. 181; Tetsuya's: pp. 182, 185 (above right and
below), 186; Rex Features: pp. 228, 233 (above right, below), 234; Arzak:
pp. 240–245, 246; Corbis: pp. 4, 8, 19, 20, 22, 28, 31 (above left and below),
32 (above), 36, 38, 39, 46, 52, 55 (above right, below), 56, 57, 74, 79 (above
left), 80, 85, 86–93, 95, 97, 110, 117, 120, 128, 131, 140, 145, 146, 149, 154/5,
158, 161 (above left and below), 163, 164, 168, 170, 173 (above left),177,
187, 188, 200, 211, 214, 220 (above right), 222 (below), 227, 229, 235, 236,
238/239, 246; Getty Images: pp. 13, 27, 33, 34, 36, 37, 49, 58, 63, 69–72, 79
(above right), 81, 82, 94, 105, 111, 118, 139, 142, 143, 152, 161 (above right),
169, 170, 175, 179, 191–193, 197 (above right), 205, 206, 210, 212, 216–218,
222, 224, 238–9 (below), 221 (above left and below), 247, 254; Photolibrary:
pp. 11, 23, 26, 31 (above right), 32 (below), 43 (above right), 45, 50, 51, 55
(above left), 60–62, 100, 106–108, 127, 176, 197 (above left and below), 198,
204, 209, 215, 223, 230, 248, 251–253.

National Library of Australia Cataloguing-in-Publication Data

ISBN 978-0-9804667-2-0
Gubler, Fritz
Great, Grand & Famous Chefs
Printed in China by Guangdong Xinyuan Color Printing Co. Ltd
through YES Printing (Xinyuan) Australia

GREAT, GRAND & FAMOUS
CHEFS
AND THEIR SIGNATURE DISHES

With many thanks
and best wishes

Peter.

*Every morning one must start from scratch,
with nothing on the stoves. That is cuisine.*

FERNAND POINT

L'entrée

BY FRITZ GUBLER

hen I published *Great, Grand & Famous Hotels*, it was to share my enthusiasm for the world's great hotels. Now, with *Great, Grand & Famous Chefs and Their Signature Dishes*, I am returning to my first love, the subject of my earliest training – the world of the chef.

While the first book was four years in the making, this book could be said to have taken 40 years, for that's how long it's been since I did my chef's apprenticeship. Since that time, food has been my passion, my religion.

Throughout my years in the hospitality industry, travelling the globe professionally, I have had the opportunity to eat the food of many different countries, both local and *haute cuisine*, which fed my passion, so to speak. As my career advanced, I was able to widen my culinary horizons even further, making pilgrimages to the more famous restaurants, following the chefs of the moment.

I have been fortunate to enjoy the food of several of the chefs in this book, and I still have a long wish list of restaurants not yet visited, signature dishes not yet tasted. Some of the featured chefs have provided meals that have been highlights to me in the past. I will forever remember Anton Mosimann's mushroom risotto, and the foie gras terrine at Gordon Ramsay's restaurant at Claridge's. The famous *soufflé Suissesse* at Le Gavroche had a texture that is a testimony to an absolute master. At Maison Boulud in Beijing, the chilled salad of Alaskan king crab paired with grapefruit gelée created a perfect balance of flavours. Special mention goes to this book's one Australian chef, Tetsuya Wakuda, whose newest creation–scallops with foie gras–is a very happy marriage of aromas and textures. Eating *baba au rhum* at Ducasse's Jules Verne in the Eiffel Tower, with its panoramic view of Paris, is probably the closest one can get to heaven without dying first. Meeting Heston Blumenthal at the Melbourne Food and Wine Festival makes me determined to visit the Fat Duck in Bray, continuing my pilgrimage to the world's great temples of food, and I hope that through this book I can encourage many readers to follow me.

A WORD ON OUR CHOICES

There are bookshops full of cookbooks featuring the recipes of great chefs, and these books are bought by hobby chefs and chefs who try to replicate the food by following their recipes. However, it is my belief that in order to cook their food we must know where the great chefs came from and we must gain insight into their passion, their belief in the food.

With so many fantastic chefs around the world, the selection of the chefs portrayed in the book was difficult. We decided to focus on the 'iconic' chefs—chefs who have developed their own trends, created remarkable signature dishes and through their experience, their talent and creativity inspired generations of young chefs to follow them.

The restaurants I have visited not only deserve their stars and hats, but their chefs deserve their fame. They are obsessed with perfection and they expect that all around them share their care for the smallest detail. They seek perfection, not just once but for every dish on every day, they are true masters of their craft; they are regarded as legends by their customers, their critics and even by their peers. Some have attained 'superstar' status which has made the professional career as a cook much more popular among young people. I was privileged to meet some of these iconic chefs while preparing this book and I was impressed with the passion and dedication they devote to their profession. They are indeed extraordinary people with the stamina of oxen, the tenacity of Olympic champions and the souls of artists.

A WORD ON FOOD FASHIONS

Food innovation has become very fashionable and an interest in food trends is now part of the modern lifestyle. Today's cuisine has gone through an exciting evolution over the past 100 years. At the beginning of last century there was only one cuisine, defined by one chef, Escoffier,

and later perfected by Monsieur Point. But then the pupils of Point used their experience, talent and passion to create their own trends, developing new cuisines—*naturelle*, *minceur*, *nouvelle*, *actuelle* and, most recently, molecular cuisine. Some have indeed revolutionised cooking with their innovative approach and in turn contributed to the evolution of cuisine. Their restaurants are often booked for months in advance – some even for a whole year.

Today, exciting new trends are developed and enthusiastically accepted by customers. For example, in a trend I return to in my comments at the end of the book, exotic salts are being used by many chefs to give food a fresh finishing touch and enhance the original flavor of the ingredients.

Great, Grand & Famous Chefs and Their Signature Dishes is a celebration of the iconic chefs who have given food lovers like myself so much pleasure. It is a recognition of their absolute talent and an appreciation of what they have contributed to their profession. Their hard work over many years has provided us with many hours in food heaven and for that we will love them forever. Unfortunately, many people have not had the opportunity to be introduced to these chefs that I admire so much. With this book, I give you, the reader, that opportunity.

Previous spread: French chef Joël Robuchon stands in the empty kitchen of his Avenue Poincaré restaurant, Paris 1994.

Above: The *baba au rhum*, an Alain Ducasse signature dish, as served at Restaurant Jules Verne, Eiffel Tower, Paris.

Contents

Opposite: Langoustines and rice vermicelli, a dish from Restaurant Arzak, the 3-Michelin-star restaurant in San Sebastian, Spain, that features the food of father-and-daughter team Juan Mari and Elena Arzak.

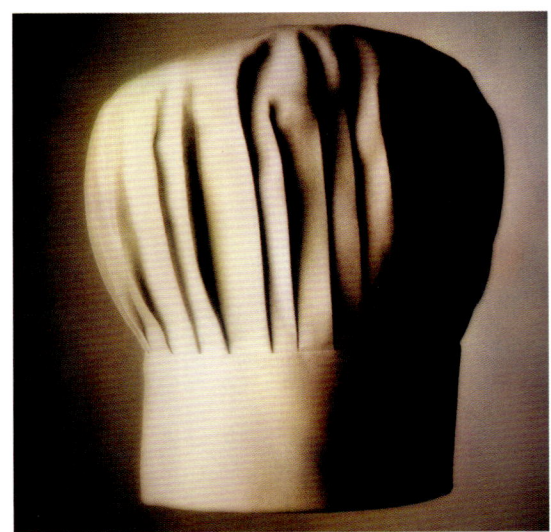

Escoffier's children

THOSE WHO WEAR THE HAT

"You must shake the saucepan lightly—see, like this …" And with those words the great Carême fell to the floor. He never regained consciousness, and died the next day. He was the greatest chef of his age, as famous as the kings and emperors for whom he cooked. He was the first to wear the hat.

But Marie-Antoine Carême did not, as is often claimed, invent the toque, the white, pleated hat which has come to symbolise his profession. He simply made it taller, adding a circle of stiffening cardboard to the flattened, starched white hat which in the early 19th century had replaced the *casque a meche*, the stocking cap whose various colours denoted a chef's ranking in the kitchen.

It was but one of Carême's innovations; it would be no exaggeration to say that Carême invented the very concept of the modern chef, along with the style of cooking we know as *haute cuisine*. Without him, things would indeed be different, and it is supremely fitting that his

last words should have been to his favourite pupil, for in a way it was he who taught the world to cook.

THE GREAT ESCOFFIER

Yet it is probably not Carême we picture when we think of the archetypal chef. He lived too long ago, and remains for us an historical figure. It is more likely that we see the great Escoffier, a small, dapper man in a tall, stiffly starched and neatly pleated white hat—the *toque blanche*—commanding his kitchen with dignity and decorum, and producing the kind of food we may still eat today. His signature dishes—peach Melba, tournedos Rossini—can be found still on menus all over the world, just as his influence is still felt in every restaurant kitchen.

In a way, each of the chefs in this book is one of Escoffier's children. Each, like Escoffier before them, is an artist working within the traditions of European culinary history, and each has contributed to it in some profound way. Each has developed a signature style that reflects both their personality and their place in that history. Each of them wears the hat.

But what, if anything, does the chef's hat signify?

It is is commonly held that the 100 pleats of the *toque blanche* represent the notion that the master chef could cook an egg at least one hundred ways. That may be so, though it is unlikely that any chef would now be called upon to prove this statement.

Carême had to. His great patron, the French diplomat and gourmand Charles Maurice de Talleyrand-Périgord, once set him a task: to create a whole year's worth of menus, without repetition, and using only seasonal produce. Carême of course succeeded, and it was perhaps this experience more than any other that set him on the path to greatness. Escoffier compiled a list of more than 7,000 recipes over the course of his lifetime, and in doing so set the path for cooking even into the twenty-first century.

A CHEF'S SIGNATURE

Each of the chefs in this book has chosen that same path. Yet each has arrived at a slightly different place; though all wear the same hat their signatures are all distinct, unique.

Gordon Ramsay's signature, for example, now lies more in his fame and his empire building than in his cooking. So if you should dine at his flagship restaurant on Royal Hospital Road, currently the only three-star establishment in London, you can order his signature dish, the cappuccino of white beans, knowing that the man himself has played no physical part in its creation.

Pierre Gagnaire, when asked what his signature dish is, replies, "My signature lies in the attention to details."

Ferran Adrià on the other hand changes his menu so regularly that it makes defining a signature dish all but impossible. "One of elBulli's rules is not to know what you are going to dine on," he says, virtually making change itself his signature.

And in Sydney, Tetsuya's restaurant goes through an average of almost a hundred Tasmanian ocean trout every week in order to satisfy the demands of the customers who would no doubt be sorely disappointed if they found that his signature dish was not on the menu that night.

THE PATH TO THE PLATE

"If the divine creator has taken pains to give us delicious and exquisite things, to eat," wrote Fernand Point, the first and arguably the greatest of Escoffier's children, "the least we can do is prepare them well and serve them with ceremony."

In essence, this is what great chefs do. The hat they wear represents many things: passion, excellence, commitment, care. In fact Escoffier himself wrote that "In cooking, care is half the battle."

Yet it is passion that above all else separates the great from the good. Talent helps. Willpower is essential, for the path to greatness is long and hard. And the value of a great teacher cannot be underestimated. But it is passion that we see on the plate, and passion that we celebrate here in this book.

Above: Auguste Escoffier (1846–1935). A restaurateur and culinary writer as well as a chef, he popularised and updated traditional French cooking methods.

THE RECIPES

Fernand Point called the recipes in his famous cream notebook, published as *Ma Gastronomie*, "abbreviations for the working cuisinier." Written in a concise, narrative shorthand, they presume a familiarity with the kitchen and an understanding of the basic cooking processes. Exact cooking times and quantities are often not mentioned. Here, for example, is his recipe for a 'simple omelette.'

Whip the yolks and white of the eggs separately. Add the beaten egg yolks, salt and pepper to sizzling butter in a skillet. When the eggs begin to set, add a good spoonful of crème fraîche and the beaten egg whites. Keep the pan moving over a high heat to avoid having the omelette stick to the pan.

Which tells you all you need to know, and nothing you do not. And it is this approach we too have taken. Cooking is an interpretive art, and no recipe is ever written to be followed to the letter: there are too many variables in the kitchen. So we have presented the recipes as Monsieur Point would have, as a guide, and a guide only, to the creation of the dish.

After all, no one would expect to recreate a dish such as Thomas Keller's 'Oysters and Pearls' exactly as he presents it. But that does not mean we may not experience something similar.

Not all of us may be able to dine at the French Laundry or The Fat Duck, but by using these recipes as a guide, the food of the gods may still be within our reach.

Opposite: When it comes to reproducing the dishes of great chefs, restaurants have the advantage of well-drilled brigades. Here we see the brigade in the kitchen of La Pyramide, the restaurant established by Fernand Point in Lyon, France.

Left: Chefs are often evangelical about the use of local, seasonal, sustainable produce. The food of Alice Waters of Chez Panisse exemplifies this philosophy.

Fernand Point

THE COLOSSUS

"His passion, above all else, was for the produce he was about to cook. He felt that if the Creator took the trouble to give us these exquisite things, we should prepare them with care and present them with ceremony."

Point

In the town of Vienne, 40 miles (64 km) south of Lyon, two pyramids stand in close proximity. The first, a Roman monument dating back to before the Caesars, marks the centre of an arena where chariot races once were held. The second, La Pyramide, is the place in which modern cuisine was born. Its father was Fernand Point.

He was born three years shy of the twentieth century. His father, Auguste, was the tenant of a railway station hotel-buffet where his mother and grandmother cooked *cordon bleu* food. By the time he was eighteen Fernand's calling was clear.

After his training—first as a *saucier* and then a *poissonnier*—it was apparent that his talents were too great for a modest station-buffet. With his father he decamped to Lyon, but there was no restaurant for them. Instead they found themselves in Vienne, where a small provincial house was for sale. There La Pyramide was born.

In the beginning there were not even inside lavatories. But when Auguste died in 1925 they had already built a fine new kitchen, and over the next five years Fernand's reputation throughout the region was assured. Still it was hardly a glamorous house, and when in 1930 he married, the young Madame Point refused to even enter the establishment while it was in such a state. They shut the restaurant, employed an architect to redecorate, and on the new land which Point had bought beside the house built a new terrace and garden.

With this Point's singular originality was liberated. Until then he had produced traditional, albeit superb, Lyonnais food. But there was no room for individuality, and Point was bored.

BEHIND EVERY GREAT MAN

It is a cliché, of course. It is also true. Before her marriage Madame Point had been a *coiffeuse*: she was used to dealing with clients. She had drive. And she understood how to run a business. Not only that, but both luck and the times were in their favour. The motor car was just beginning to become commonplace. The wealthy had taken to driving down to the South of France and Vienne, still a pretty Roman town, made for a delightful stop.

More importantly, people wanted something different. The heavy meals, the grand restaurants, the formality; all of these things belonged to a tradition that was stagnant, one that Point would forever change.

He was perfectly capable of creating showpieces, like the *filets de sole Brillat-Savarin*, a creamy lobster mousse jacketed in sliced truffles, surrounded by poached filets of sole on puff-pastry croustades, each filet topped with a lobster tail scallop and another, ruinously thick, slice of truffle. But his innovation, his genius, was to strip away the superfluous, the dogmatic, and to replace them with common sense. "Success," he said, "is a lot of small things correctly done."

By 1933, three years after his marriage, Point had three Michelin stars, and his restaurant was known around the world. Two years later the great Escoffier was dead and La Pyramide was, as Prince Curnonsky pronounced it, "the summit of culinary art."

LA CUISINE DU MOMENT

The dishes that today are identified with Point's heritage are the simple regional specialties that he brought to their apotheosis: gratin of crayfish tails, roast truffled chicken, foie gras encased in brioche. Nor did he fear to go simpler still, happily serving various omelettes, *truite au bleu,* or just a hot Lyonnais sausage accompanied by cubed potatoes. His passion, above all else, was for the produce he was about to cook. He felt that if the Creator took the trouble to give us these exquisite things, we should prepare them with care and present them with ceremony.

Paul Bocuse, Point's favorite apprentice and heir apparent, called it "la cuisine du moment." The market was everything. Cooking, for Point, was to simply capture the taste of the food, then to enhance it. The chicken on the customer's plate should taste of chicken—the very best,

most perfect chicken, prepared with meticulous care and cooked in such a manner that none of its essence be lost. Each ingredient was treated thus, so that no vegetable should lose its juice, no fish its firmness. Nothing would be done one moment before it *had* to be done.

"Every morning one must start from scratch, with nothing on the stoves. That is cuisine."

But Point's cuisine was in no way rushed. He experimented with his *gratin de queues d'ecrevisses* for years before he and his wife agreed that it was ready to appear on the menu. Mado, as he called her, was the only person he deferred to: she would test all of his creations, just as every day she would write out the new menu in her large, fine script. Neither was elaboration the mark of Point's cooking. Art, in the words of Saint-Exupéry, is not when there is nothing more that you can add, it is when there is nothing more you can take away.

THE ESSENTIAL

"Butter," Point insisted. "Give me butter and then more butter."

He was merely emphasising a fundamental truth. Much fine cooking can be done without butter, but French cuisine lives and breathes it. It is essential to what gave Point's food its luxurious and polished simplicity—the sauce. Never something used to conceal or mask a deficiency, but rather a complement to the perfection of his materials. "It is the sauce that distinguishes a good chef. The *saucier* is a soloist in the orchestra of a great kitchen."

The greatness of his kitchen was denied by no-one.

In the years before the war, (and before the questionable benefits of television, or advertising) Point and his team were famous around the world. He enchanted everybody with the immense warmth of his personality, refusing to make any distinction between the famous and the unknown. He also had that love of practical jokes which seems to characterise great chefs: he was forever putting the lights out in the cellar when people were down there, and

Previous spread:
A portrait of Fernand Point (1897 – 1955) hangs in La Pyramide Fernand Point, the restaurant he founded. La Pyramide, which has 2 Michelin stars, is now owned and run by chef Patrick Henriroux.

Opposite: Point and his brigade at La Pyramide. Point's reputation as the 'father' of modern French cuisine was based in part on the numerous great chefs that he influenced and trained.

one April 1 when he telephoned the fire brigade to insist that this time there really *was* a fire in his staff cloakroom, they simply laughed.

His genius with food, then, was maybe just a reflection of his belief in living well. His greatest pleasure of all was champagne, which was always left open on ice for at least a minute before being poured, and it is said that in the company of his friend and cellarman, Pierre Chauvon, they could get through seven or eight bottles in a day.

But the war troubled him. He was essentially a man of peace and kindness, and war revolted him possibly more than it did other people. Still, he was willing to defy the occupiers if that was what it took to get black market butter. He worked with the Resistance, often hiding escaped Allied soldiers and airmen in the attics while Germans dined downstairs. Those five years were an intolerable misery which undoubtedly contributed to his early death.

After the war he and his wife were decorated by the British. But for Point, things could never be the same. The grand style which he enjoyed and at which he excelled, was finished.

THE DUTY OF CHEFS

It was perhaps in the last ten years of his life that Point contributed most to cuisine. He always said that it was the duty of chefs to teach and to train the young, and it was in Vienne under Point that Paul Bocuse and a band of brothers learned the sophisticated simplicity that was to become the guiding principle of modern cooking. He was a superb teacher, knowing exactly how to encourage enthusiasm whilst instilling the benefits of experience.

He loved maxims and aphorisms, and never tired of telling his pupils that it is the simplest dishes that are the hardest to master. "Take a *béarnaise* … what is it? A yolk of egg, a shallot, some tarragon. But, believe me, it takes years of practice before the result is perfect. Let your eyes wander for a moment and the sauce is unusable."

To this end, he devised an infallible test for any who entertained the idea of perhaps coming to work for him: he asked them to fry an egg.

Faced with the invariable failure, Point would cry "Stop, unhappy man—you are making a dog's breakfast of it!" And then he would proceed to demonstrate the only right way to treat an egg:

Place a lump of fresh butter in a pan or egg dish and let it melt—that is, just enough for it to spread, never to crackle or spit. Open a very fresh egg onto a small plate or saucer and slide it carefully into the pan. Cook it on heat so low that the white barely turns creamy, and the yolk becomes hot but remains liquid. In a separate saucepan, melt another lump of fresh butter. Remove the egg onto a lightly heated serving plate. Salt it and pepper it, then very gently pour this fresh, warm butter over it. Serve.

COAGULATED SUNSHINE

Perhaps it was because Point was first and foremost a *saucier* that his enthusiasm for butter was so great, for all you need do is melt it and, voila, you have a sauce. Heat it a little further and you have *beurre noisette* or *beurre noir*. Less heat but a few small additions—shallots, herbs, vinegar—gives you *beurre blanc*, which is of course a *béarnaise* without the eggs. Take away the herbs and add lemon juice instead of the vinegar and now you have *hollandaise*. These are the tip of the iceberg. Without butter, this 'coagulated sunshine' as the poet Seamus Heaney called it, the glories of French cuisine are all but inconceivable.

Nor would we have Point's signature *gratin de queues d'ecrevisse*, a dish that has endured for more than seventy years. Though it may nowadays seem excessive—the crayfish cooked in butter, the sauce thickened with butter *and* enriched with hollandaise—the dish still conforms to Point's fundamental philosophy: good quality food enhanced by careful cooking and meticulous preparation.

One of Point's own maxims put it another way: "A good meal must be as harmonious as a symphony and as well-constructed as a Norman cathedral."

Fernand Point, the greatest chef of the twentieth century, died in 1955. He had already given birth to modern cooking, and each and every chef that follows owes to him a debt.

This page: Fernand Point was known for his love of butter and the ease with which it could be transformed into sauces. Overleaf: The freshest ingredients sourced at nearby markets were the foundation of Point's cuisine.

Gratin de Queues d'Ecrivesses

Plunge two crayfish in boiling water for five minutes. Drain immediately and remove the flesh from the tails and claws. Cut the flesh into medallions. Crush and reserve the shells.

In a saucepan, sweat the crushed shells with a knob of butter. Add onions and carrots cut into small dice and sauté. When the vegetables are lightly coloured, flame with cognac, then add white wine and a little water to bathe everything. Add puréed tomatoes and a bouquet garni. Season with salt, pepper and a dash of cayenne.

Cook over low heat for 20 minutes, then pass through a fine sieve. Thicken the sauce with a little beurre manié.

Sweat the crayfish flesh in butter. Remove and keep warm. Deglaze the pan with cognac. Add the sauce, along with some cream. After incorporating a julienne of truffles, bring to the boil. After a few minutes remove from the heat and bind together with sauce hollandaise.

Divide the crayfish among individual gratin dishes. After correcting the seasoning, cover the crayfish with the sauce and flash under the salamander.

CARÊME, COAL AND THE FRENCH KITCHEN

In 1833, exactly a century before Point opened La Pyramide, the most famous chef in the world died. At forty-nine he was still young, and though his doctors diagnosed intestinal tuberculosis acquired from unpasteurised milk, his final symptoms—incremental weakening over the last years of his life, and a final, stroke-like paralysis—suggested that he was also suffering from low-level carbon monoxide poisoning. It was a demise he had all but predicted.

"The coal kills us, but what matter? Fewer days, more glory."

Such were the words of Antonin Carême, who knew that it was all worth it. For although cooking had helped kill him, it had also given him fame, and riches. It had carved his name into posterity. It had literally saved his life.

He was born into turbulent times. In the words of Talleyrand, one of Europe's greatest diplomats (and Carême's greatest patron), no one born after the Revolution could know how sweet life had been before it. Certainly young Marie-Antoine Carême did not, for at the tender age of eight his father sent him, with these improbably florid words, into the world.

"*Go, go and fare thee well, my child. The world is large; chances are many. Leave us to our squalid poverty; it is our lot. Die we must as we have lived, penniless. This is the age of quick fortunes. There are splendid opportunities for all who, like thee, have a ready wit.*"

The year was 1792. Terror, as Robiespierre had commanded, was the order of the day. Heads and body parts were paraded through the same Paris streets that young Antonin (Marie-Antoine being no longer a politic name) now found himself abandoned on. Terrified he undoubtedly was. But salvation soon appeared, and it was in the shape of a cook. The boy was plucked from the street, taken in and put to work.

THE FRENCH KITCHEN

Talleyrand may have been right. But then, he was both an aristocrat and a clergyman; the pleasures of pre-revolutionary life were his for the taking. And of those pleasures the greatest, by far, was food.

By the time of Louis XIV (whose autopsy revealed a stomach and bowel twice the size of any normal man!) French cooking was on its way to becoming an art. All of the basic cooking methods had been devised—the first definitive French cookery book was published in 1651, eight years after the Sun King's accession—and those techniques were being constantly refined. "There is today no longer a prodigious overflowing of dishes, no confused piling of diverse varieties, mountains of roasts, all bizarrely served," one writer noted in 1674. "Instead there is an exquisite choice of meats, finesse in their seasoning, politeness and propriety in serving them."

But cuisine was not solely the preserve of the aristocracy, and it was as much the aspirations of an ever-increasing bourgeoisie which drove development in cooking: their desire for aristocratic refinement coupled with more modest resources tempered many of the court's excesses. And by the time this new, tempered sophistication reached the provinces, with their abundance of produce, a distinctly French cuisine appeared that was the property of all classes.

The middle-class, of course, were the biggest growth market, and by the middle of the 18th century cookbooks catering to their particular demands were being published, and books such as Menon's *La Cuisinière Bourgeoise* (1746) present a cuisine which most of us would find perfectly acceptable. One book, by François Marin, lists at least a hundred sauces. Here we find the first evidence of what was to become the hallmark of classical French cuisine. Where once sauces had been used merely to bind, moisten or mask ingredients, now chefs were using sauce to complement, to make interesting, dishes that were themselves plainly cooked.

And in Marin's very first sauce, *béchamel*, the tradition of naming dishes after famous people—in this case Louis XIV's *maître de hotel*—rather than the chefs who actually devised them, is continued. Such is the way. There is an endless array of dishes to which great names—Talleyrand, Pompadour, Richelieu—are attached. But the names of their true creators are forgotten. Food was all-important; chefs were but functionaries. A handful are remembered because they produced cookbooks. One, Vatel, is remembered because, bewildered by lack of sleep after organising a lavish banquet to be attended by the Sun King himself, he could not recall if he had correctly ordered the fish. He saw a delivery boy come with only two small packets and, distraught that he had erred so terribly, went to his room and ran himself through with his sword, just as the rest of the order was arriving. He was buried promptly, so as not to offend the King, in an unmarked grave, and the party continued without a hitch, just as Vatel had arranged it.

THE STOVE

And so it was not a glamorous profession in which young Carême found himself. French cuisine, according to Quentin Blake in his

Opposite: Anthony Bourdain cooking over a gas flame. Many chefs value the 'magic' of the flame in their kitchens.

Below: Marie Antoine Carême (1784–1833), arguably the world's first celebrity chef.

in these establishments was cooked, just as the gastronomic masterpieces of the Sun King's court had been, over open hearths.

The cooks were being cooked. Not only that, but valuable fuel was going to waste. And then an American solved the problem.

Benjamin Thompson, better known as Count Rumford, was a shopkeeper, schoolteacher and self-educated inventor who served George III of England and then became war minister for the Elector of Bavaria. In 1787 he published "On the Management of Fire and the Economy of Fuel," in which he described a boxy, insulated iron stove which he had designed and installed in various kitchens. He also designed a coffee percolator, invented a form of baking powder and a forerunner to the hot-air convection oven, among other things. But it was his stoves, first of brick and then of iron, which changed cooking forever.

A typical early arrangement consisted of a brick range that enclosed a number of separate fires. Above each a pan or pot was fitted into a circular, iron-rimmed opening. Flues carried the smoke to the main chimney, and each fire could be regulated by controlling the draught through the ash-pit door, or capped by an earthenware cover when not in use. Fuel waste was reduced, heat was where the chef needed it, and his job became infinitely more bearable.

Kitchen ranges built according to Rumford's designs were soon in use throughout Europe. In France, chefs took advantage of their even heat production to invent new sauces and smoother *roux*, and devised a new tool, the sauté pan, to use on it. By 1800 the modern kitchen was all but complete. It awaited only the modern chef.

THE CELEBRITY

Carême's father was right, insofar as Carême *was* possessed of ready wit, and indeed went on to make his fortune. In 1802, by which time he was 18, he says "I was earning quite a lot of money, better proof than all the compliments paid me that there was in my work something original which pleased and upon which was built my reputation."

groundbreaking book *Great Chefs of France*, 'had reached perfection in all its essentials.' Paris was now home to more than a hundred restaurants, from lowly chop-houses to Beauvilliers' La Grande Taverne de Londres, where what remained of the aristocracy dined. The modern chef—or diner—would have felt essentially at home, save for one thing: the food

The spectacular career on which Carême's reputation is based cannot, or at least should not, be reduced to a few paragraphs. Nevertheless, we may point out some of its highlights. The first of these, after his training as a *pâtissier*, were the extraordinary *pièces montées* which made him famous. These remarkable architectural centrepieces made from pastry, marzipan and meringue and decorated with coloured icing and spun sugar could be Athenian ruins, turning globes, Roman temples or ships in sail, depending on the occasion. They were usually several feet high and often took days to assemble. Nor were they designed to be eaten, and some survived Carême 'by a generation'.

It was through these *pièces montées* that Carême found his great patron, Talleyrand. During his service at the master-diplomats estate he was compelled to compile a menu for every day of the year, and had the opportunity to cater for Napoleon. He served the Prince Regent of England, the Tsar of Russia and Baron Rothschild. He invented the chef's hat. He invented the vol-au-vent. He was proclaimed a genius, and was paid like one—the Rothschild's paid the equivalent of £125,000 per annum for Carême's occasional services. He once catered a military banquet for 10,000 men. He wrote eight books, the last of which he was still reciting on his deathbed.

This was *The Art of French Cuisine in the Nineteenth Century*, in five volumes, in which Carême details an entire culinary system—a body of knowledge and a repertory of techniques—that could be put into practice by anyone who had mastered the principles. In it, and in his other works, Carême created the vehicle that took French cuisine around the world. No less than Escoffier said, "The fundamental principles of the science [of cooking], which we owe to Carême … will last as long as cooking itself."

Indeed, Carême was the first celebrity chef, cooking's first media star. But we must remember that despite his seeming modernity, things were different then. Let Carême himself set the scene.

"Picture a large kitchen at the hour of a grand dinner. See twenty chefs coming and going, moving with haste in this furnace of heat; look at the great mass of charcoals, a cubic metre for cooking the entrées, and another mass on the oven-tops for cooking the soups, sauces, ragoûts, for frying and for the bain-maries. Add a heap of glowing wood before which turn four spits, one bearing a sirloin of one hundred kilos, another the poultry and game. In this inferno everyone moves quickly, not a sound is heard. Only the chef has a right to be heard, and at his words everyone jumps to obey. Then the last straw—for about half an hour the windows are shut so that no air shall cool the dishes as they are served. This is how we spend the best years of our lives. We must obey even when our physical strength fails, but it is the burning charcoal that kills us."

Maybe not so much different. The old charcoal stoves at La Pyramide were replaced with gas and electricity only in 1976. Madame Point had carried on—La Pyramide was too great a house to die along with its patron—and for seven years Paul Mercier, Point's *chef de cuisine*, carried on his exact traditions, until he too died. His place was taken by a young man, Guy Thivard, who was part of Mercier's brigade, and *he* cooked for fifteen years on the type of coal range that Carême would have known intimately.

It is this tradition, spanning centuries, that kept French cuisine alive; on that same coal range Point's many pupils learned the magic of the flame. For some, even now, it remains the only way. "I would never use electricity," says Paul Bocuse, Point's greatest pupil. "It has no magic. I have gas and the spit because a flame is alive. How could you be a blacksmith with no flame? Think what a poor fellow the Devil would be if all he had was electricity…"

Opposite: This sugar sculpture in the style of Carême stands 4.4 metres (14 feet 4 inches) high and took 8 months to create. Carême's original sculptures were completed in days rather than months.

Paul Bocuse

THE RINGMASTER

" While his contemporaries stayed mostly in their kitchens, Bocuse took himself to the world, built the first real culinary empire and invented the concept of the celebrity chef. "

Bocuse

There are certain photographs of Monsieur Bocuse in which he resembles no-one so much as Napoleon. The same aquiline nose and deep, black eyes project that same force of personality, that same will to dominate.

There are other pictures, too. There's his face on the cover of *Time* in an era when no American could have given you the name of a single other chef, and on the postcards he has had made of the dozens of other magazine covers on which he has starred. On advertisements for everything from champagne to mineral water, and on his own brand of kitchen wares. Unremarkable, it's true, in this age of the chef as celebrity. But then you remember that it was Bocuse alone who made it so.

"I am as old," he likes to say, "as Mickey Mouse." And, we are to understand, just as famous.

THE ROAD TO STARDOM

In fact, the mouse is two years younger. Ten generations of Bocuses had been chefs in the small village of Collonges–au–Mont–d'Or before Paul was born in 1926. His father had been apprenticed in the same kitchen as Point. Bocuse would be apprenticed *to* him. His destiny was almost assured.

The war interrupted his training. Still a teenager, he fought with the Free French Army until he was wounded by German machine gun fire. Then, in 1948, he found himself in the kitchen of La Pyramide, learning from the master.

Instead of taking steps to curb Bocuse's natural exuberance—as would normally be the case between a master-chef and a spirited apprentice—Point gave it every encouragement. But we might imagine the scenes, knowing that a young Bocuse had once revenged himself on a bullying chef by sneaking a human skull into the stockpot. Still, it is clear that along with spirit there was talent and application, for there are no shortcuts to stardom in *haute cuisine*. And stardom, it seems, was inevitable.

Though not without further trial. His father's tiny hotel had been damaged in the war and only roughly restored. Worse, his impecunious grandfather had sold not only the family restaurant but also the rights to the family name. But from such difficult circumstances a man might still become the greatest chef in France, if he so willed.

THE LIGHTNING STRIKE

The Roman historian Plutarch surmised that truffles were produced when lightning struck the ground; with a little imagination we might still believe it. Something about the mysterious, ineffable *Tuber melanosporum*, the 'black diamond of cuisine', suggests that it *could* have sprung into existence in just so dramatic a circumstance. Its elusiveness, perhaps, or the way its pungent yet subtle odour will insinuate itself into anything the truffle touches.

The presence of Fernand Point in Lyon proved to be just such a lightning bolt. Almost all of the great Lyonnais *chefs-patrons*—of which Bocuse was merely the most driven—felt the touch of his hand. Not only Bocuse but Alain Chapel, Françoise Bise, the Troisgros brothers, Louis Outhier and Raymond Thuilier all apprenticed to him. Those like Jacques Pic and Roger Vergé that did not train under him absorbed his dictates at only one remove.

More than anything they learned the true value of produce. Point's practice of personally going around the markets of Lyon was passed on to Bocuse *et al*, and Bocuse maintained this habit long after he became famous. His mission was always to encourage a return to the intrinsic taste of produce, enhanced by ingenuity and subtle skill. He did not claim novelty, and felt that a great chef is one who finds maybe two new dishes in a lifetime. He knew that a *truly* great chef is one who, like Point, inspires a generation of pupils. And with all his soul he believed in the integrity of French cuisine.

THE MEDAL OF HONOUR

He also believed in Paul Bocuse. That was what he called his restaurant, long before such practice was commonplace. He had his third Michelin star by 1965, yet still had the bravado to serve the prominent French food critic Henri Gault a dish of fresh haricots verts he picked from his garden that morning, simply boiled and dressed with olive oil, shallots and salt. For Mr. Gault it was a revelation. For the rest of the world, it was perhaps the beginning of *nouvelle cuisine*.

That bravado remains. You can see it in a picture of Bocuse in his mid-seventies, the sleeve of his black shirt pulled up to expose a particularly erect French *coq* tattooed on a burly upper arm and an almost juvenile smirk on his age-worn face. But this is also a man who by his own admission never plays games—"because I hate to lose."

It is obvious that the personality such an attitude expresses was forged, as most are, early in life. Yet one may wonder if that personality—along with his fame—was not fully cemented until President Giscard d'Estaing's famous luncheon, which Bocuse catered, where he was presented with the *Légion d'Honneur* and at which he, in turn, presented what was to become his most famous dish.

THE LADIES MAN

As well as speculation as to their source, it has been said of truffles that, due to their hefty price, they were seen only on the tables of notable men—or kept women. Given that Bocuse is reported to have kept not one but two mistresses, is seems appropriate that his signature is a soup of black truffles.

Appropriate, too, that the dish should offer some reflection of the contradictions evident in the man himself. For all the luxury of its key ingredients, truffle and foie gras, it remains a soup, and a relatively simple one at that, just as the man with two mistresses remains happily married to his wife (only in France, perhaps…) yet is still much given to saucy chat and pinching girls' behinds.

Opposite: Paul Bocuse (born 1926) pictured outside his three-star Michelin-rated restaurant l'Auberge du Pont de Collonges near Lyon. Bocuse, considered an ambassador of modern French Cuisine, was honoured in 1961 with the title Meilleur Ouvrier de France.

Or the way the driven and self-promoting Bocuse accepted the Legion of Honour not for himself but on behalf of French cuisine. What's more, it serves to highlight the undeniable connection between the classic techniques of Escoffier, the innovations of Point and the revolutions of the *nouvelle cuisine* that Bocuse and his fellow chefs championed.

Finally, it features that little touch of personal genius that Bocuse undoubtedly brought to cooking: the pastry lid that seals in the essential aroma of truffle, so that when the diner plunges in with the spoon he or she is for a moment literally overwhelmed by its impact.

THE COST

Of course there is no free lunch. The qualities of leadership that Bocuse possessed (and at eighty-one still possesses) are likely to prompt others to jealously and resentment. After representing himself well on a television show, he received a letter from a man saying, 'I hated you before I saw you on that programme. Now I quite like you, but I think you make too much money.'

Money he has certainly made. While his contemporaries stayed mostly in their kitchens, Bocuse took himself to the world, built the first real culinary empire and invented the concept of the celebrity chef into the bargain. The criticisms quickly followed: that he was too commercial, that he was too often absent from his restaurant, and that lending his name to products and to advertising was unbecoming. But for a man of such relentless drive, one kitchen was never likely to be enough. Now he has a kitchen at Disneyland.

If Bocuse suffered such accusations in his prime, worse has been levelled at him in the twilight of his career. A 2003 review in *GQ* magazine dismissed him as "the Flying Dutchman of French cuisine, sailing aimlessly through his premises." It dismissed the food as laughable, and accused the Michelin judges of lowering standards in the case of Bocuse, not for payoffs or for advertising but for sentiment, where other less revered chefs had had to suffer for any drop in quality.

THE RINGMASTER

These accusations undoubtedly have some merit. Bocuse *is* regarded with much sentiment, and not only by chefs and critics—he tells of a friend travelling in California who was let off a speeding fine because he knew Bocuse. For his eightieth birthday Alain Ducasse organised a three-day celebration in Monte Carlo attended by 350 guests, 80 of them chefs, including Ferran Adria. Entertainment was provided by acrobats and go-go dancers, and in the words of a journalist in attendance, "if the sedate world of fine dining has become a circus, no chef has a better claim to the title of ringmaster than the guest of honor, Paul Bocuse."

No one would deny it.

But there are other pictures, too: The chef, his daughter, his wife, his mother and a grand-daughter sat down to lunch on a simple *pot-au-feu* he has prepared. Or a man who friends say could not bear to sleep alone; he would rather sleep on a chair in a friend's room. A man who says, "If you have guests, you want them to sit in your kitchen and dip their fingers in the food. In many ways that is the kind of restaurant I would like to run, a little one where people eat in the kitchen." A man who, if he saw a young couple in his restaurant that obviously understood food, was quite likely to give them their dinner gratis. A man whose practical jokes are legion, and legendary.

Monsieur Bocuse has been all of these men, and more. But he does not take himself too seriously. "Life is a farce," he says. "That is why I like jokes. Imagine, when the President of the Republic invites the President of the United States to dine, he also invites me. It is ridiculous."

This page and overleaf, below: Like Point before him, Bocuse stresses the importance of fresh ingredients of the highest quality.

Overleaf, above: Chef Paul Bocuse in his restaurant in Collonges-au-Mont-d'Or, Lyon, France.

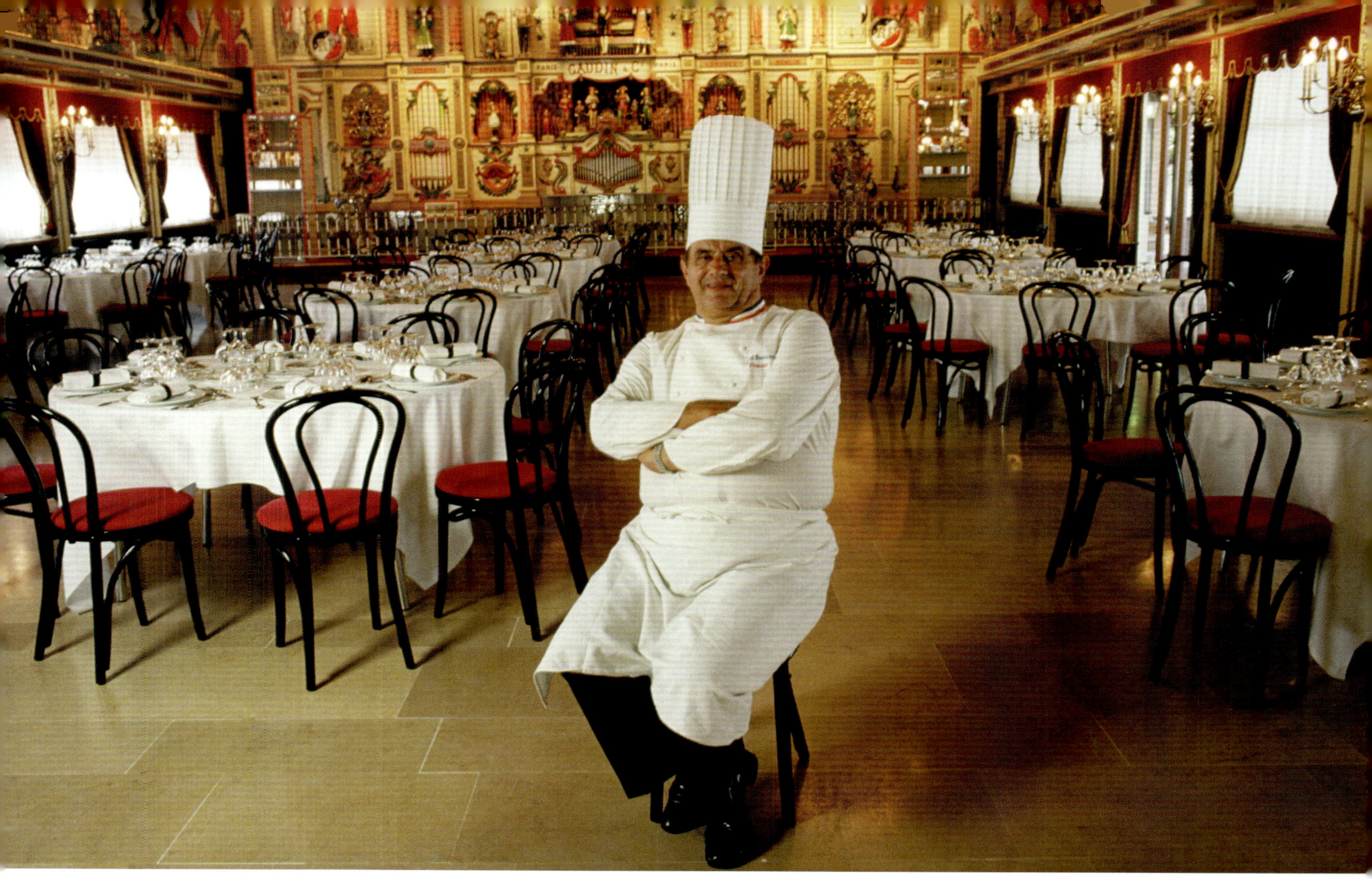

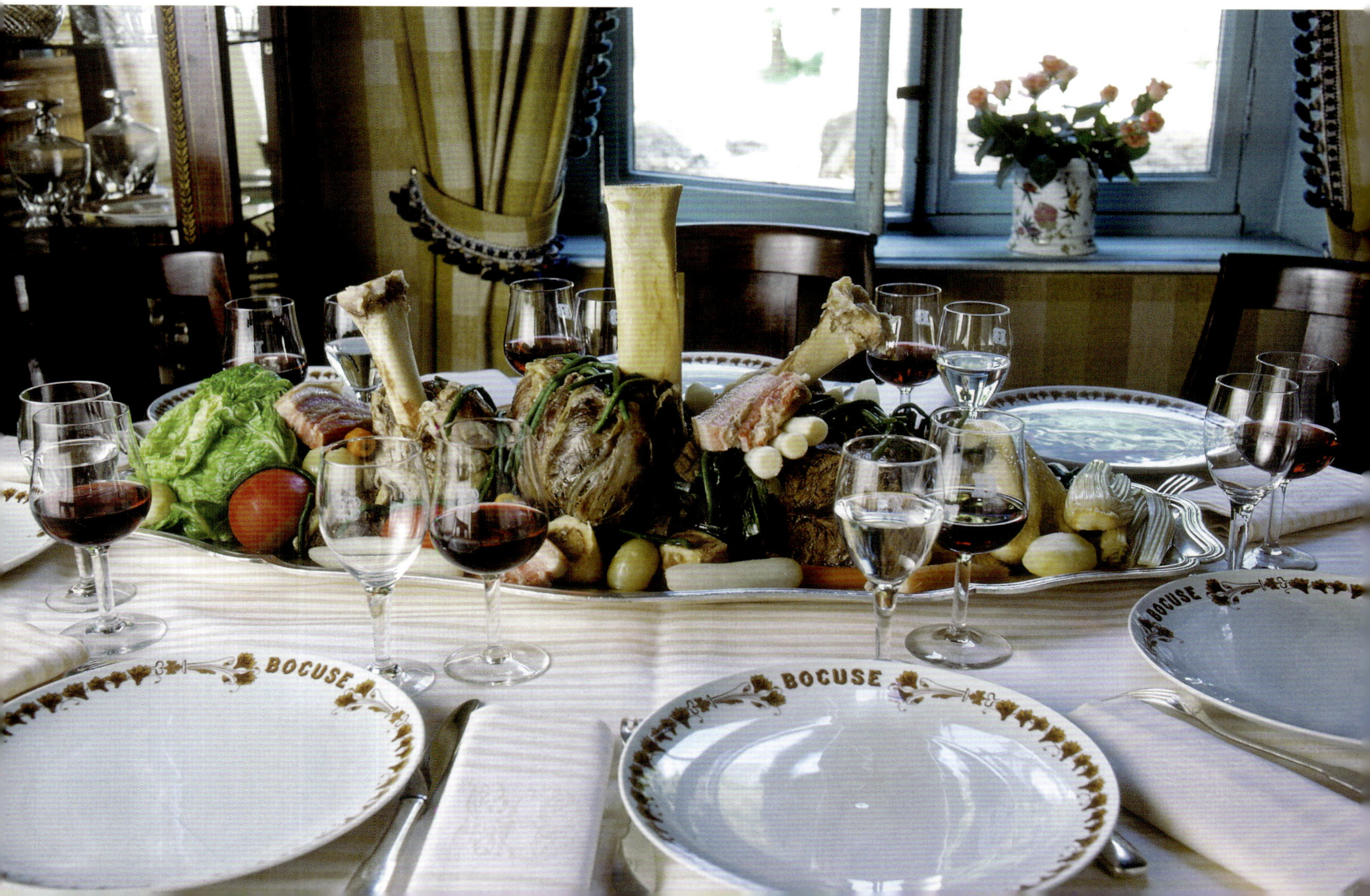
BOCUSE
BOCUSE
BOCUSE

Black Truffle Soup Elysée

Divide four tablespoons of white vermouth and some strong chicken consommé among four small ovenproof soup bowls.

Sautée in butter a mixture of very finely chopped carrot, onion, celery and mushroom in equal proportion. Divide this among the soup bowls, then add thinly sliced black truffles, diced foie gras and thinly sliced cooked chicken breast.

Season with salt and pepper. Place rounds of puff pastry on top of the bowls, pressing well on the edges so that all the flavors are sealed inside.

Brush with egg yolk and place in a preheated 220° C (450° F) oven for 18–20 minutes. When the pastry is puffed and golden, remove from the oven and serve.

Hierarchy

REFORM AND THE KITCHEN BRIGADE

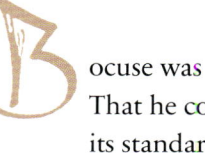 ocuse was the first great chef to leave the kitchen. That he could, and expect his cuisine to maintain its standard, was due to a force of personality that reigned even in his absence. Even so, he could never have done it without Escoffier.

Isaac Newton once claimed that he was standing on the shoulders of giants. So too were Point and Bocuse. But giants come in different sizes. Georges Auguste Escoffier was short. He needed built-up shoes so that he did not burn himself on the stoves. Yet his influence was—is—greater even than Carême's. No less a person than Kaiser Wilhelm, Emperor of Germany called him 'the emperor of chefs.' For almost half a century Escoffier *was* cuisine, and even today every kitchen, grand or small, runs the way it does because of him.

A PROVENÇAL LINEAGE

Young Auguste was an artistic boy, born into a modest family in the South of France. His father was a blacksmith, schoolteacher, and the village mayor, and his grandmother a fine Provençal cook, whose recipes Escoffier used throughout his life. At thirteen, his education complete, he was apprenticed to his uncle, who owned a restaurant in nearby Nice.

The uncle was hard, but fair. Escoffier was a talented pupil. Then in 1865, at the age of nineteen, he went to Paris to work at the celebrated restaurant Le Petit Moulin Rouge. It was a shock.

"The kitchen was like nothing I had ever seen or imagined—a stifling, low-ceilinged inferno of a cellar, red-lit from the fires, and deafening with oaths and the clanging of pots and pans. It was so hot that all the metal-work except the stoves had to be covered with cloth. In the middle were furnaces, where twelve cooks skipped to and fro, their faces dripping sweat in spite of their white caps. Round that were counters where a mob of waiters and *plongeur* clamoured with trays. Scullions, naked to the waist, were stoking the fires and scouring huge copper saucepans with sand. Everyone seemed to be in a hurry and a rage. The head cook, a fine, scarlet man with big moustachios, stood in the middle booming continuously, '*CA MARCHE DEUX ŒUFS BROUILLES! CA MARCHE UN CHATEAUBRIAND AUX POMMES SAUTEES!*' except when he broke off to curse at a *plongeur*.'

These are not Escoffier's words. They were written by George Orwell in *Down and Out in Paris and London*, published nearly 70 years after Escoffier's first real experience of the day-to-day brutality of kitchen life. Conditions which Escoffier had vowed to reform.

Since the glory days of Carême the status of the chef had been directly tied to his visibility: the rise of the restaurant gained some, such as the lofty Adolphe Dugléré, a certain regard from their customers, but over time the demands of cooking chained them to the stoves, and once hidden again their social standing dwindled. The conditions in which they worked, even with the advent of Rumford's enclosed stoves, were still extreme. Because of the heat they drank too much. Most kitchens were badly organised, and the head chef invariably maintained order with curses, blows and kicks. The work itself was hazardous, and serious burns were common. But Escoffier was committed to changing all that.

He never stayed in one place for too long, and in each of his kitchens he persevered in trying to improve the chef's working conditions, and their public image. He forbade chefs from going outside in their uniforms. He prohibited alcohol, supplying his chefs instead with copious amounts of barley-water. There was no smoking. There was not even shouting; orders were to be spoken—loudly if necessary, but spoken nonetheless.

THE BRIGADE

These reforms alone would have ensured that his name was remembered, among chefs at least. But the wider public may never have come to know Escoffier had he not had the good fortune to encounter another man whose name would also go down in history.

César Ritz was Swiss. As a boy he had herded his father's cows. He was then apprenticed as wine waiter in a hotel restaurant. In less than a decade he was a hotelier. Soon he was the greatest hotel-keeper of all, his name synonymous with luxury.

In 1883 Ritz was working at Monte Carlo's Grand Hotel when his chef was poached by a rival hotel. The departing man recommended Escoffier, and the two were a match made in heaven. Ritz, too, was an innovator. He had radical ideas on how a luxury hotel should be run, requiring new standards of efficiency and hygiene, and Escoffier shared his views.

He first tackled cleanliness—kitchens were scrupulously cleaned every day and kept spotless. Then there was issue of getting large quantities of food to diners, efficiently and at the correct temperature.

The system by which chefs worked was antiquated and confused. Different jobs were apportioned to the separate *parties*, as they are now, but the allotment of a task might not make any rational sense. The *rôtisseur*, whose job was the grilling of meat and fish, had to make the pastry for his *boeuf-en-croûte* himself, even though it was far more sensible for the *pâtissier* to do it. During service that same *rôtisseur* may have been grilling fish while the *poissonnier* was standing idle.

Logical it was not. Escoffier had an analytical mind, and he could clearly see what needed to be done. He divided his staff into teams, each headed by a chef, called *brigade de cuisines*. He rationalised the tasks of each of the *parties* into separate, logical groups—fish, meat and vegetable preparation, *saucier* and *garde-manger*—and, long before Henry Ford, instituted an assembly line. To compose a single dish each *brigade* prepared their item at roughly the same time, adding it to the dish as the plate was passed to them. The *chef-de-cuisine* approved the dish at the pass, and then it was sent to the table. This was Escoffier's method, and more than a century on it is the standard for kitchens around the world.

Opposite: *Brigade de cuisine* is a structured team system which delegates responsibilities to individuals, each with their own specialised tasks. While the concept was refined by Auguste Escoffier, evidence of brigade-style culinary arrangements can be found in late medieval French and English sources.

SAUCE

By the time Ritz and Escoffier moved to London's Savoy Hotel in 1890 they were both on their way to becoming as famous as their patrons. But Escoffier did not yet have time to enjoy his growing celebrity. His approach to his art was alway more intellectual than intuitive; many sleepless nights were spent thinking up new and innovative combinations—his fashionable customers demanded novelty—and his days were taken up with creating them.

It was not novelty for its own sake that drove him to innovate, however. He believed that the foundations of cuisine, particularly as laid down by Carême, were eternal. Yet he knew the world had changed, was changing still, and the cuisine had to reflect that. Modern palates were becoming more refined, therefore his dishes must become more refined. In the end, on the matter of sauce, he broke with Carême profoundly.

Carême believed that there were four grand sauces—*velouté*, *béchamel*, *allemande* and *espagnole*—from which all the hundreds of variations derived. Escoffier concluded that this was two too many, and that *allemande* and *espagnole*, a *sauce blonde* and *sauce brune* respectively were old-fashioned and no longer relevant. He denounced them and, in the words of André Simon, "their bastard progeny," substituting the lighter and more fragrant *fumets* made from the concentrated natural juices of meat, fish or vegetables and the water, broth, butter or oil in which they were cooked.

A tradition he did retain, of course, was the naming of dishes after famous clients, of which his peach Melba and *tournedos Rossini* are only the two most famous.

Both are firmly part of the modern repertoire. Indeed, the name Escoffier may still not have become synonymous with *haute cuisine* if he had not been such a prodigious writer.

LE GUIDE CULINAIRE

Published in 1903, *Le Guide Culinaire* was in Escoffier's words merely an '*aide-mémoire de cuisine pratique*'. Considering that it contains at least 5,000 recipes we must consider it a little more than just a memory aid, even it did arise simply from Escoffier's habit of trying to get everything down on paper in an orderly way.

And though it may have come from humble intentions, *Le Guide Culinaire* served to codify almost everything to do with cooking, taking the experience of the previous century, explaining it in detail, updating much of was old-fashioned, and of course cataloguing a vast number of recipes. Not all of them were his, nor did he claim they were. Even so, Escoffier's extraordinary flair was applied to creations that were both his own and other peoples, and for the chefs that followed the book became a bible—and a straitjacket—for decades to come.

But rules, as they say, are made to be broken. It just remains to decide which are the ones worth breaking. "Cuisine," Point said, "is not invariable like a Codex formula." At the same

time he warned against tampering with the essentials. Michel Guérard believes it impossible to create cuisine of any quality without having studied Escoffier, and Bocuse, like everyone else, runs his kitchen in *brigades* just as the great man specified. His genius for systemising means that a chef like Bocuse *could* leave his kitchen, safe in the knowledge that the structure would remain sound, and the cuisine retain its integrity.

Integrity, in the end, was one of Escoffier's hallmarks. In his later years this dapper, fastidious man used his reknown in favour of social causes, calling for aid for the poor and personally helping a number of charitable organisations. He even helped care for one Ulysse Rohan, the chef whose violent treatment of him as a young man had set him on the path to reform.

As has been said, for almost fifty years Escoffier *was* cuisine, and his influence, whether one chooses to embrace it or reject it, simply cannot be ignored.

Opposite: César Ritz (1850–1918), the Swiss hotelier who collaborated with Auguste Escoffier to create the modern hotel, pictured with his wife Marie.

Above: Chefs at work in a kitchen at the Savoy Hotel, London, 1928. Ritz and Escoffier insisted that the Savoy kitchens be kept scrupulously clean.

Michel Guérard

THE THIN MAN

"The revolutionary extremes of *cuisine minceur* were in a way just a reaction to his circumstance: if one is running a health spa one has no choice but to offer healthy food."

Guérard

"henever I go to a restaurant I don't know," Fernand Point would say, "I always ask to meet the chef before I eat. For I know that if he is thin, I won't eat well. And if he is thin and sad, there is nothing for it but to go. But," he would add, wryly, "before misjudging a thin man one should make an enquiry or two—he may be a formerly fat man."

Michel Guérard is such a man, insofar as he was once fat. No one has accused him of being sad (he shares with many great chefs an enthusiasm for practical jokes), but by the time his famous bistro Pot-au-Feu was compulsorily purchased to make way for a new road he was both unhealthy and unhappy.

Not through lack of success: his tiny restaurant in a rundown Paris suburb had become the haunt of ministers, film stars and socialites, and it had already made him famous, if not rich. The turnover was too small to cover the costs, and Guérard's routine was to go to

bed at 2am, barely three hours before he rose again to get to the markets. And then a bureaucrat's whim relieved him of the burden. His reputation was such that he was offered, among other jobs, the kitchen at Maxim's, where he had once trained. He toyed with the idea of buying a place on the Champs-Elysées.

Then love, as it so often will, intervened.

THE OUTSIDER

Unlike Bocuse and the other pupils of Fernand Point, Michel Guérard hailed not from around Lyon but rather a town north of Paris. Still, though he started from a different point, he managed to arrive at much the same place as them, at much the same time.

His training was relatively traditional—he befriended Bocuse and Pierre Troisgros while at the Lucas-Carton—yet when it was complete he took the unusual step of going to work for a private family. He had always felt that the rules imposed by Escoffier, while in no way wrong, had been followed too slavishly. Now, with private employers, he could begin experimenting with a lighter, more natural kind of cuisine. In a way, it was Guérard who was the true revolutionary, and the success of Pot-au-Feu confirmed his approach. His vegetables, one writer has claimed, had the superb quality of being cooked, yet tasting as if they were raw. Already he had two Michelin stars.

He also had a weight problem, and when Pierre Troisgros introduced him to a young woman named Christine Barthélémy, whose father owned a chain of health spas, slimming was naturally a topic of conversation. Love seemed naturally to follow.

They married in 1972. Guérard now had an interest in one of the family's hydros, a rather tired watering-place, once patronised by the Empress Eugénie, in a sleepy corner of southern France. It was the ideal spot from which to foment a small revolution.

THIN COOKING

Guérard's revolution was *cuisine minceur*, which admittedly sounds better in the French than in English. And for the French public, assailed by both the best and the worst of *nouvelle cuisine*, the idea of 'thin cooking' must have seemed a particularly unfunny joke.

For the slimmers who came to shed weight, however, the food at Le Pres d'Eugenie probably seemed miraculous. Here was a famous, Michelin-starred chef dedicating his energy to creating such dishes as the famed *vollaile 'truffee' au persil*—in deference to slimmers he trims the fat from inside the chicken, uses no butter or sauce and discards the fat from the roasting pan—or a baby rabbit cooked for barely ten minutes and presented on a bed of fresh spinach and baby turnips. Food that was profoundly healthy yet still flavourful and satisfying.

Well, some of his energy, at least. The revolutionary extremes of *cuisine minceur* were in a way just a reaction to his circumstance: if one is running a health spa one has no choice but to offer healthy food.

But just as in every fat chef there is a thin one trying to get out, perhaps in this thin chef there is a fat one trying to get back in. In 1977 Guérard was awarded his third Michelin star. In his autobiography of 2000, Michel Roux stated that, if given the choice, he would eat his final meal *chez* Guérard. Many other starred chefs, one suspects, would choose the same. It is not 'thin' cooking that gets such acclaim.

LA CARTE GOURMANDE

"I cook as the bird sings," the chef declares on his website, and indeed this claim is accompanied by bird song. Amongst the poetry and pictures of pretty gardens he also lists three separate cuisines on offer at the hotel—*minceur, gourmande* and *terroir*.

It is his *gourmande* style that won him his stars, offering as it does both lightness and substance, both song *and* bird, if you will. Guérard's *soupe aux écrevisses de riviére* blends crayfish with vegetables and herbs, cream and butter, dry white wine, Armagnac and port, for example, and in his own words, 'blossoms in the mouth.' His *deux oeufs poule au caviar*, lightly scrambled eggs mixed with chopped onion, chives and cream, put back in their shells and topped with caviar, are a delightful flight of fancy. The *trois feuilletés legers de saison* are pastry leaves which may contain anything from asparagus to oysters, foie gras to cocks' crests and kidneys, depending on the season.

THE SHOCK OF THE NEW

If dishes such as these gave Guérard his Michelin stars, it was his association with *nouvelle cuisine* that in the 1970s bought him an international fame almost as great as that of his friend Bocuse.

Of course, the new is never really 'new' at all. "Modern cuisine, built on the foundations of the old, with less fuss, less equipment and quite as much variety, is simpler, cleaner and perhaps more knowledgeable." This a quote from 1739. The Roman writer Apicius spoke of a new cuisine in the first century AD.

Previous spread: Chef Michel Guérard (right) in the kitchen of his three star Michelin rated restaurant, Les Pres d'Eugenie in Eugenie-les-Bains, France.

Opposite: Chef Michel Guérard with his *brigade de cuisine*.

Even so, that a change had taken place could not be denied. The 'rules' of *nouvelle cuisine* were defined in a series of articles in 1972 by authors and food critics Henri Gault and Christian Millau. In reality they were simply codifying the practices that the pupils of Point (*les petits Point*, Bocuse called them) had made standard, above all of which was the utmost respect, almost veneration, of produce. The rest was mainly a process of reduction, simplification, and common sense.

What drove the movement, primarily, was that the chefs who were its vanguard—Roger Vergé, the Troisgros and Haeberlin brothers, Jacques Pic, Alain Chapel, Françoise Bise, Louis Outhier and Raymond Thuilier—were all possessed by a touch of genius.

But Bocuse and Guérard were its stars, and of the two Guérard was also by far the most inventive. The irreverence that is an essential part of his personality (he wanted to be a comedian, and his wife says he missed his calling) came out in his cooking. So much so, in fact, that the exploratory side of what became *nouvelle cuisine* was closely associated with his name. That he had also, by necessity, invented *cuisine minceur* was enough to confuse a great many people, and some would lay the blame for the worst excesses of *nouvelle cuisine* firmly at his door.

Indeed, there was much that came to be bad about *nouvelle cuisine*; meagre portions arranged artfully over huge plates, the combining of inappropriate ingredients, the assumption that everything must be low-calorie. For this, responsibility lies in a combination of overenthusiastic journalists, greedy restauranteurs, confused chefs, and a public eager for novelty. In a telling anecdote, Charles Barrier recalls seeing an American chef putting paprika on a sole: "I asked him what on earth he was doing; he said that he thought it *looked* nice. What a monstrous betrayal."

Guérard's cooking manages none of these crimes. From his beginnings at Pot-au-Feu it has always been honest, direct … modern.

In many ways it has become the acme of modernity. Take his *vollaile 'truffé' au persil*—almost everything that health- and environmentally-conscious cooks strive towards in the twenty-first century is exemplified by this simple dish.

THE BIRD

The bird is the poulet de Bresse, the one that Brillat-Savarin called 'the queen of chickens and the chicken of kings.' It is the only chicken to be protected by an *Appellation d'Origine Controlée*, and invariably it is the poulet de Bresse that is served in any Michelin-starred restaurant.

But why is *this* chicken so special? Insofar as the unique clay-rich soil of the region, the temperate climate, the proven purity of the breed and the specific rearing procedures combine to produce a particular and specific bird, it is deemed by French law to be unique. Yet that still doesn't quite explain it.

The reason is that it tastes like chicken. And even if the only chicken we have ever eaten is the factory farmed, pale-fleshed and insipid tasting version the modern consumer has perforce gotten used to, we still know instinctively what chicken *should* taste like. Its flesh should be firm and richly coloured, and its taste should reflect the way it lived and what it ate. It should, in all senses of the word, be *organic*, which means it should taste as chicken tasted before that term ever needed to be used.

And if we should have the good fortune to have such a chicken in front of us? It is unlikely we would be inspired, as generations of French chefs have been, to 'truffle' it, for that would be a crime against both chicken and truffle. Rather we might do as Michel Guérard, and with the simple additions of herbs, seasoning and some low-fat cheese allow all of that marvelous flavour to shine. But we would not call that *cuisine minceur* or even *nouvelle cuisine*. We would just call it good food.

This page: Michel Guérard developed the 'light' style of cooking, *cuisine minceur*, in the 1970s. His approach includes less butter and cream, more vegetables and vegetable sauces and lean cuts of meat and poultry.

Overleaf: Guérard and his wife Christine own three restaurants in Eugénie des Bains, transforming the tiny village into a significant tourist destination. Les Prés d'Eugénie, part of the main spa hotel, has received three stars in the Michelin Guide since 1977.

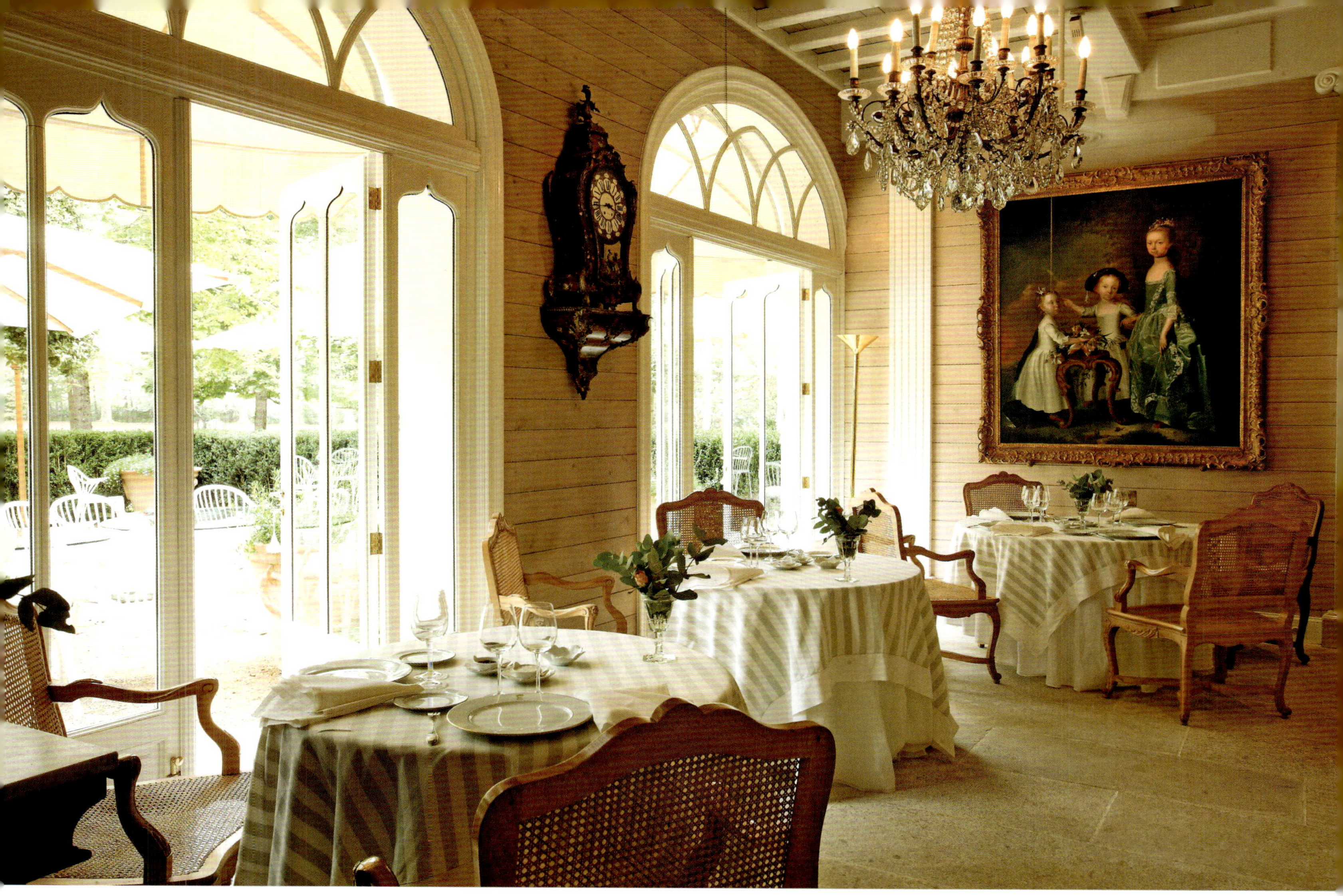

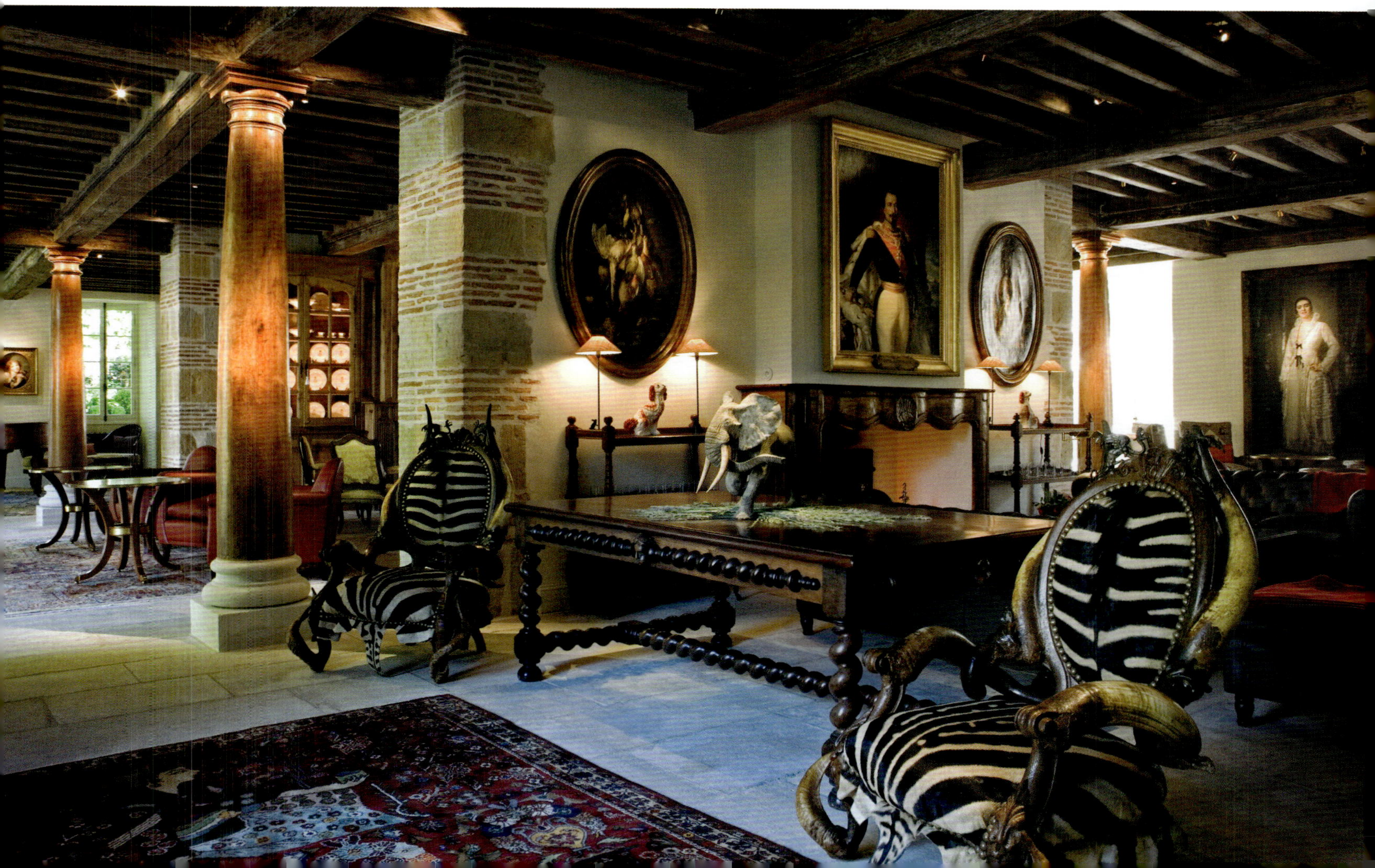

Vollaille 'Truffé' au Persil

Chop together some fresh parsley, chives, tarragon, shallots and mushrooms. Bind this together with fromage blanc to make the stuffing.

Clean and dry the chicken. Gently loosen the skin from the breast meat to make space for the stuffing—the flavour is cooked into the meat by direct contact. Spread the stuffing evenly over the breast, then roast the chicken in a copper pan with a lid in a hot oven until the juices run clean.

The finished chicken may be served with a simple garnish of young carrots, baby turnips and chives.

Le patrons

THE RISE OF THE *CHEFS-PATRON*

The story goes that it all started with soup, but the dish in question was in fact sheep's feet in white sauce—not really a soup at all. The magistrate, however, ruled in favour of M. Boulanger, and the restaurant was born.

The year was 1765. Public dining was strictly controlled; only inns and the *traiteurs* (caterers) were permitted to cook and sell food. The *traiteurs* were protected by restrictive guild practices, and sold mainly cooked meats, *ragoûts* and *pâtisseries*. But the vending of soups was unrestricted, and one such soup vendor, Boulanger, served alongside his *bouillons* and *potages* the above-mentioned dish. The *traiteurs* sued to prevent him from doing so. They lost. Boulanger was permitted to keep serving his restorative meals, *restaurants*, as he called them.

The idea quickly caught on; the word 'restaurant' followed more slowly. When in 1782 Antoine Beauvilliers, who had long served in royal households, opened what would become Paris's pre-eminent eating establishment, he called it La Grande Taverne de Londres, because the English taverns still defined the popular idea of 'eating out.'

ELITE DINING

But Beauvilliers had assuredly opened a restaurant —it catered to the elite, offering a choice of dishes served to them at individual tables—and many were to follow. By 1789 there were about a hundred in Paris, and by the turn of the century there were five or six times that many. The Revolution had bought many politicians, diplomats and legislators to the capital, and those without homes there needed somewhere to dine. The great aristocratic houses had been broken up, and their chefs needed somewhere to ply their trade. And those men that had made fortunes during the Revolution chose to spend their money in restaurants: ironically they did not want to draw attention to themselves by enjoying lavish entertainments at home.

As always, the middle classes followed this lead. Even so, Beauvilliers knew where the money was. The consummate restaurateur, he was "the first to combine an elegant dining room, smart waiters, and a choice cellar with superior cooking," wrote Brillat-Savarin. The man himself held to the respectable traditions of the *Ancien Regime*, and would walk around his restaurant with a sword buckled at his side which, having been an officer, was his privilege. And here Brillat-Savarin is worth quoting at length, to illustrate just how consummate a restaurateur Beauvilliers was:

"He also had a method of procedure peculiar to himself. When he was told that a party of wealthy people had sat down at one of his tables, he would approach them with an obliging air, kiss the ladies hands, and appear to honour his guests with special attention.

"He would point out here a dish to be avoided and there one to be ordered at once, before it was too late; a third which nobody dreamed of ordering, he would himself, at the same time sending for wine from a cellar to which he alone had the key; in a word, he assumed so gracious and engaging a tone, that all these additional items seemed so many favours on his part. But this role of Amphitryon lasted only a moment; having played it, he withdrew from the scene; and before long the swollen bill, and the bitterness of Rabelais's quarter of an hour, amply demonstrated the difference between a host and a restaurateur."

The contrast between Beauvilliers and his near contemporary, Carême, also illustrates the difference between restaurateur and chef. Carême once toyed with the idea of opening a restaurant; Beauvilliers was seen as his chief rival, and he wished to outdo the older man. But Carême was wedded to his own independence, and he was a freelance chef almost his entire life. "The chef who is a man of routine lacks courage," he wrote, "his life drips away in mediocrity."

THE *CHEFS-PATRON*

Carême, being a genius, could say such things. We, however, must be less quick to conflate routine with mediocrity. Point, for example, could not be accused of the second, even though his life was typified by the first (the same man came to shave him at the same time every morning), and he came to revile the idea of 'progress', and had no desire whatsoever to travel beyond his restaurant.

The truth is that cuisine is a product of routine. Indeed, Quentin Crewe and Anthony Blake's *Great Chefs of France* opens with a description of the very routines that these chefs and their *brigades* undertake every day; Bocuse at the market, Jacques Pic briefing his team, Alain Chapel checking the place-settings in his dining room. Crewe describes the kitchen during the heat of service: "Pierre Troisgros chases after a dish which a waiter is carrying, to wipe a drop of sauce from the rim of the plate. Bise rejects a piece of toast which he judges to be slightly burnt." Then the pace begins to slacken. Desserts are going out. Soon the *chefs-patron* say goodbye to their customers "as if the day were over." But of course it is not. That was only lunch—everything must be done again for dinner.

Published in 1978, *Great Chefs of France* took readers into the kitchens of Frances twelve provincial three-star restaurants for the first time, and remains unrivalled as a study of France's heroic chefs at the height of their powers. After Point, who is represented by his still-living wife, the chefs are presented in alphabetical order—Charles Barrier, Françoise Bise, Paul Bocuse, Alain Chapel, Michel Guérard, Paul and Jean-Pierre Haeberlin, Louis Outhier, Jacques Pic, Raymond Thuilier, Jean and Pierre Troisgros and Roger Vergé—all interviewed by Crewe and photographed by Blake. It is a remarkable document, capturing as it does a moment in time when a dozen provincial restaurants were at the centre of the gastronomic world. Paris in 1977 had half as many three-star establishments.

Opposite: Chefs Michel Troisgros (left) and his father Pierre Troisgros in the Troisgros restaurant, Roanne. The restaurant has had three Michelin stars awarded to it since 1968.

REVOLUTION

Every generation experiences some small revolution, because change, both from within and without, is the natural order of things: Escoffier himself said that cuisine was at the mercy of fashion "and equally inconstant." So what is revolutionary about these *chefs-patron* is perhaps less the cuisine and more the way they managed to set themselves free.

Even up until World War II a restaurant was nearly always run by a *maître d'hôtel* who in turn employed a chef, and only the greatest chefs—names such as Nignon, Dumaine, and André Pic—were held in any regard. Indeed, at the time of Crewe's book there were still chefs who in their youth had been embarassed to admit their profession.

The rise of the *chefs-patron* and their 'new' cuisine reflected the changes not just in cooking but in society itself. The motor car meant more customers were discovering regional cooking. The pace of life had grown more rapid, and big, heavy meals were suddenly outmoded, now that people had no time to exercise away (or sleep off) excess calories. And chefs, after a long history of secrecy and competitiveness, seemed suddenly to develop a new camaraderie, to band together, and to share ideas.

But the thing that truly set them apart was the fact that they were *chefs-patron*; they owned their own restaurants, and with that came the freedom to become jet-setters like Bocuse or stay-at-home perfectionists such as Chapel. Where once chefs had been near slaves, now they could, if they wished, be stars.

Tempting as it may be to lay all of this at the feet of Bocuse's relentless self-promotion, and to assume he dragged his companions (Crewe called them the *bande à Bocuse*) unwillingly into the limelight, ultimately one cannot. Each of the fourteen men featured in *Great Chefs of France* contributed in their own way to making the restaurants of regional France famous, and for the *nouvelle cuisine* which took the world by storm. Those like Pic and Chapel whose own private pursuit of perfection worked in virtual isolation, or Vergé, who was going to be an aviation mechanic but instead found himself flying around the world alongsided Bocuse, each brought a different personality to their *métier*. Each excelled in their own particular way. Each, in their own way, was a star.

Most of those featured in Crewe's book would refute that. Vergé 'admits to enjoying this status enormously, while Bocuse is disengenuous: "While the tap is running," he says, "I might as well sit under it." For the others the only thing which counts is being true to their *métier*, their customers, and above all else their food.

THEY CAME FOR THE FOOD

It was for the food that the world came to these men and their restaurants. After all, three stars in the Guide Michelin indicates that 'here one will find the best cooking in France, worthy of a special journey.'

The world came to them because it had no choice: the food they were making could not be transported, predicated as it was on the daily selection of seasonal ingredients chosen by the chefs themselves (or at least their trusted suppliers) and cooked in a style that combined a classical repertoire with local techniques that, like the restaurant buildings themselves, were handed down through generations.

It was these dozen restaurants which first inspired the notion of the 'gourmet traveller,' because if one wanted to eat Alain Chapel's food, or that of the Troisgros brothers, one had to go to Mionnay or Roanne. They would not come to you.

Things were changing, however, and two chefs in particular, Bocuse and Roger Vergé, were intent on taking their cusine out in to the world, travelling to such far flung places as Japan, Denmark or Mexico in order to consult at restaurants, train chefs or cook one-off meals. Still, they were only ever visitors, and they would always return to their restaurants. But there were others who were prepared to stay.

This page: Chef and restaurant owner Alexandre Dumaine, in his restaurant Hotel De La Cote D'or, Burgundy, 1956.

Salvador Dali once announced a visit to La Cote D'or months ahead. "I shall be coming in the spring." he wrote. "I am Spanish and I want to eat what my king ate in the spring season." He was served a cold saddle of hare accompanied by gooseberry jelly, which, according to the restaurant's files, had been a great hit with Alfonse XIII.

Gualtiero Marchesi

THE ARTIST

" As the father of *nuova cucina*, it was Marchesi who brought the advances of *nouvelle cuisine* to Italy; Marchesi who raised the humble risotto to the level of high art; Marchesi who deconstructed ravioli. "

Marchesi

The title of one of his dishes translates into English as 'fish dripping'. The inspiration behind it, when you see it on the plate, is obvious: the small pieces of fish arranged over a bed of bright yellow sauce and swirled around with touches of iridescent red, vivid green and glistening black are indeed a culinary manifestation of Jackson Pollock's abstract expressionism. Art, it must be acknowledged, is very important to Gualtiero Marchesi.

"I have attempted to bear in mind," he says, "Goethe's assertion that artists 'are not those that say something new but those who know how to say a well-known thing as if it had never been said before."

That Signor Marchesi has certainly done. As the father of *nuova cucina*, it was Marchesi who brought the advances of nouvelle cuisine to Italy; Marchesi who raised the humble risotto to the level of high art; Marchesi who deconstructed ravioli.

"To us," says Giorgio Locatelli, speaking on behalf of all the Italian chefs who follow in his wake, "Gualtiero Marchesi is God."

BETTER LATE THAN NEVER

Even so, he was a late bloomer. Though he was born into a catering family, and by seventeen was cooking ossobuco and risotto alla Milanese in the family's Milan hotel, it was not until 1985, when he was 55 years old, that Marchesi became the first Italian to be awarded three Michelin stars.

It was a long journey, one that took him through his early training in Switzerland and through years of providing traditional food to the vendors at the marketplace opposite the family hotel. Then came what Marchesi calls his 'university education' in Paris, Dijon and, finally the kitchen of the famed Troisgros brothers in Roanne. On the way he met and married a young woman of Sicilian origin, the daughter of a famous soprano, and flirted with the idea of becoming a concert pianist. But in the end cooking was his destiny.

He opened his first restaurant in 1977, on Via Bonvesin de la Riva in Milan, and within six months Michelin had given him his first star. He was the vanguard of the new cuisine. He had travelled to Japan by then, and brought back with him radical ideas of presentation, and was filtering the French techniques he had learned at Troisgros through the traditions of his homeland and his own desire to combine simplicity and complexity in pursuit of the new, the beautiful.

Lofty aims, indeed. But Marchesi has ever been unafraid to make bold statements, both on and off the plate. He is quite happy to claim that a chef "becomes accomplished when he can recognize the quality of a dish without even tasting it, when he simply looks at the plate, because a dish is beautiful if it is good. Beauty is goodness, not beauty *per se*! We are not merchandising mere aesthetics; this Kierkegaardian is interested in the ethical as well—that is, the beautiful that must be good."

It must be said that few chefs would refer to themselves as 'Kierkegaardian', and one wonders what Marchesi's mentors, Jean and Pierre Troisgros, brothers famed for their joviality and lack of pretension, even as they cooked at the pinnacle of *haute cuisine*, would make of it.

But then few chefs would take a dish as traditional, as humble even, as risotto and turn it into art.

RICE BECOMES RISOTTO

Rice was brought to Europe by the Moors, and came to Italy, along with oranges and sugar cane, via their conquest of Sicily in the 9th century. By the 15th century it was growing on the plains of Lombardy, and in 1543 a dish of 'Sicilian-style rice' was served at a banquet organised by one Cristoforo da Messisbugo, a steward of the Este family in Ferrara—a dish which contained egg yolks, grated cheese, pepper, saffron and sugar.

A myth, more charming than plausible, claims that the dish now known as *risotto alla milanese* was created in 1574 by the artist responsible for the stained glass windows in the Cathedral of Milan. Legend has it that he added some saffron, used by him as a pigment, to a dish of rice for his daughter's wedding, and that the guests at the wedding pronounced the result to be 'risus optimus', excellent rice. Which, over time, became 'risotto', defined somewhat vaguely by the Oxford English Dictionary as "a stew or broth made with rice, chicken, onions, butter, etc."

That crucial 'et cetera'. One may make a *risotto al Barolo* using red wine and Borlotti beans, or a *risotto al nero di sepia* with cuttlefish cooked with their ink-sacs intact. The Italians will even allow a strawberry risotto. But for *risotto alla Milanese* it must be saffron, the glorious golden threads that have long been the world's costliest spice.

Marchesi's genius was to take this simple, golden dish and add … gold. A friend of his had given him some gold leaf, and by its simple addition to the presentation he created his classic, and controversial, *Riso, oro, e zefferano*. Rice, gold, and saffron. It became the most controversial, and certainly the most photographed, dish of the *nuova cucina*.

"The work of art," Marchesi says, invoking the spirit of Michelangelo, "is already there: you have to remove the superfluous, not add, to find the essence, or the heart of the essence."

For Marchesi this means taking away the beef stock of the traditional Milanese risotto, along with most of the cheese. And instead of the *mantecatura*, that part of the process where chilled butter and Parmegiano-Reggiano are beaten into the rice, Marchesi mixes in a *beurre blanc* instead. In this way, a little of the cuisine of France comes to Italy.

A few of the pretensions, too, of the *nouvelle cuisine*, and for this Marchesi was derided by some critics. Gold leaf on risotto! Or four mouthfuls of different pasta plated on a mirror. Perhaps not surprising then that his third Michelin star took seven years to come.

Previous spread: Gualtiero Marchesi and chefs in the kitchen of his restaurant in the L'Alberato hotel, Erbusco, in the wine-growing region of Franciacorta, Lombardy.

Opposite: Dripping fish, a 'gastronomic painting' inspired by Jackson Pollock, comprises liquid yellow mayonnaise, liquid green pesto mayonnaise, tomato sauce, black sauce from squid ink, calamari and cockles.

MIRTHFUL MENTORS

But it is somewhat surprising that Marchesi's spiritual fathers should have been the *frères* Troisgros. It is true that their training reflected his own, learning to cook for workmen and travellers in the hotel run by their father in the town of Roanne, central France. From there they were sent to the kitchens of the Lucas-Carton and La Pyramide, still under Point, where humour and unpretentiousness, as well as formidable cooking, were inculcated in them. For example, when asked how they achieved three Michelin stars, Pierre was apt to laugh, saying "It has something to do with the cooking, I believe."

Yet learn Marchesi did. "While I was there," he recalls, "everything they did was like going to school for me, down to the way they handled a frying pan." Nor should it be implied that Marchesi is without humour. His 2006 book, which encapsulates his career and his philosophy, bears the title 'The Marchesi Code'. But it seems unlikely that a customer ever left his restaurant with a champagne cork tied with string to the belt of his raincoat, such as many a patron of *Les Freres Troisgros* did. Their legacy, continued in a direct line from the great Point himself, lives on in Marchesi's passion for his art.

"Whatever ingredients I'm using," he says, "I want to give them a certain nobility, and I feel that this is how this can best be expressed … when I visit a museum and see something I like, I'll try to translate the feeling that it gives me directly onto the plate."

A maxim from one of his favourite artists, Paul Klee, who maintained that art was found 'between the paint and the canvas' best sums up Marchesi's approach. That, and an example.

One day, he was served some overcooked ravioli, which split open on his plate. Marchesi was struck then by the idea that things, traditions, could be modified. No longer need ravioli be a vehicle for using up the leftover meat from the day before. It could be the vehicle for something new, literally and figuratively. The result was his groundbreaking open ravioli—two superimposed squares of pasta filled scallops—which in turn opened up even further vistas of what pasta could be. It could be served with foie gras, truffles, caviar or raw seafood. It might even be served cold, shocking indeed in a culture where pasta is always—always—served hot.

And in another unexpected move, Marchesi closed the doors of his three-star restaurant in 1993 and moved to the country, sixty kilometres east of Milan in the heart of rural Lombardy. At the Ristorante di Erbusco in the small, luxurious Albareta Hotel, he created a forum where he might pursue his vision of a 'total cuisine' that is typified by attention to every detail and inspired by his love of art and his desire to reinterpret the traditional and familiar in a new light. "It is important to respect tradition," he says. "Only then can you move forward."

This page: Skewered snails with polenta and fennel (far left); cold spaghetti with caviar and chives (left); serving turbot baked in a salt crust (below).

Overleaf: A selection of appetisers served in the dining room of the Restaurant Gualtiero Marchesi. The restaurant is in the L'Alberata hotel, a nineteenth century luxury villa.

Rice, Gold & Saffron

Melt six tablespoons of butter in a medium saucepan and sauté a small onion that has been finely diced. Add 2½ cups of Carnaroli rice and stir to coat with the butter. Stir in some dry white wine and allow to evaporate.

Heat a good quantity of light vegetable stock and add a quarter of a teaspoon of saffron. Add the stock to the rice one cupful at a time, stirring constantly, until it has been absorbed. The risotto should be still slightly liquid, the grains of rice firm to the bite.

Add two tablespoons of Parmigiano-Reggiano and some ground white pepper. Spread the risotto over four flat plates and arrange a square of 24 carat gold leaf in the centre of each plate. Serve warm.

Form

THE ART OF CUISINE

On a hot, sunny day in 1931 an artist, at home with a headache while his wife was out shopping, found himself staring at a half-eaten round of Camembert that had gone runny in the heat. That night he dreamed of clocks. The next day he returned to an unfinished painting on which he had been working, a bare landscape with some rocky cliffs in the background and a tree on a platform, and added to it the draped and melted faces of pocket watches, thus creating one of the most striking images of the twentieth century.

If this anecdote illustrates anything at all, it is that an artist will take his or her inspiration from wherever it might be found. A chef may be inspired by a painting just as a painter may be inspired by cheese. Indeed, Henri de Toulouse-Lautrec was as passionate about food as he was about painting. And where Salvador Dali, in the spirit of surrealism, may have claimed that his favourite food was lobster with chocolate sauce, Toulouse-Lautrec was far more serious, to

the point that he intended to bring out his own book of recipes.

Unfortunately he died--at only 36, of a combination of alcoholism and syphilis--before his book came to pass. But his art dealer, Maurice Joyant, found Toulouse-Lautrec's recipes among his papers, and eventually they were published as *The Art of Cuisine*. In it are recipes for such exotic fare as a heron cooked over a fire of vine leaves, fresh squirrel, and even "Saint sur le Gril", Saint on the Grill, which requires the assistance of the Vatican in procuring a real saint, along with more genteel dishes: calves liver with prunes, young wild pigeon with olives, or steak à la Toulouse.

The recipe for steak à la Toulouse gives an indication of Lautrec's culinary style. One requires three *tranches* of sirloin. Smother the steaks in Dijon mustard, then pile them up, one on top of the other, and grill them in unison on a vine-wood fire until their edges begin to blacken. Now take them all out, and throw away the top steak and the bottom steak. Because, according to Lautrec, only the one in the middle will be perfectly cooked.

ART OR ARCHITECTURE

Lautrec was an artist who liked to cook. Carême believed that cooking was in fact a branch of architecture, which he believed to be the most noble of the arts. Escoffier more than anything believed that cooking was a noble *profession*, and by his efforts made it so.

For most of *le Patrons*, just as for Signor Marchesi, cooking was something they were born into. To define what it was that began to elevate *their* cooking into the realms of art is perhaps as difficult as defining what art itself is. Which is "one of the most elusive of the traditional problems of human culture," according to British philosopher Richard Wollheim.

But Wikipedia, the fount of all modern knowledge, does a reasonable job of it. "Art is the process or product of deliberately arranging elements in a way that appeals to the senses or emotions," it says, and by this definition the cooking of the great chefs more than qualifies. A modern commentator on Marchesi's dish of egg, truffle and leek with herb sauce, for example, omits any talk of taste: "the orange of the egg yolk, the black of the truffle and the precise folds of the leek, like contours on a map, creating an amazing visual expression." Though of course we presume it tastes amazing, too.

Still there are many who would argue that cooking—mere *food*—might aspire to the condition of art. Clive Bell, in his book *Art* of 1914, coined the term 'significant form' to describe a certain, distinctive "combination of lines and colours" which makes an object a work of art.

Bell was only concerned with the visual arts, and their ability to produce a distinctive aesthetic experience in the viewer. He called this feeling "aesthetic emotion." He also believed that, ultimately, the value of anything whatever lies only in its being a means to "good states of mind."

Combinations of lines and colours. Aesthetic emotion. Good states of mind. All of which, as anyone who has dined on the results of a great chef's work knows, are all intrinsic to that experience. And though Mr Bell would doubtless have been aghast at the thought, cooking is one of the few ways in which all five of the human senses may be excited simultaneously, contributing to the 'aesthetic emotion' in all the possible, or at least physical, ways.

THE 'GOLD LEAF' FACTOR

But it is only 'artists' who aspire to be artists. A chef, even one such as Marchesi, still wants only to cook. To have fun. (Jean Troisgros believed that he lived better than a Rothschild. Who else, he would say, can sit down at any moment of the day and say, 'Bring me a pot of caviar and a bottle of champagne.') The art comes simply as a result of flawless technique applied to superlative ingredients.

No … it is not that simple. There is another element to the equation, that indefinable "x" factor which, in every field of human endeavour, separates the great from the merely good. The 'gold leaf' factor, in the case of Marchesi. The showmanship of Bocuse. Indeed each *le Patrons* had or still have it, and they in turn handed it down to the best of their disciples.

An artist, Andy Warhol once said, is someone who produces things that people don't need to have but that he or she—for some reason—thinks it would be a good idea to give them. Alain Chapel, who many consider the greatest of all the chefs-patrons, and who died tragically young, in 1990 at the age of 53, decided that people needed a *gateau de foies blonds,* a silken, creamy, mousselike creation made with pureed chicken livers and beef marrow and served with a sauce combining lobster and cream. In 1977, a review for the *New York Times* called the dish "one of the absolute cooking glories of this generation," claiming the dish to be Chapel's "ultimate triumph."

We notice that the reviewer did not once mention art. He did not need to.

Dramatic black and white presentations from two contemporary Italian chefs.

Opposite: Tongue-fish, crème fraîche and caviar, David Scavin chef, Combal. Zero restaurant in Rivoli, Piedmont, Italy.

Left: Cuttlefish with liquorice and minced olives, Emanuele Scarello chef, Agli Amici restaurant, Godia, Friuli Venezia Giulia, Italy.

Albert & Michel Roux

THE BROTHERS

" The reputation of the brothers Roux rests on a few essential things, not least their ability to cook in the grand style. "

Roux

If it had not been Albert and Michel Roux then it would have been someone else; the English channel is only 21 miles (34 kilometres) wide between Dover and Calais, and sooner or later another Frenchman would have crossed it, determined to bring gastronomy to the United Kingdom. But would that Frenchman have eventually been awarded an OBE, or voted the most influential chef in Britain? One wonders. Certainly the task of teaching the British how to cook—and eat—must have seemed a daunting one, and perhaps it could never have been achieved by one single man. After all, as Michel notes, "it was the culinary Stone Age."

But Mike and Bert, as the vendors at London's markets affectionately called them, turned out to be just the men for the job.

CHICKEN AND EGG

It has been claimed that the chicken is simply the egg's way of producing another egg. That may even be true. We do know that the word 'egg' derives from an Indo-European root which means 'bird', and that each is contained in the other, which is why the egg is the perfect vehicle to carry the weight of religious symbolism that is attached to it. It is also a perfectly proportioned package of nutrition that comes in its own convenient carry-case.

You could argue that the Roux brothers' restaurants, first Le Gavroche and then the Waterside Inn, were simply means for them to create more great chefs. You could even argue, not too fancifully, that Albert and Michel are essentially the same chef divided into two separate bodies.

Witness their careers. Born five years apart, both trained first as *patissiers* before serving in the French army in Algeria. Both were employed at the British Embassy in Paris. Each then went to cook for a wealthy private employer, Albert for Peter Cazalet, the Queen Mother's horse trainer, and Michel for Cécile de Rothschild. After opening Le Gavroche they would rotate between kitchen and front of house week by week, until the time Michel took over the Waterside Inn. The egg, finally, had cracked.

There was plenty of work to do before then. "We knew nothing of the British indifference to food," Albert says, "because we had only cooked for the rich."

AWAITING THE SOUFFLÉ

They were bankrolled by the rich, too. The Cazalet's had invested in Le Gavroche, and on its opening night in 1967, situated as it was then in a small building on the corner of Lower Sloane Street, it is claimed that Ava Gardner, Robert Redford and Charlie Chaplin were among the 150 in attendance.

Whether they indeed were scarcely matters. The place was packed with society *demi-monde*, and the soon to be British Ambassador to France predicted a radiant future. He was not wrong. It was the first restaurant in Britain to be awarded one, two, then three Michelin stars, and has been continuously successful now for forty years. The British may have been indifferent to food, but they were not indifferent to Le Gavroche.

An anecdote from Michel's autobiography serves to illustrate. Albert had created the twice-cooked *soufflé Suissesse* that was to become a signature, and already it was wildly popular. One regular customer did not even bother to order, but simply sat at their regular table and waited for it to come. On a particular evening in their first year, when Michel's English had improved just enough that he was prepared to put on his dinner jacket and welcome customers, an elegant and determined young woman came thrusting in, even though the restaurant was full. "I pursued her and even took her by the arm. I told her she could not come in, but she replied, 'I'll

have my usual table,' pointing to one that was already occupied." A horrified *maitre d'* had to intervene, explaining that this was the Queen's sister. Michel, however, would not be swayed. She had not booked. He was sorry, but…

Despite such treatment, Princess Margaret continued to be a regular customer. Such is the power of success, and of soufflé.

A CRIME TO EAT WELL

The food at Le Gavroche—'the urchin'—has always been in the grand French style. Dishes like lobster mousse with caviar and champagne butter sauce, duck foie gras with truffles, and omelette Rothschild have been on the menu for much of its forty years. It hasn't always been easy preparing them. In the 1960s and 1970s it was literally a crime to eat well in Britain.

"When we opened up you couldn't get foie gras or poulet de Bresse in this country," Albert recalls, "so my wife drove to France to smuggle it back in." Sometimes Madame Roux was stopped by customs; she would simply turn around and try again through a different port. Compare that with Bocuse, who is reported to have hauled great slabs of American beef past French customs officers that, because of his enormous public stature, simply turned their heads, and you will appreciate their tenacity.

The Rouxs had stature, too. The newspapers reported Le Gavroche's opening as one of the events of the year. But then, in terms of British gastronomy, they had no competition, and in Albert they had a man whose business mind has been likened to a steel trap.

"You have know whether there is demand for the product," he says. "Then you've got to build up your staff because they are the ones who make it." Silvano Giraldin, the *maitre d',* is a case in point. He has been there for 39 of its 40 years, winning as many awards for his front-of-house skills as the kitchen has for its food.

Indeed, as Point had done a half-century earlier, the Roux brothers have trained the generation of young chefs who went on dominate, indeed reinvent, British cooking. Marco Pierre White, Gordon Ramsay and

Opposite: French-born restaurateur brothers Albert and Michel Roux (centre left and right respectively), with their sons Michel Jr (far left) and Alain (far right), 1998.

Pierre Koffman of La Tante Claire are only the three most famous of their protegées. There are many, many more, including those who were never employees but trained in France under the Roux Brothers Scholarship. It is for this, more so than their food, that they will likely be remembered most.

BREAKING EGGS

Ultimately a single restaurant, for Albert at least, was not enough. They had already opened a *charcuterie* and two more restaurants when in 1972 they purchased the lease on a Thames-side pub in the village of Bray called the Waterside Inn. They installed a gifted young Pierre Koffman as chef, and the restaurant's reputation quickly grew. Fortunate, for the family itself was fracturing. Indeed the rivalry between them—the sort of rivalry that only two brothers are capable of—is legendary.

"I am the entrepreneur of the family," Albert says, "much against the will of my brother. His idea was one restaurant with his brother until he died. Michel was devastated when I started opening new places." Or perhaps it was when he chose to take sole credit for Le Gavroche's newly-acquired third star.

Whichever. By 1986 they had decided to separate out the business; Albert would take Le Gavroche and the other holdings, and Michel would get the Waterside Inn. The deal, it is said, was sealed with a kiss.

The Waterside Inn had by then become Britain's second three-star restaurant. It had hosted private parties for the British Royal family, catered to guests from King Hussein of Jordan to the Rolling Stones. Michel wasn't getting a *bad* deal, exactly; in 1990 he was able

to purchase the property freehold, and it has maintained its reputation as one of Britain's great restaurants.

Le Gavroche fared less well. In 1991, on his fifty-fifth birthday, Albert Roux handed over the kitchen to his son—ironically named Michel, Jr.—and a mere two years later the restaurant had been downgraded to two stars. As things rise, so must they fall. But not too far.

ALL RISE

The reputation of the brothers Roux rests on a few essential things, not least their ability to cook in the grand style. Certainly they were not innovators. But then they did not need to be; there are certain fundamentals that will not be denied.

Take the soufflé. It always seems a challenge, an event, and so to diners it is always a delight; there is this idea that its preparation is difficult, its chemistry volatile, and should you open the oven door for *one second* the enterprise is doomed. But this simply isn't so: soufflés are reliable and resistant. One of the miracles of the egg, and there are many, is that once air is trapped within the beaten whites it wants very much to stay there. What's more, it is the air *and* the moisture within the mixture that causes it to rise. Once the correct mixture is made one need not be precious.

This is why Albert Roux's *soufflé Suissesse* has stayed upright, so to speak, for forty years. You can, as he did, bake them once briefly to set them. Then, if you wish to unmould them, set them in a small dish in a sea of cream, sprinkle them with Cheddar and Gruyère or Emmenthal cheeses and then bake them again until golden and airy, you can. Just like you can teach the British to cook.

This page:
Le Gavroche, founded
by Albert and Michel
Roux in 1967, is now run
by Michel Roux Jr. Dishes
served include lobster
and roquefort gratin (left),
souffle suissesse (right)
and spice-crusted foie gras
(below).

Overleaf: Originally
located in Lower Sloane
Street, Chelsea,
Le Gavroche is now
in Upper Brook Street,
London W1. It is luxurious
yet comfortable, as befits
a 40-yr-old institution.

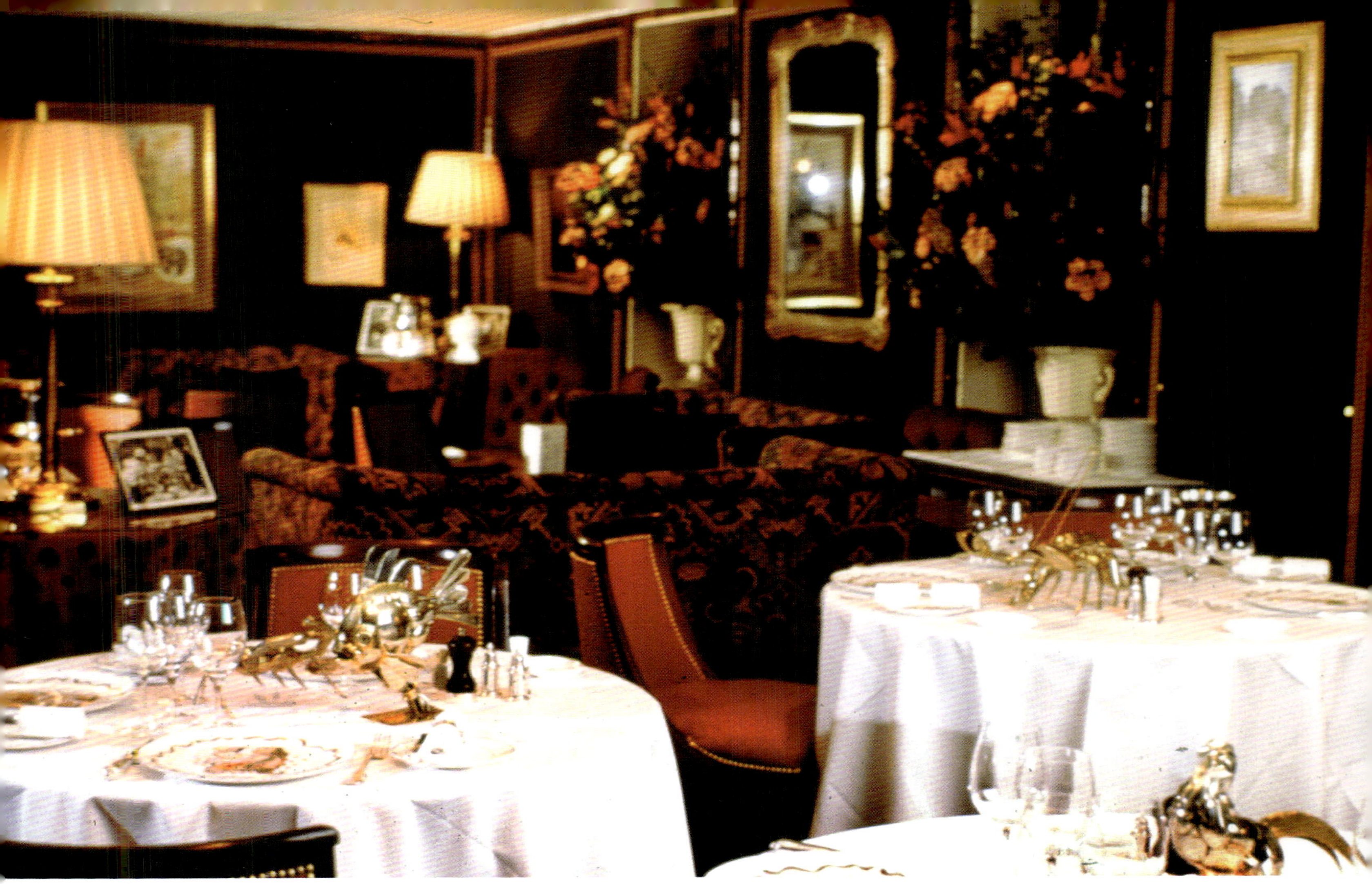

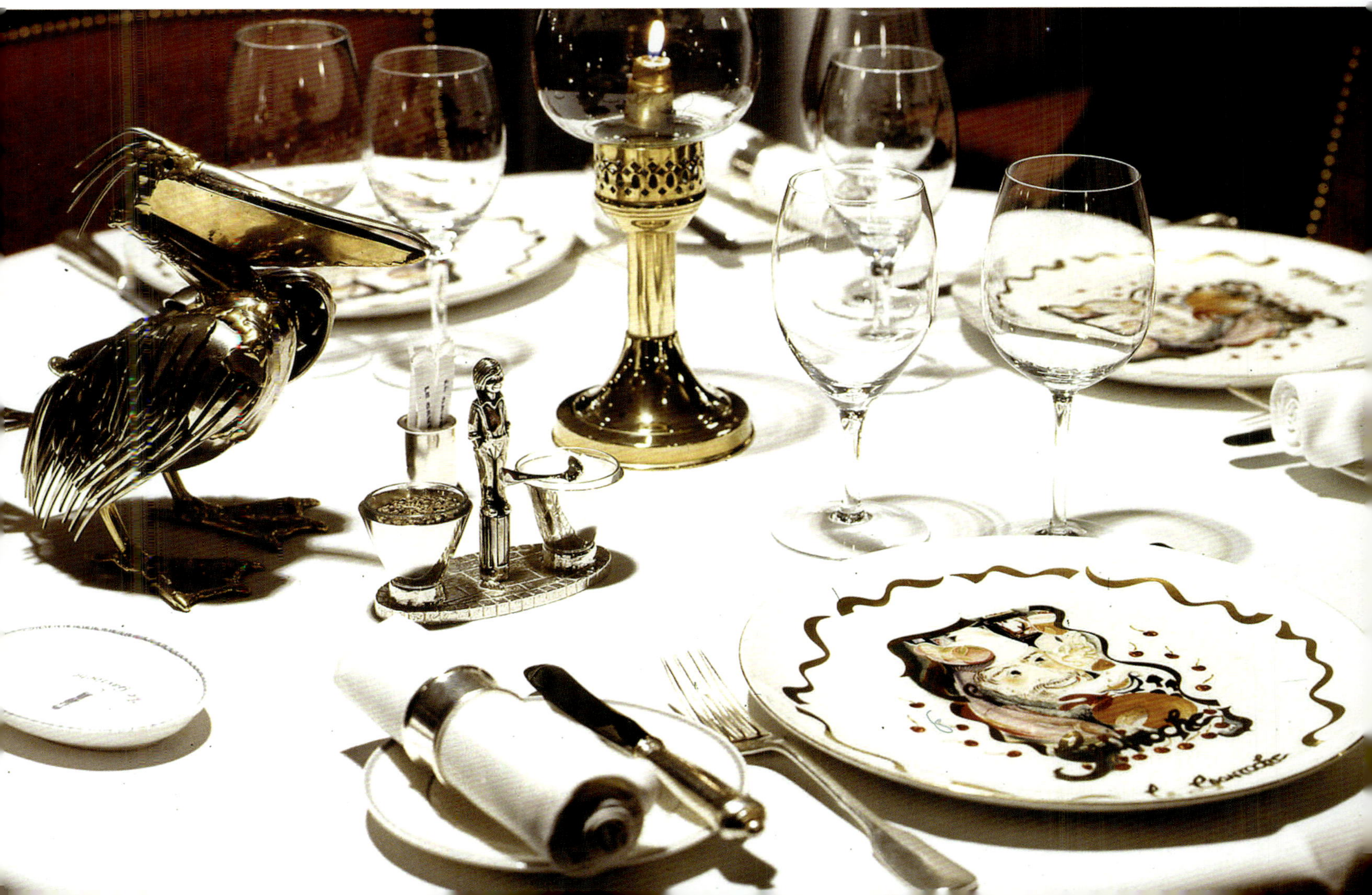

Soufflé Suissesse

Preheat the oven to 200° C (400° F). Melt 65 g butter in a small saucepan set over low heat. Using a small wire whisk, stir an equal amount of flour. Cook gently for 2 to 3 minutes, stirring continously. Take the pan off the heat and leave the roux to cool slightly. Bring 700 ml of milk to the boil, then pour it over the cooled roux, whisking all the time. Set the pan over a high heat and, stirring continuously, bring the mixture to the boil and cook for 3 minutes.

Take the pan off the heat and stir in 5 egg yolks. Season to taste with salt and pepper. Dot the surface with 1 tablespoon of butter cut into small pieces to prevent a skin from forming. Set aside at room temperature.

Meanwhile, chill 12 round 8 cm tartlet tins in the refrigerator or freezer for a few minutes, Remove and immediately grease them generously with softened butter and arrange on a baking sheet.

Pour 1 litre of double cream into a large gratin dish. Lightly salt the cream, then warm it gently without allowing it to boil. Beat 6 egg whites with a pinch of salt until they form stiff peaks. Pour the soufflé mixture into a wide-mouthed bowl. Using a whisk, quickly beat in about one-third of the beaten egg, then using a spatula, carefully fold in the remainder. Using a tablespoon, heap up the mixture in the tartlet tins to form 12 moulds.

Bake the soufflés in the preheated oven for 3 minutes, until the tops begin to turn golden. Remove from the oven and, protecting your hands, turn each soufflés into the dish of warm cream. Sprinkle grated Gruyère or Emmenthal cheese over the soufflés and return to the oven for 5 minutes.

Serve immediately.

Technique

WHY THE MARKET IS NOT ENOUGH

 for all the others, I used to think that, with their humourless expressions, they had missed their vocation. They would have made good undertakers."

Such were the traders at London's Covent Garden vegetable market, according to Michel Roux. Almost to a man, he says, they seemed lazy, with little interest in their customers. It was reflected in their produce, which was "enormous and lifeless," where it was available at all. Even in 1969, he tells us, courgettes were considered a luxury, and therefore unavailable. So too were many other things that he had known in France: button mushrooms, tiny onions, fresh young carrots, little blue turnips or extra-fine beans were not to be had for love nor money.

The Billingsgate fish market and the meat market at Smithfield fared better in his estimation. Billingsgate offered monkfish, salmon, sole, turbot, bass, eels and carp, all fresh-eyed and pink-gilled, direct from the sea. Shellfish was plentiful and cheap—the domestic demand was then so small that much, ironically, ended up on the Continent. The vendors there were cheerier, too, and the porters, dressed in waterproof coats, fisherman's boots and flat, rigid hats, still carried the lighter items perched on their heads.

At Smithfield, the porters pulled carts laden with half a tonne of meat down narrow aisles, and one needed one's wits about one. The produce was of a standard, with vendors putting aside a case of plump squab pigeons or a particularly good lamb for a customer who wanted only the best. A jerrycan of pig's blood saved from the abbatoir might also be had, though "only at the offal counters was I disappointed," Roux says, with sweetbreads and kidneys often old, shrivelled and unappetising.

SOMETHING FROM NOTHING

The French provincial chefs had no such problem. Those that were situated near Lyon had access to one of the country's great markets (now renamed *Les Halles de Lyon-Paul Bocuse*), while those that were not still had access to the finest produce the growers of France had to offer. Suppliers could be relied upon to deliver only the freshest fish, fruit, and vegetables. Even the chickens were guaranteed to be at their peak—producers of Bresse chickens test that their birds are ready by parting the breast feathers and blowing onto the breast; if a certain vein bulges then the bird is ready for the table. Truffles and foie gras could be sourced without difficulty.

Such luxuries were unavailable to the Roux brothers. They took what they could get, sourced those items such as vegetables which they could get legitimately from France, and took to smuggling for the rest. And if they were forced to make do with what produce they found, at least they had what they brought with them: technique.

Carême's *L'Art de la cuisine* ran to five thick volumes. Escoffier's great work compiled over 5,000 recipes. Even Julia Child's 1961 consolidation of French technique for the American public, *Mastering the Art of French Cooking*, ran to almost seven hundred pages. (Her instructions for making an omelette took up twelve of those!) And as she writes in her introduction to the anniversary edition, many of the more onerous tasks and techniques have been simplified by the arrival of machines such as the food processor.

Michel and Albert Roux were steeped in those techniques, and in an England where food was dramatically less sophisticated— the core of the culinary tradition was home cooking—it was only natural that they would stand out.

Of course, the traffic had never been only one way: both Carême and Escoffier had cooked in England. Indeed Escoffier was there for twenty years, though it must be remembered that in that time he refused to learn English, for fear that it might coarsen his cooking! Even so, the French had long admired the skill of the English in roasting meat, which they called *rosbif*, even if the meat in question happened to

be lamb. The words *à l'anglais* became common on menus, used to describe vegetables, meat and fish prepared in a variety of straightforward ways. *Crème anglaise*, English custard, is a fundamental preparation in classic cuisine. And perhaps most ironically, an Englishman named Richard Lucas opened a *Taverne anglaise* in Paris in 1832, its menu featuring roast beef and Yorkshire pudding. The establishment became the Restaurant Lucas and subsequently the Lucas-Carton, where Bocuse himself, among a number of others, trained.

1001 TECHNIQUES

Yet no one could deny the superiority of French technique. Talleyrand himself, enlarging on a quote of Voltaire's, claimed that "England has three sauces and three hundred and sixty religions, whereas France has three religions and three hundred and sixty sauces."

A less exaggerated comparison might be cuts of meat: an English butcher would separate a pig into nine distinct cuts, while a Frenchman would create sixteen; a Frenchman could expect to use one of twenty-four cuts of beef, while an English chef had only fifteen.

And if thanks to Escoffier there were no longer three hundred and sixty sauces, there were at least that many techniques for a French chef to master. The making of quenelles, those elongated ovals shaped using two spoons, for example. Or rillettes, a preparation of pork,

rabbit or poultry cooked in lard, pounded to a smooth paste, then potted and served cold—the trick being to achieve a fine texture and deep colour by virtually caramelizing the meat during the cooking. Mousses, galantines, terrines or *pâté en croute* all employed different techniques.

To illustrate, the *pâté de canard en croûte* is a boned duck stuffed with forcemeat, sewn up again, browned, wrapped in pastry and then baked. But if the same boned and stuffed duck were instead wrapped in a damp towel, poached in meat stock, cooled with a weight over it, chilled, and then glazed with jellied stock, it would be rather a *galantine de canard*.

The classical repertoire is filled with such dishes, many of them far more complicated. As Michel Roux writes in his autobiography, 'It was only in the great private houses such as

recipes as *Millefeuille d'ecrevisses*, which is a simple crayfish cream layered between sheets of puff pastry, or fresh foie gras cooked and then served cold inside a pepper jelly, a simpler and more effective version of the galantine above.

THE OLD AND THE NEW

The Roux brothers did not take *nouvelle cuisine* to England; their cooking, though not necessarily old-fashioned, did not reflect the same kind of adventurousness that Guérard's possessed. It was not what their customers wanted. Unused to eating good French food, they wanted the traditional—twice-baked *soufflés*, *pot-au-feu*, jugged hare—before moving on to the cutting-edge.

In Lyons, having sought out Paul Bocuse, Michel Roux recalls accompanying him to the market, and how the vendors were devoted to him and would reserve the best of their produce just for him. In the same way, the English traders at Smithfield and Billingsgate had begun to do the same, putting aside a case of red mullet or some fresh sardines that they could have sold a hundred times over, because they recognised that the Roux brothers' success and inspiration depended on the variety, quality and freshness of their raw materials.

Ingredients, technique and inspiration. These are the three pillars of cuisine. Only the most partisan would insist that French cuisine is superior to all others, for this is patently untrue. But as Julia Child wrote some forty years after her first, and most important, book was published, "if you are thoroughly skilled in French techniques, because the repertoire is so vast, you have the background for almost any type of cuisine. In other words, and at the risk of creating mayhem in some circles, I think you are better as an Italian, Mexican, or even Chinese cook when you have a solid French foundation."

Julia Child did not create mayhem, because her comment is eminently reasonable. What she did do, however, was help plant the seed of cuisine in America just as surely as the brothers Roux had done in England.

[the Rothschilds], where time and money were irrelevant, that many dishes of the past would be cooked. Many would be wonderful to recreate today if we had the time…' He tells of a favourite *hors d'oeuvre* of his employer, which she would call 'an easy little dish,' that involved making brioches, a chicken purée, poached eggs and a truffle sauce that alone took about two hours to make, as one of its ingredients was veal stock. Only *then* could the whole thing be assembled.

It was elaborate constructions such as these that Point and his followers had succeeded in doing away with, even though they retained the essential techniques used in creating their separate elements. Mainly they simplified, reducing the number of elements in any given dish, or applying unusual techniques to new ingredients. In Michel Guérard's *Cuisine Gourmande*, published in 1978, he gives such

Left: Chefs Michel Guerard and Paul Bocuse test cheeses at a French market.

Alice Waters

THE EARTH MOTHER

"For its entire life Chez Panisse has been for Waters a platform from which to push one irreducible message: food should be local, organic and beautiful."

There is a story of a young woman and her travelling companion who, somewhere on the high plains of Anatolia, pitched their tent beside a herd of goats. The young woman had a degree in French Cultural Studies from Berkeley. She had recently completed training at the Montessori School in London. She was going to be a high school teacher back in America. But first she was going to France. Everyone knows that the quickest way from London to France is not through Turkey. But Alice Waters chose to take the long way—they were driving a Morris Minor!—and by the time she returned to California all thoughts of being a teacher had vanished.

A small token of charity had forever changed her perspective. "Somebody had put a bowl of fresh goat's milk under the flap of our tent," she recalled in 2006. "We never saw who."

She remembers being deeply affected by the anonymous gift. The occasion for this recollection, and others, was the 35th birthday of her restaurant, Chez Panisse. It had recently been awarded its first Michelin star. "You know, I've always wanted a little one-star restaurant," she said. "When I was in France, they were the ones I loved the most."

IT'S A LIVING THING

A cheesemaker will tell you that cheese is a living, growing organism. A nutritionist will tell you that a live dairy animal will produce the nutritional equivalent, or more, of that same animal slaughtered for meat, every year. A historian will tell you that evidence of dairying can be traced back to 5000 BC, at least. And every one will agree with renowned food writer and scientist Harold McGee that, of humankind's great achievements, cheese is one of the greatest.

It is almost too simple. The earliest of shepherds would have discovered that the milk which remains after the cream has been separated will naturally curdle into a thick yoghurt. Draining separates this into solid curds and liquid whey. Add salt to the fresh curd and, presto, you have a simple, long-keeping cheese. Then it takes only a few refinements of technique—and four or five millenia—and you have before you the glory that is Stilton. (Or Roquefort. Or Camembert, depending on your taste.)

COME BACK

Alice Waters came back to Berkeley a changed woman. With a small group of friends, all of whom knew nothing about running a restaurant, she borrowed $10,000 from her father and opened Chez Panisse on August 28, 1971. It offered a single *prix-fixe* menu which cost $3.95. Dessert on one early menu was a single peach.

"I don't think she single-handedly changed the way America eats," says one critic. Which is true: she couldn't have done it without her father. And the times *were* right: this *was* Berkeley, California in the early 1970s, the very epicentre of the American cultural revolution.

"It's hard to know whether we were just expressing what was there or whether we started it all, but something happened back then that none of us could have predicted," says one of Waters' early partners. Certainly no one knew then that Alice Waters would become the most politically powerful chef in America, with celebrity patrons from Bill Clinton to the Dalai Lama counted as regulars.

As she says, "I never imagined it anything beyond a little neighborhood restaurant."

THE BIRTH OF CHEESE

Not long after the discovery of the basic process of cheese-making in Central Asia and the Middle East it became apparent that the texture of the curd became more pliable, more cohesive, if curdling took place in an animal stomach, or even with pieces of stomach in the same container; such cheeses probably resembled a modern brine-cured feta.

The technique, and the stomach extract, now called rennet, made its way west and north into Europe. And in these cooler regions it was slowly realised that the curds would keep just as well with less souring of the milk, less brining or salting. In the presence of this lowered acidity and salt the natural microbes and their enzymes could flourish, and in the words of Harold McGee, cheese became "capable of pronounced development and change; it entered the cyclical world of birth, maturation and decline." By Roman times cheese as we know it had been born.

CALIFORNIA CUISINE

A grilled sardine wrapped in a fig leaf; a small pile of pinto beans covered by a slice of pork that has been roasted in olive oil; ice milk infused with peach leaves; each ingredient the best in California, probably organic, and probably from a small farm no more than an hour or two away.

"She is utterly medieval in her resistance to the idea of bigger is better," says one supplier.

It is true. For its entire life Chez Panisse has been for Waters a platform from which to push one irreducible message: food should be local, organic and beautiful. To Waters, food is politics, and politics is food. If you change how people eat, you change a nation. And many would argue that she has.

Today, thanks largely to Waters' original emphasis on the importance of locally grown produce, thousands of community farmers' markets are strung from Miami, Florida to Anchorage, Alaska. But it is the personal relationship with her suppliers—75 on the approved list—that is most important.

"I eat a piece of bread knowing that the wheat is produced in a way that is sustainable, that the starter for the bread and the salt are produced in a way that is sustainable, and the people that are producing these products are being paid a living wage. The values of the food have to be understood to make that food real food… nourishing food."

Opposite: Chez Panisse, in Berkeley, California, is known as the birthplace of California cuisine, a style credited to its co-founder Alice Waters.

Michelin awarded Chez Panisse a one-star rating in its guide to San Francisco Bay Area dining in 2006 and 2007.

DIVERSITY RULES

Like any art, cheesemaking progressed. The monasteries and feudal estates worked steadily at clearing land for grazing, and by the Middle Ages communities across all of Europe had developed cheesemaking techniques to suit their particular landscape, climate and market. The small, soft, perishable cheeses could be made from the milk from a single farm, and did not travel far. Large, hard cheeses needed the volumes that only a cooperative such as the Gruyère *fruiteries* could provide; but they kept indefinitely, and could be sold in distant regions.

The result was diversity—one will find up to 50 traditional cheeses in any given country. France, thanks to its size and range of climates, has several hundred. And cheese travelled; the French court received shipments from Germany, and cheeses from Parma in Italy were already renowned throughout Europe. By Elizabethan times Cheddar, Stilton and Cheshire were famous. In the 19th century Brillat-Savarin expressed his famous dictum that a dessert without cheese "is like a beautiful woman who is missing an eye."

SHE'S ALRIGHT

"If it were up to Alice, she wouldn't charge anything," says Chez Panisse's service manager. "She just wants everyone to have a good, pure meal."

But she wants more than that, this petite sixty-something woman in a cloche hat who has more than once been called 'the mother of American cooking.' Her Chez Panisse Foundation, patrons of which include Mikhail Baryshnikov and Meryl Streep, now spends a million dollars annually on its various programmes, the most important being the Edible Schoolyard, that puts gardens and kitchens in to schools to teach children where food *really* comes from.

"Really, this is about the human values we all have in common," Waters says. "We all have to eat, and if we eat within a certain set of values, we begin to communicate those values to one another."

THE CYCLE OF LIFE

If cheese had a 'golden age' it was probably between the late 19th and early 20th centuries; techniques were perfected, local styles had reached their apotheosis, and the railroads transported country-made products to the city while they were still at their best.

Decline was inevitable. The rise in industrialisation, particularly in the United States, saw cheese become mass-produced, while science bought standardisation in the form of pure microbial cultures for curdling and ripening cheese. What had once been a truly organic process, where each cheese was essentially an expression of local conditions and regional flora, was now the province of the factory. And after World War II, when agricultural lands as well as economies had been ravaged, consumers were grateful for whatever they could get. Inexpensive, standardised cheese was here to stay.

But there were people who believed things didn't have to be that way.

In Sonoma, California, in the late 1970s there was a young woman who kept some pet goats. Inspired by a home-style French *chevre* she had tasted, she decided to milk her goats and handcraft some cheese herself. Not long afterwards, a chef called Alice Waters discovered that cheese and put it on the menu at her Berkeley restaurant.

Time went by.

Thirty years later that same handcrafted cheese from Sonoma is in supermarkets and on plates all across America. That Berkeley restaurant remains a beacon. On the high plains of Anatolia tents are still pitched beside herds of goats. The circle remains unbroken.

ALICE WATERS

THE ART OF SIMPLE FOOD

Notes, Lessons, and Recipes from a Delicious Revolution

This page and overleaf: Alice Waters is a strong proponent of using farm-raised, seasonally fresh ingredients in her French-meets-Californian cuisine.

Overleaf, below: Alice Waters helped create The Edible Schoolyard at the Martin Luther King, Jr. Middle School, in Berkeley, California, consisting of a one-acre organic garden and a kitchen-classroom.

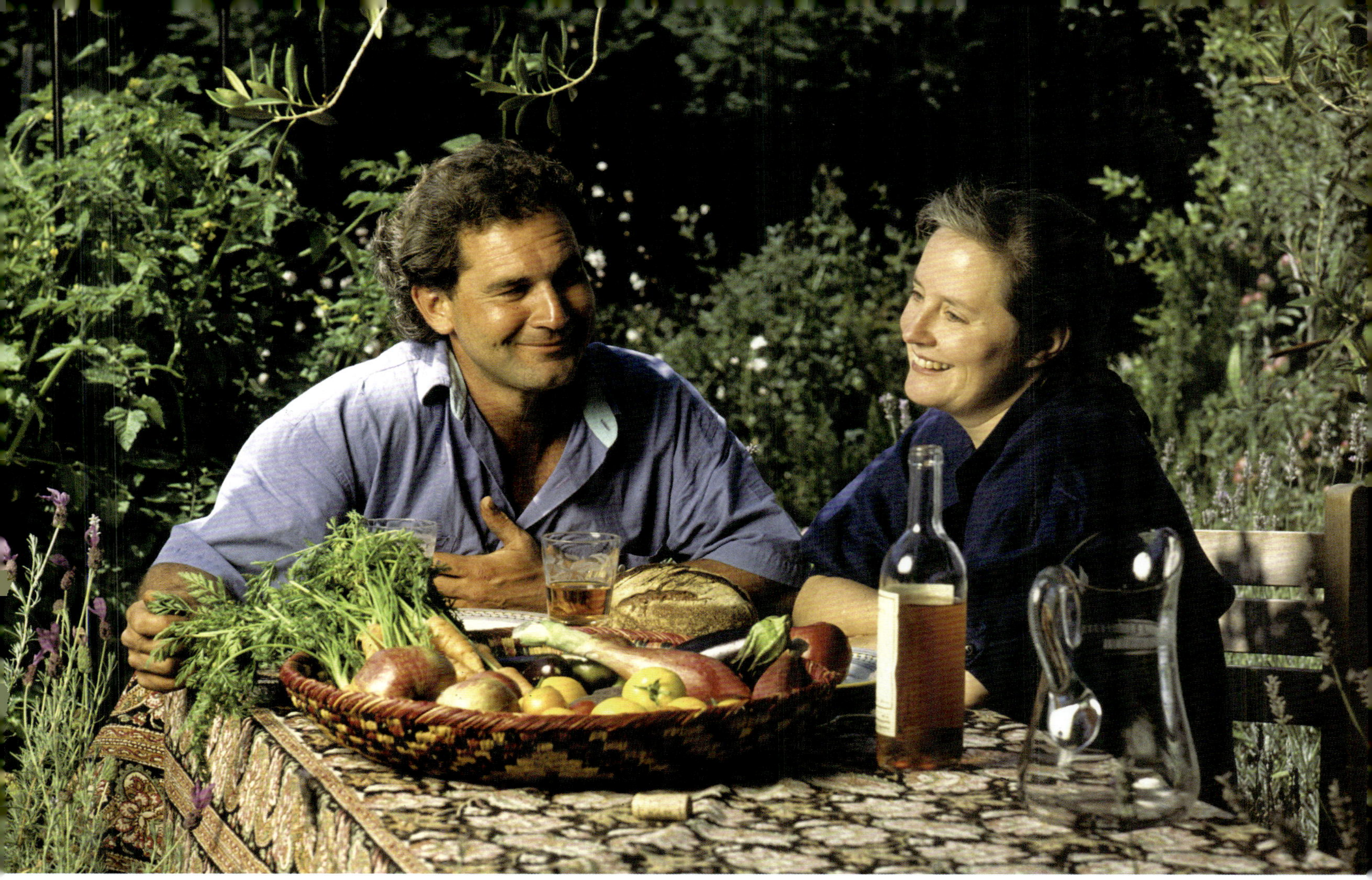

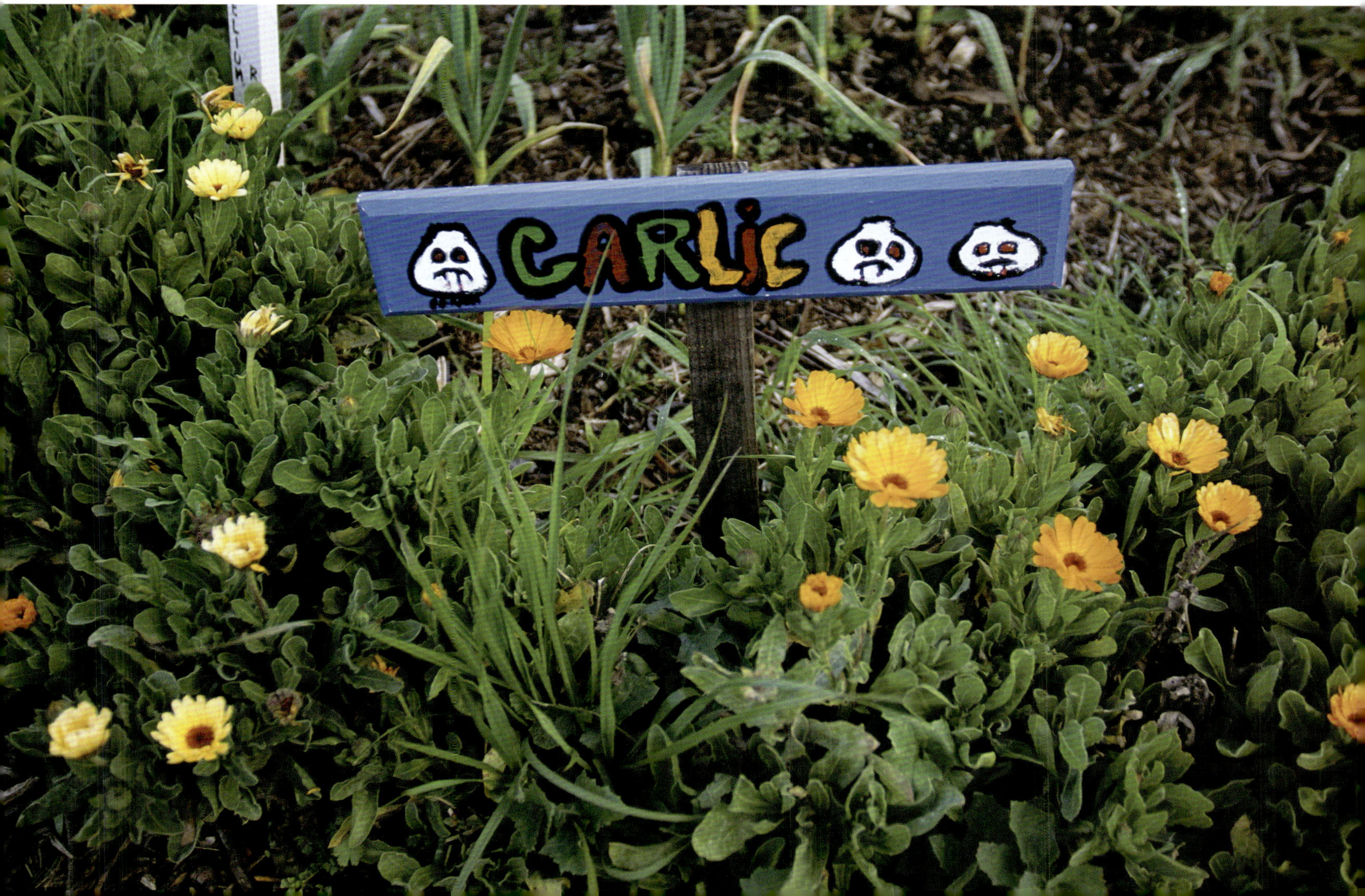
GARLIC

Baked Goat's Cheese with Garden Lettuce

Carefully cut fresh goat cheese into discs about half an inch thick. Pour over good extra virgin olive oil and sprinkle with chopped thyme and rosemary. Cover and store in a cool place for up to a week.

Cut a day-old baguette in half lengthwise and dry out in the oven until dry and lightly coloured. Using a grater or food processor, process into breadcrumbs.

Preheat the oven to 200° C (400° F). Remove the cheese from the marinade and roll in the breadcrumbs, coating them thoroughly Place the cheeses on a small baking sheet and bake for about 6 minutes, until the cheese is warm.

Measure the 1 tablespoon each of red wine and sherry vinegar into a small bowl and add a big pinch of salt. Whisk in olive oil or walnut oil and a little freshly ground pepper to make a vinaigrette.

Toss a variety of garden lettuces lightly with the vinaigrette and arrange on salad plates. With a metal spatula, carefully place 2 discs of the baked cheese on each plate and serve.

Women

FROM CORDON-BLEU TO THE LAND OF THE FREE

Julia Child. Isabella Beeton. Elisabeth David. Betty Crocker. M. F. K. Fisher. These are the most famous women in cooking, yet none owned a restaurant. None were chefs. And one of them was made up.

Of course all of them, save Betty Crocker, were cooks. All contributed to revolutions in cooking. All were writers in some form or another (Julia Child became a television star due to the success of her first book), and it is through books about food that their influence prevailed—the first print run of the *Betty Crocker Picture Cook Book* was an astonishing 950,000 copies. It hardly mattered that she had been invented by a flour company. By 1954, according to a company survey, 99 percent of American housewives were familiar with her name.

But as far as women *chefs* went, there were barely any to be familiar with. Chefs were men. Many of the great chefs were inspired by formative experiences in their mother's, or grandmother's kitchens. Often those women were *cordon-bleu* cooks themselves, running the kitchen of the family *auberge*. Still, they were not chefs.

At least it was acknowledged that they could cook. Louis XV had insisted that cookery was the province of men. His mistress, Madame du Barry, sought to prove otherwise, and arranged secretly for a woman to cook the King's dinner, which was of course a success. The King insisted on seeing the man, perhaps to poach him for the royal kitchens. "Right, France, I have you," said Madame du Barry, "it wasn't a chef who cooked dinner, it was a woman." She required that her *cuisinière* be recognised. "I cannot accept less than a *cordon bleu*."

The title was from the *Ordre du Saint Esprit* whose members were called after the broad blue ribbons they wore, and came to apply to any individual that excelled in their chosen field. Thanks to the wit of Madame du Barry, the term 'cordon-bleu cook' was historically applied only to women.

THE JOY OF COOKING

And so it remained—men were chefs and women were cooks. Doubtless the brutal conditions in eighteenth and nineteenth century kitchens contributed as much as anything, for we cannot imagine many women aspiring to enter the kind of inferno described by Carême. Even in the twentieth century, as we have seen from Orwell, the French kitchen— even after Escoffier's reforms—could still be a hellish place.

So, women cooked, as they had always done, in the home. In Victorian England they were guided by Mrs Beeton's *Book of Household Management* (though it was more compiled and presented in Isabella Beeton's name than actually written by her), and in America by Lydia Maria Child's equally famous *The American Frugal Housewife*. The fictional Betty Crocker began her radio broadcasts in America in 1924, and Irma Rombauer published *The Joy of Cooking* (18 million copies and counting) in 1936. Then, in the middle years of the twentieth century, the triumvirate of M. F. K. Fisher, Elisabeth David and Julia Child opened up a whole new world to English-speaking women everywhere.

Fisher's earlier writings were more personal, more esoteric, and it was David's *A Book of Mediterranean Food*, published in 1950, and Child's *Mastering the Art of French Cooking* which set off their tidal wave of influence. "Julia Child paved the way for Chez Panisse and so many others," writes Alice Waters, "by demystifying French food and by reconnecting pleasure and delight with cooking and eating at the table. She brought forth a culture of American ingredients and gave us all the confidence to cook with them in the pursuit of flavour."

It was not just Julia Child that was promoting French cuisine. The Kennedys were in the White House and they had a talented French chef, René Verdon, in residence; Jacqueline Kennedy in particular was intent on proving that America was no cultural backwater, and the spectacular dinners that she organised, with French cuisine at their heart, were frequently in the news. And with affordable air travel Europe was accessible now in a way it had never been before, so that the average American could, if they so wished, experience such food first hand. Many did.

THE WIND OF CHANGE

A new generation had been inspired, as much by the films of Godard and Truffaut as by the writing of Julia Child and the aspirations of Jackie Kennedy. But the result was the same. Young Americans took themselves out into the world, and came back with new ideas, new intentions, and new possibilities. The times were indeed changing.

By the early 1970s America was a far different place than the one it had been two decades earlier. Simone de Beauvoir's *The Second Sex* had been translated into English and the women's liberation movement was in full flight. The rise of a new type of cooking, at the forefront of which was a woman, is unsurprising.

According to Marion Cunningham, home-cooking guru and longtime friend of Waters, Chez Panisse was about much more than food. She recalls bringing James Beard, doyenne of American cooking, to the restaurant in the mid-1970s, a visit that helped Waters gain her first national attention. "We went for lunch," Cunningham says. "The very first sentence he said was, 'This is not a real restaurant …,' meaning that it was a home that took in money for food. And it really still is."

In that way, Waters and Chez Panisse remain something of an oddity. Although Waters is frequently credited with creating 'California cuisine,' it is chefs like Wolfgang Puck and Jeremiah Tower who in the 1980s took the idea and parlayed it into fortunes.

Waters' motives were as much social—political, even—as culinary, and in that she was always part of a wider movement. Women could do anything they wished. They could even become chefs. By 1977, for example, the Troisgros brothers had seen four women train in their kitchen; it was by no means an avalanche, but it was a start.

Left: Julia Child (1912 – 2004) was an American cook, author and television personality. She introduced French cuisine and cooking techniques to the American mainstream, through her many cookbooks and television programs. Her most famous works are the 1961 cookbook *Mastering the Art of French Cooking* and the television series *The French Chef*, which premiered in 1963.

And here it must be remembered that the conviction that women cannot be great chefs had become so much a part of French culture that it has long been institutionalised in the French language: even though the word for cook, *le cuisinièr* has its feminine counterpart, *la cuisintère*, there is still no feminine counterpart to *le chef*.

ARDENT DESIRE DENIED

The fact is that for two millenia men had simply not allowed women to become chefs. In the societies of ancient Greece and Rome elegant dining had already come to symbolise social status and economic success, and women were already being excluded from cooking—it was the male slaves who prepared the great banquets.

By the time of Julius Caesar it was accepted that male servants, including cooks, possessed more status than females. And over time being a chef became a way for a man to dramatically improve his social standing. Taillevant, cook to King Charles V, was given both a title and an estate in recognition of his services. Carême was the son of an itinerant stonemason, and Escoffier's father was a blacksmith.

It was in the interests of such men to guard jealously their new and hard-won status. It was necessary that they been seen as different, better, than ordinary cooks (who were women), as artists and creators rather than mere artisans or servants (again, women). The formation of the guilds and the use of emblematic status symbols—think of the chef's *tocque*, and how high it rises—served to further differentiate them.

So it went. A woman's place was in the home, either as mistress or servant, and only with the advent of feminism did things finally change for the better. Ironic, then, that independent career-minded women such as Julia Child, Elisabeth David and M. F. K. Fisher should use cooking as vehicle to further the cause. Ironic, too, that so many of the great male chefs should have been inspired by their humble, hardworking mothers and grandmothers to excel in such a masculine domain.

In 1867 the English philosopher John Stuart Mill wrote that society did not "allow women to have that ardent desire for celebrity" that was necessary to success in any profession. But that 'ardent desire' may not necessarily be for mere celebrity, even among men.

Left: Alice Waters pictured in 1982 with the newly-published *Chez Panisse Menu Cookbook*.

Michel Bras

THE NATIVE SON

"Speaking of my feeling of love for Aubrac is like speaking about everything, it is like speaking about the world. It is speaking about me, about mankind, about art and, of course, about cooking."

Bras

Rocambole garlic. Giant amaranth. Saint Fiacre beans. Valerian. Meadowsweet, with its taste of 'honey and seed.' Chickweed. Baldmoney, which is the emblem of the house, exuding an aroma of anise. Geslu. Bryony. Blonde and red orache. Of such things is the world of Michel Bras composed.

The first 'recipe' in his award-winning cookbook is for soft-boiled eggs and toast soldiers; in his introduction he has already recounted how he and his brother would, on the way home from school, steal and swallow the freshly laid eggs, still warm, from a neighbour's chicken.

No question, the man is unconventional.

Indeed much has been made of his 'contradictions.' He has a restless, insatiable curiosity, yet remains rooted to his native soil. His restaurant has been likened to 'a Zen retreat in a space colony,' yet beneath the building's severe formal aesthetic lies the soul of a provincial family inn. His is a sober, monkish personality that is shot through with warmth and wonder. He was going to be a scientist. Now he is both botanist and poet, artist and businessman. And, of course, chef.

"I'm open to everything," he says.

AUBRAC

It can be a forbidding place. There is still snow in April, May. For pilgrims on the route to Santiago de Compostela to visit the bones of St. James the Apostle, the crossing of Aubrac plateau, over a thousand metres high in places, was particularly testing.

But in summer there is riot, profusion. Over 2,000 plant species live here; the golden Aubrac cattle graze among fields carpeted with wild rose, narcissus, pansy and gentian, "soft grasses of every shade of green stretch as far as the eye can see, fragrant flowers blow in the wind, and the air is heavy with the scent of herbs."

Small wonder, then, that Bras has never strayed too far from home.

"Speaking of my feeling of love for Aubrac is like speaking about everything, it is like speaking about the world. It is speaking about me, about mankind, about art and, of course, about cooking."

These are strong words, to be sure; yet coming from Bras they do not seem so… fanciful as they might from another. Indeed, his life and work may be truly seen *only* through the prism of his native land; the Aubrac plateau, and the village of Laguiole, where he was born.

He is now its most famous son. Even so, this small village in a windswept part of the Auvergne, high in the Massif Central, has been reknowned for centuries—for its unique cattle, its cheese, and for the famous Laguiole knife. And just as it once played host to medieval pilgrims, now it is subject, thanks to Bras and his family, to a pilgrimage of another kind.

A FAMILY AFFAIR

His father was a blacksmith, but when in the 1960s he could no longer make a living he and his wife opened a small restaurant, Lou Mazuc, in the village. It was there, when his mother became ill, that Bras famously gave up his studies and taught himself to cook. "At first I was interested in pastry," he says, "because it's an exact science; the rest developed over several years."

He may have dreamed of apprenticing with the great chefs, but he never did. Instead he married, and with his wife Ginette turned the family restaurant into a unique gastronomic destination: in 1987 they were awarded two Michelin stars and 19/20, the highest possible rating, from Gault & Millau, who praised the 'simplicity and grace' of his cuisine. Remarkable, almost incredible, for a man with no formal training.

"I take joy in cooking and I like to share that joy," Bras says, simply.

To do so, however, soon required a greater forum than the small village restaurant was able to provide.

'WHY DID HE BUILD THAT THING THERE?'

It has been likened to a 'shard of crystal' plunged into the hillside, though it is rather a collection of buildings than a single structure. Built of basalt, schist, granite and glass, the restaurant Michel Bras and accompanying hotel opened in 1992. Its design has been mildly controversial (few things excite controversy quite the way architecture does), but despite its modernist angles the structure still manages to echo the age-old buron, the squat, slate-roofed shepherd huts, unique to Aubrac, which dot the landscape, and if it does not exactly blend in, then at least it stands out with *elán*.

Tradition and modernity. Blending in and standing out. Talk of these as 'contradictions' gets us nowhere: if twice a day the matriarch of the Bras clan still cooks a family meal, what does it matter whether she prepares it on an old wooden bench or a long slab of expensive granite set in an ultra-modern kitchen. She is still preparing the same *aligot*, a traditional Aubrac dish of cheese and potatoes, that she has cooked for most of her 80 years. The family still gathers around to eat, Bras and his wife, his mother and father, his son, Sébastian, and his wife and daughter. Régis Saint-Geniez, Bras's lifelong assistant, may be there too, and some locals or suppliers who just 'happened' to drop by. A typical scene, rural, almost peasant, no matter what the architecture.

The man himself remains untypical. He had (and still has) a passion for running. And for the unique flora of his home. "During my runs I constantly marvel at my surroundings and discover new plants," he says. For this he has sometimes been caricatured as (to quote his own cookbook) a 'basket-case running through the fields picking wild herbs.'

Perhaps because it is easy to ridicule those who are so passionate. Bras simply acknowledges that gathering was our original, primal activity; for him, cooking is the celebration of ingredients which follows. "I try to make compositions that are lively and sparkling, little mixtures that awaken and tickle the tastebuds."

Previous spread: Michel Bras' mother, his culinary mentor, prepares aligot, a potato and cheese curd puree.

Opposite: French chef Michel Bras in his three-star Michelin-rated restaurant in Laguiole, South Western France. Built over 15 years ago, the restaurant is a granite and glass capsule perched on a hill amid farmland.

He succeeds. His restaurant gained its third star in 1999. It's name was changed, too, to simply Bras, reflecting the increased contribution of his Sébastian. For Bras, truly, life is a family affair.

"I can think of no greater happiness than being surrounded by my family. The love I feel for them is what enables me to create."

GARGOUILLOU

Sometimes he describes a 'fever' of creation. Other times it is more a reverie: his poached monkfish in black olive oil came to him as he watched the play of light and shadow across the Aubrac hills. His famous *coulant*, a baked lozenge of biscuit with a flowing liquid centre that has been copied by chefs around the world, had its genesis in a family skiing trip.

But his most famous composition, indeed the one that made him famous, is born every day from the land itself. Described by one commentator as 'perhaps the greatest achievement of culinary abstract art of our time', the *gargouillou* of young vegetables is a fantastic agglomeration of fresh, seasonal, local ingredients, each cooked individually to maintain their perfect taste and texture and then assembled with the eye of a painter, the soul of a poet. Its creator compares it to jazz, with tones both sonorous and dissonant. Yet where the musician has only the twelve tones of music, Bras claims the use of up to 350 types of herb and vegetable, seed and fungus, to be played with in infinite combination. Not for nothing has the *gargouillou* been called his daily love song to the land.

"The creation of the *gargouillou* is the culmination of my art. It is the core of the music I bring to the table, rising from the bottom of my heart to the tip of my tongue."

A TRUE KNIFE NEVER HURTS WHAT IT CUTS

If all of this sounds a little… esoteric, then it should be remembered that the origins of the *gargouillou* were a simple country dish of ham and potatoes that bears the same name. Just as the sleek, black, razor-sharp Japanese carbon knives that remain on the table throughout ones meal at reataurant Bras are an homage to the Laguiole knife that his village has long been famous for.

In the 14th century the shepherds of Aubrac used a short knife called the capujadou; these were hung around the waist and served for everything from whittling wood to cutting bread and cheese to serving as a makeshift altar; at the end of the working day the shepherds would stick their knives into the ground and recite their evening prayers in front of them.

The Laguiole knife was invented by a local cutler in the early 19th century, combining the traditional capujadou with a contemporary Catalonian curved and folding knife called a navaja to create something unique.

Michel Bras has done much the same thing. His edifice of stone and glass, stuck immovable into the rocky soil of Aubrac, offers just such a synthesis. It provides just as serviceable an altar. And if there is no worship as such, then those that come may still be afforded an opportunity to eat, and to give thanks.

"We always have something to learn from the riches nature spreads before us: Alpine fennel and the almondy flavor of meadowsweet, prized for its medicinal properties; elderflowers fragrant with the heady scent of nutmeg. Vegetables too: basella with its sticky leaves; the delicate flavor of chickweed; and 'tanous' or cabbage shoots. Anything crisp, crackly, crunchy, sharp or sweet-smelling winds up decorating the plates. To all those who make the friendly gesture of sharing our love for Aubrac, we give the best that we and the region can offer. The intensity of these moments will linger on, the gift of a place which makes you forget all else but which will stay bright in your mind forever."

Because it is the land, alone, which abides.

This page: Michel Bras' cuisine draws on the produce and history of the Laguiole region, with a strong emphasis on local herbs and vegetables.

Overleaf: The interior of the restaurant Michel Bras.

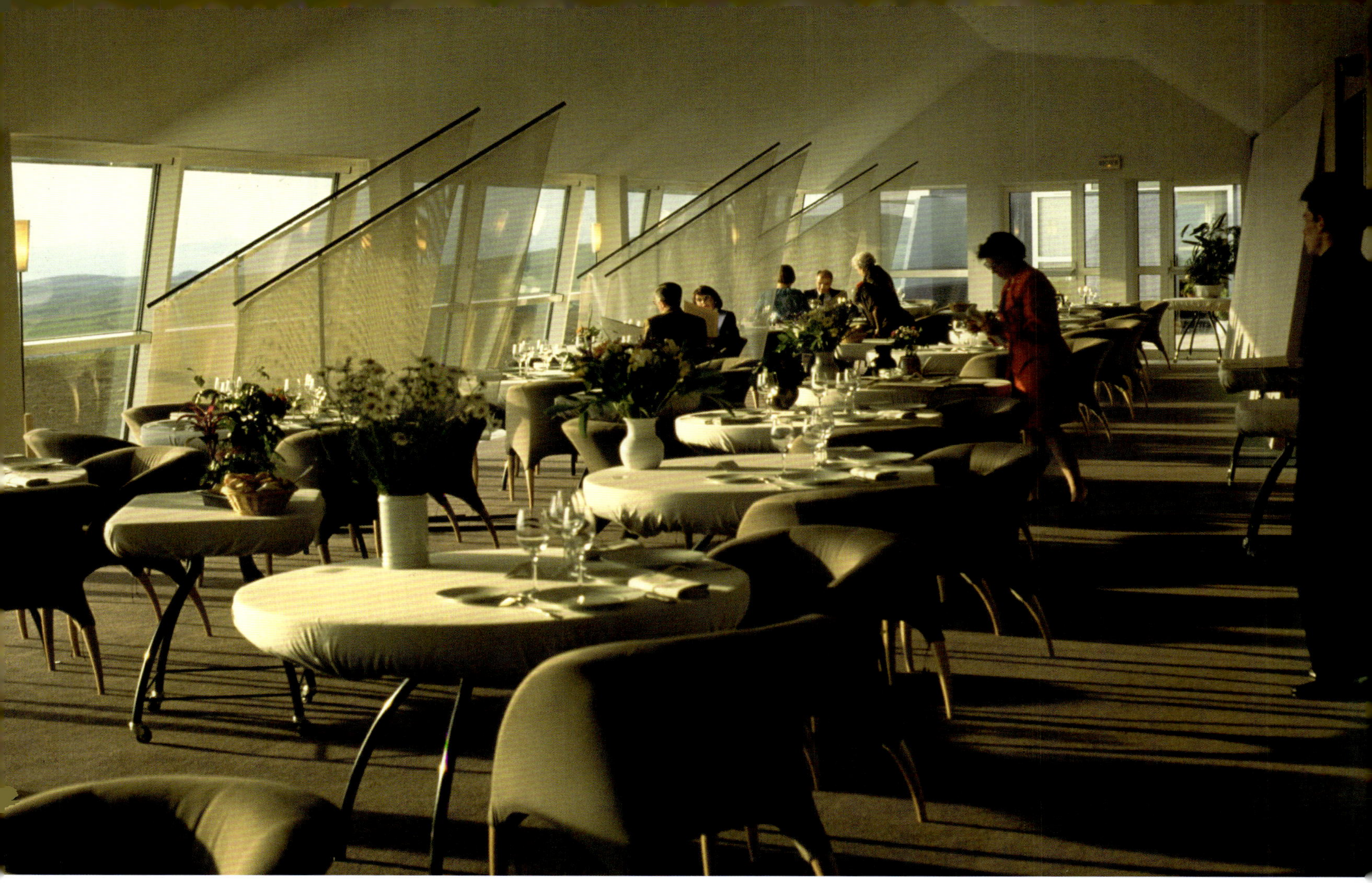
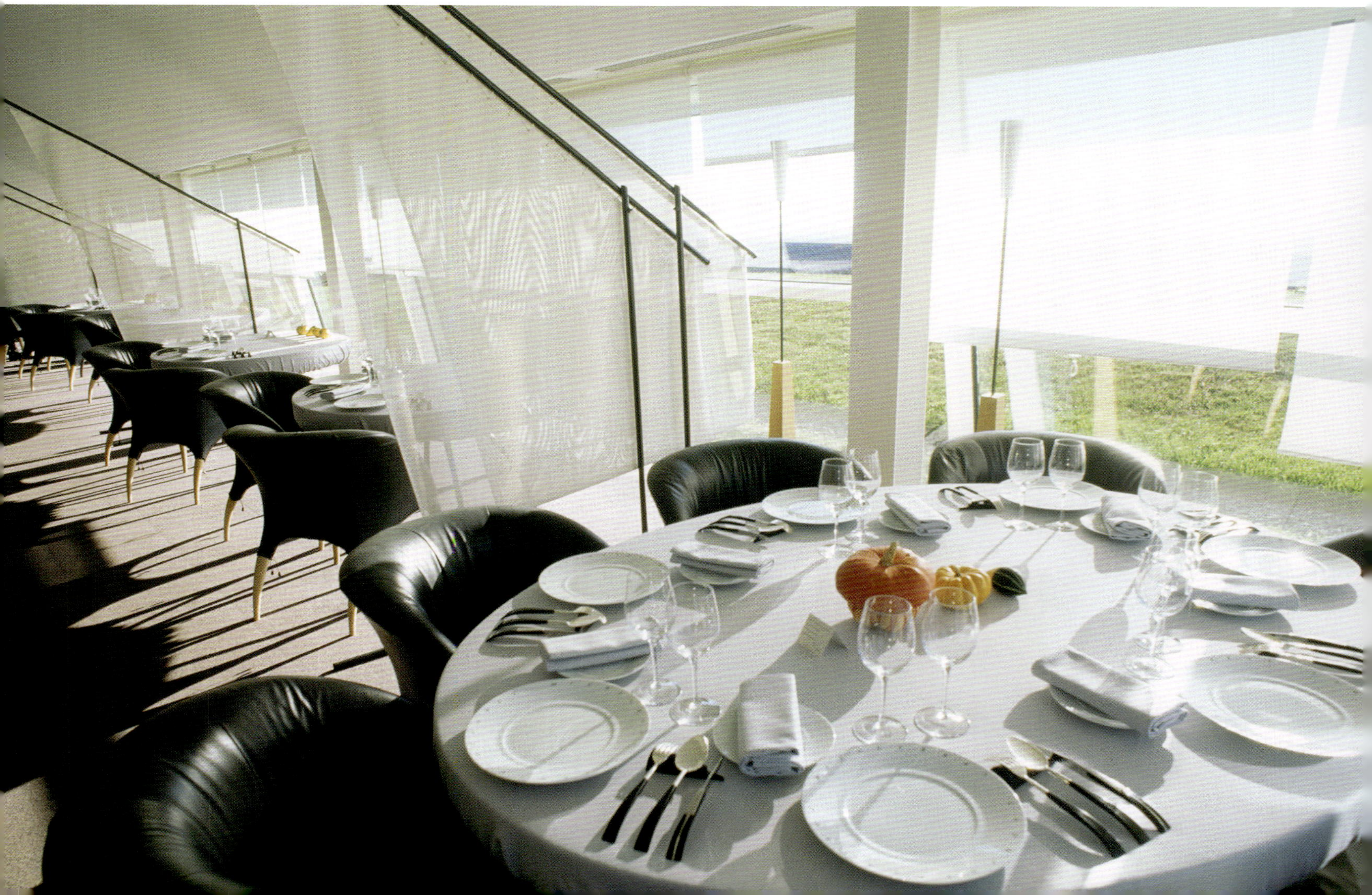

'Gargouillou' of Young Vegetables

Individually cook and season a
seasonal selection of between 30
and 40 types of fresh leafy vegetables,
root vegetables, herbs, flowers and
mushrooms, and arrange attractively
over large plates.

To finish, fry slices of country ham in a
deep frying pan. Skim off the fat and
deglaze with vegetable broth. Add a
pat of butter and toss the vegetables
to heat them.

Arrange the vegetables on a plate
to give an impression of motion.
Decorate with chopped garden herbs,
country herbs, and sprouts.

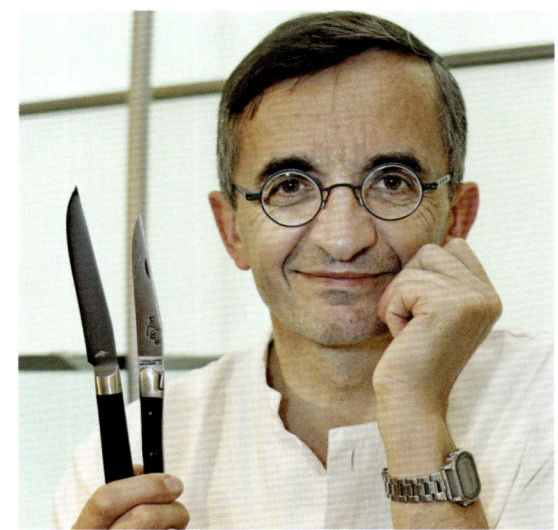

Tradition

PEASANT COOKING AND THE RULE OF THE KNIFE

Garlic, writes a fifteenth century Italian scholar, is "always rustic food, but at times becomes artfully civilised when thrust into the body of a roasted duck."

The key word here is 'artfully'. Products of humble origin can be ennobled not just by association with more expensive ingredients—rich meat, spices—but also by art.

But we must not forget the words 'rustic' and 'civilised', either. Another Italian scholar, the culinary historian Massimo Montanari, notes the 'wholly lower-class popular tradition of greens in the kitchen: cabbage, turnips, fennel, mushrooms, pumpkin, lettuce, parsley, and all sorts of herbs, as well as such vegetables as beans and peas.' Yet these are the basis, he says, of dishes offered by the cookbook of Maestro Martino, 'the most prestigious Italian cook of the fifteenth century'. He seems to be surprised.

For Montanari, this intersection of a 'written' cuisine, intended for the ruling classes, and the 'oral cooking' of the peasantry is of much cultural significance. For us, the issue is less important: we need only look at *Essential Cuisine* by Michel Bras to see how art can transform humble ingredients and basic techniques into something far greater than the sum of their parts. And perhaps, we might think, this Martino also began his culinary career in an unpretentious family restaurant located in a small village, and by his own art raised himself to become the most prestigious chef of his day.

ART AND ARTIFICE

Actually, not all of Bras' techniques are basic. Many of the dishes in *Essential Cuisine* contain elements such as milk skin, potato and mushroom powder, duck emulsion or milk tuiles that are time-consuming even where they are not elaborate—certainly each implies an amount of preparation that is completely alien to 'peasant' cooking.

For Mantonari, such refined cooking was the province first of the great families and then

the great restaurants, and was characterised not only by the complexity of its final phases— the construction of the dish—but also the labour involved in the preparatory stage. The innovations of the French in the seventeenth and eighteenth centuries, which underpin the modern culinary method, were largely in the area of 'preps' such as court-bouillon, roux, and brunoise. These changed the character of the dishes from the outset, altering the flavour, texture and consistency of things as they cooked.

Carême, Escoffier and Julia Child have already exemplified the written cuisine that these techniques are part of. Michel Bras exemplifies the merging of written cuisine and oral cooking in much of his work, and nowhere more so than in his liberal use of *aïgo boulido*, the Provençal soup made from boiled water and garlic.

One of the oldest culinary traditions of the region (there is a saying there that garlic soup saves one's life), it is traditionally served thickened with an egg yolk and poured over

bread that has been sprinkled with olive oil. For Bras it is used as the base for emulsions or jus, to soak bread for garnish, for poaching or to create a bouillon: it has become part of cuisine, and features throughout his book. In contrast, the traditional *aligot* that is served at the restaurant is unmediated by any alteration or technique and makes little pretence at being cuisine. It is what it is—hearty peasant fare.

In fact it has been commented that the food Bras actually serves in his restaurant is far more rustic than the elaborate and artistic arrangements that are presented in *Essential Cuisine*. Perhaps when Mantonari writes that 'the visibility of peasant cuisine … in the cookbooks of the medieval and Renaissance elites … was enhanced by the specific modalities of the cook's work', he is saying much the same thing?

It's hard to say. It is probably more helpful to remember that Escoffier's father was a blacksmith, just as Michel Bras' father was, and that all his life Escoffier used his grandmother's

Opposite: Michel Bras displays cooking knives of his own design, produced by Kai, a Japanese cutlery manufacturer.

Above: Aligot, a hearty French peasant dish from the Auvergne which is traditionally made with fresh Cantal cheese.

Provençal dishes as a jumping-off point for his own cuisine. And we must doubt that any of her recipes were ever written down.

THE KNIFE

Bras' parents opened their *auberge* when his father's blacksmithing could no longer support the family. Bras entered the kitchen as a young man only when his mother became ill. He learned to cook not through books but through application.

In this regard cooking, as a profession, is unique: in virtually no other endeavour can one reach the top without instruction. One does not *need* training to be a chef. It helps. But common sense, enthusiasm, application and a good sense of taste are essentially all that is required.

And some tools, though not too many. Michel Guérard, who like Bocuse still keeps an open fire in his kitchen, has said that if there is one thing above all that he would teach a young apprentice, it is how to cook on an open fire. Then, he says, you can see what kind of strength they have. "When you provide a person with everything—whether produce or machinery or utensils—it can make him lazy. Faced with the restrictions imposed by an open fire, the imagination soars."

So, a flame, a pot, and a knife. Most of all, the knife. "If a knife has become a part of your hand, you can cut … without thinking," Bras says. You can chop, mince, dice, fillet, score, peel, crush, de-bone, slice, carve, core, julienne, shred, spread, scrape and even flute. If pressed, the knife may take the place of virtually any other kitchen implement, and in the hands of a great chef they can weave magic.

A chef without a knife is like a musician without an instrument. They are highly personal, only used by their owner, and usually bought to the kitchen in the morning and taken home again at the end of the day. Good knives must be jealously guarded: Anton Mosimann tells of working in St. Moritz under a Monsieur DeFrance, who was old enough to have worked under Escoffier. Once Mosimann was careless enough to leave his knives out after lunch and they disappeared. It turns out that the chef had a tradition of collecting knives to sell in Paris at the end of the season.

Such traditions continue—only now chefs sell their own knives. At the restaurant Bras one may buy the same Japanese carbon steel knife that the chef uses (for only €200) or a replica of the Laguiole knife which graces his tables. The knives are created by a traditional Japanese knifemaker, and on their combined website Bras speaks of visiting the craftsmen at their work. "When I heard the sound of the blacksmith's hammer striking the anvil, I was reminded of my father's workshop, with the same sounds and the same atmosphere."

Because certain things remain the same, even as the world changes around them. The *aligot* can only be made in one way—the cheese must be beaten into the mashed potato by hand, with a wooden spoon. Only then will it form a smooth, flowing, elastic purée. Such traditions cannot be altered, which is why they have prevailed. They come down through generations, just as they mingle with cuisine, because those such as Bras and Guérard retain the fascination for them that they possessed as children. As Michel Guérard writes in the foreword to his *Cuisine Gourmande*, "I learned to listen to the musical murmur of *ragoûts* acquiring their musky flavours beneath the golden oil, to dip my finger into stews brimming over with intoxicating aromas, to watch over wild rabbits as they were toasted to a deep golden brown by the heat of the fire."

And in the end it does not really matter *how* the traditions are passed from one generation to the next. It is simply enough that they are. But some lessons are learned more easily than others, and a good teacher often the single greatest blessing a young man or woman can be given at the start of their career. And yes, one can learn at home, but sometimes a young man has to go a long way to get what he needs.

Above: Chef Michel
Guérard cooks over
an open fire in the
kitchen of his restaurant,
Les Prés d'Eugenie.

Anton Mosimann

THE DRIVER

"My approach to food was a bit radical. I introduced a lighter menu and all the food was freshly cooked."

*H*ere is a man who owns 365 bow ties. He counts Prince Charles as a personal friend. At last count his private dining club had over 2,000 members. He became famous for teaching a lorry driver's family from Sheffield how to cook a full Sunday roast for under £10, and in doing so paved the way for both Jamie Oliver and Gordon Ramsay. His signature dish is bread and butter pudding. His name is Anton Mosimann, and he is Swiss.

We first encounter him at barely five years old. His parents have bought a restaurant in a small village outside Berne. From there he walks the five miles to school and back, accompanied by his dog; we can see him in the dark of a Swiss winter, trudging through the snow; we can see the soft, golden light spilling through the restaurant's windows as the small boy sits on the great carved chairs to do his homework, everything going on around him.

By six we see him already in the kitchen, cooking cheese fondue and spaghetti bolognaise.

At twelve he encounters the most beautiful thing he has ever seen: a shiny new Chevrolet Corvair. He is transfixed. He vows then and there that he will one day own such a car.

From that day forth he is possessed. He sells old newspapers. He breeds rabbits and sells them to the local butcher. Soon he is trading in bicycles and radios, employing school friends so that he has the time to excel at running and wrestling as well as work even harder himself. He passes his driving test and, with a little help from his mother, buys a brand new Triumph Spitfire.

He is eighteen years old. At nineteen we see him trade in his car so that he may invest in property: the owner of the farmhouse he buys has to wait a year before Mosimann is old enough to legally sign the contract.

THAT'S DEDICATION

He is already five years in the trade. "It was, I am still certain, one of the hardest apprenticeships imaginable … I worked six days a week, scrubbing floors, cleaning copper pans and doing any general kitchen work, from eight in the morning and rarely did I finish before eleven at night." Sometimes he cries himself to sleep.

But Anton Mosimann, as we have seen, is nothing if not determined.

"From the very beginning I recognised that I had to learn the basics of the profession. It is these basic methods of preparation that form the mulitiplication tables of cookery. Without a comprehensive, practical understanding of elementary culinary skills it is not possible to progress."

Very determined.

"As I worked in the kitchen I would look out and notice guests arriving in their cars—young men driving impressive, open-topped cars with beautiful women at their sides. The ambition to have a fine car and to escort a beautiful girl made me work even harder. Not many years passed before I bought a red E-type Jaguar."

Unstoppable, even. At twenty-five he gains the *Chef de Cuisine Diplôme*—the youngest chef ever to do so. He has already worked in Switzerland, Rome, Canada, and Belgium: at Expo 70 in Osaka he is head chef at the Swiss pavilion. But his life's great challenge is yet to come.

THE DORCHESTER

He is appointed *sous chef* under Eugéne Käufeler, *Maître Chef des Cuisines* at the Dorchester for twenty-five years. Standards, it would seem, are not high.

"The first banquet I experienced at the Dorchester, the meat was roasted, a saddle of lamb, in the oven at five in the morning. It was carved, put back on the carcasses and covered in foil. The meat was served at eight o'clock that night. It was very unhappy looking meat."

In 1976 he succeeds Käufeler. He is now all of 28 years old. But he still has a lot of work to do. He has to teach a nation how to eat. There is

the concept of the television chef to invent, and a young Heston Blumenthal to inspire. *And* he has to make 26 soufflées, one for each letter of the alphabet. So he gets to work.

"The chef's profession demands a single-minded approach," he says, "almost a holy devotion."

THE WAY WE LIVE NOW

There are 132 cooks at the Dorchester, many who have been there twenty, thirty years. Every one of them joins the union, just in case. But every morning Anton Mosimann shakes hands with every member of his brigade. Soon he knows the name of each of their wives. At the end of that first year, only seven remain in the union.

"It was not an easy role to fill, and at first it was a very difficult job," he says. "My determination and ambition drove me on." By the time he leaves the Dorchester there are 650 people on the waiting list to work for him.

Before he leaves, though, there are stars to get. By 1979 he has them: the only hotel restaurant outside France to have two Michelin stars. "I am still very proud of that." The Terrace Restaurant and Grill Room win restaurant of the year awards, and celebrities flock there, drawn by Mosimann's new style of cuisine.

"My approach to food was a bit radical. I introduced a lighter menu and all the food was freshly cooked."

He calls it *cuisine naturelle*. There is no more serving tired food from silver tureens. Staff are taught to cook sauces to order, and serve dishes when they are at their peak. It is the way his parents cooked at their family restaurant, not what he learned at the Palace Hotel in St. Moritz, where the chef had cooked with Escoffier himself.

"We reduced cream every day, ten to one. That's ten gallons of cream, down to one gallon. We mixed it with butter to make sauces. Unbelievable!"

So he insists on no cream, no butter, no fat. He uses the techniques he learned in Japan. He steams scallops for 15 seconds, puts in a bit of lemon juice, a bit of black bean, a few herbs. He serves a poached fillet of beef with vegetable crudités, and steamed halibut with nothing more than two complementary sauces.

"In this country a lot of things we take for granted now was a result of what he initiated," says one of his former employees. "He changed the restaurant world for the lighter, for the better."

INVENTING JAMIE
But he does more than change how the British eat.

"Anton can be celebrated as the first of the modern generation of super-chefs," says influential critic Egon Ronay. "He was the first to not just appear on TV, but also be talked about by the public, and written about all the time. He stands head and shoulders above the rest … many of the top chefs that followed owe him for creating the atmosphere in which they could thrive."

For the *The Observer* newspaper's French cookery series he prepares a soufflée for every letter of the alphabet—apple, banana, *champignon*, and so on. "Not one letter missed and every soufflée perfect," he recalls.

In 1985 Anton Goes to Sheffield is broadcast on the BBC. In the programme he is charged with teaching a working class family how to shop for and prepare their Sunday dinner for under ten pounds—including wine. Over 64,000 people write in to request the recipes. A young Heston Blumenthal takes note:

"I remember him serving bread and butter pudding. Seeing a Swiss man making bread and butter pudding fashionable was a big thing

for me. He managed to make it complex and refined … to put real emotion and passion into the sort of dish you'd previously thought was only okay in a pub."

But finally it is time to move on. He has a private club to start, and many more things to learn. He must cook for the birthday parties of Princes Charles and Philip, for Mrs Thatcher and Tony Blair, and then he must drive an old car from Peking to Paris.

THE STAFF OF LIFE
In the words of the *Larousse*, Prosper Montagne's vast edifice of culinary wisdom, "no food is so redolent of myth, tradition and rite as bread." It hardly exaggerates. Not for nothing did Jesus, who more than anyone knew the power of metaphor, say, 'I am the bread of life: he that cometh to me shall never hunger.' Nor could one imagine the ritual of the Last Supper being enacted with anything other than bread. Indeed, the concepts represented by the words 'bread' and 'life' are interchangeable.

For Anton Mosimann, it seems, those two words would be 'life' and 'drive.'

And so we see him now at sixty, in his private dining club, Mosimann's, where he works six days a week, surrounded by his 6,000 cookbooks, never ceasing, always driving, driven.

"Every morning I look forward to doing something different or better. It's essential in my profession to deliver every day. I am proud to be a perfectionist. The chef's profession is one of the few in which you do not get a second chance."

A chef may not, but at least his bread does…

This page: Anton Mosimann inspecting mushrooms at London's Borough Market (left); risotto from the menu at Mosimann's (right); demonstrating cooking techniques (below).

Overleaf: A view of the balcony inside Mosimann's London. The wine cellar can be seen in the background, on display behind glass so that diners can choose the bottles themselves.

Bread & Butter Pudding

Lightly butter a large ovenproof dish. Slice three small bread rolls and spread each slice with butter, then arrange the bread slices in the base of the dish.

Bring 250 ml of milk, 250 ml of double cream and a split vanilla pod gently to the boil with a pinch of salt. In a bowl, mix together 3 eggs and 125 g of sugar until pale.

Gradually add the milk and cream mixture to the eggs, stirring well to amalgamate. Strain into a clean pan.

Add 10 g of sultanas that have been soaked in water then drained to the bread in the dish, along with the milk mixture. The bread will float to the top.

Place the prepared dish in a bain marie on top of a folded tea towel to ensure even cooking and pour enough hot water to come halfway up the sides of the dish. Bake carefully in a 180° C (350° F) oven for 45 to 50 minutes. When the pudding is ready, it should wobble very slightly in the middle. Remove from the oven and cool a little.

Gently heat some apricot jam with a little water. Lightly brush a thin coat of the warm glaze over the top of the pudding, and then dust with icing sugar.

Serve slightly warm.

Presentation

NOUVELLE CUISINE & THE ART OF PLATING FOOD

Imagine a dish of *filets de sole Brillat-Savarin*, the creamy lobster mousse with its jacket of sliced truffles, the poached *filets* of sole on their puff-pastry *croustades*, the lobster tail scallop on top, placed just so. Truly a feast for the eye *and* the palate.

Now imagine that the *croustades* had been made a week ago and the lobster was three days old.

"In the big Paris restaurants where I worked," Bocuse says, "the chef ordered provisions to fit the pre-established specialties already printed on the menu. Each morning the *maître d'hôtel* would come into the kitchen with a ritual question: 'What should we push today?' There was always food left over from the night before that they had to get rid of on a priority basis. Monsieur Point would have none of that. He made a fresh, clean start every morning. It was *la cuisine du moment*."

La cuisine du moment. Bocuse of course had his own version, as did Michel Guérard, and these were the founding pillars of what became *la nouvelle cuisine française*. In England Anton Mosimann offered his *cuisine naturelle* to diners at The Dorchester, while Alice Waters brought California cuisine to the rest of America.

The integrity of these chefs was never in question. Even so, this new cuisine—which simply followed Point in cooking according to the day's market, cooking it at the last minute, individually for each guest, and cooking it perfectly—was not universally well-received. Some perceived it as merely an excuse to display delicate, even miserly, portions of food on oversized plates. Obviously, critics said, these chefs took themselves for *artistes*, with their insistence on pretty arrangements and 'daring' combinations of ingredients, with sauces that seemed to have been applied by a brush.

It was never meant to be so, but some got carried away. Charles Barrier, the oldest chef featured in *Great Chefs of France*, said in 1977, "There is too much talk of presentation of food.

Ten years ago, when I was still evolving, I did elaborate presentations, as I thought it was important; now I think it is … *merde*." As if to prove his point, his house specialty at that time was a simple salmon fillet cooked *en papillote* with a julienne of vegetables, a spoonful of fish gelée, butter and some fresh tarragon. The dish is perfect in its essential simplicity: as Barrier says, "Another way to betray produce is to do too much. You must not put parsley on something if it makes no contribution."

THE REBELS

It is one of the eternal themes of history: the new order built upon the rubble of the old. And in Paris in May 1968, as students manned the barricades and fought pitched battles in the streets, that rubble was not just metaphorical.

Their revolution was short-lived (and the de Gaulle government's mandate was increased in the election that followed), but even so a new spring was in the air. Radical new ideas, both social and artistic, were sweeping across Europe.

Nowhere more so than cinema, which had been invented in Lyon by the Lumiere brothers just two years before Point was born there. Now Godard, Truffaut and their friends, "*les copains*" as they called themselves, were assaulting the celluloid establishment with provocative articles which claimed that the cinematic conventions should be shattered. Stodgy scenarios shot on heavy, outmoded equipment would be replaced by imagination and ingenuity, using the new cameras which could film on the move.

Maybe it was the title of one of the ground-breaking works of this new wave of cinema— Godard's *A Bout de Souffle* (Breathless)—which helped inspire three young journalists and gourmands named André Gayot, Henri Gault and Christian Millau to begin a crusade against Michelin and its "pompous" stars. At any rate, according to Gayot, "we felt that a new era was looming behind the kitchens of France."

They were to be its polemicists, and in 1969 launched *Le Nouveau Guide*, a monthly magazine devoted to food and wine. It was the first of its kind in France, and on its first cover it proclaimed in bold type, "Michelin: Don't forget these 48 stars!" Just as the previous spring, battle lines were being drawn.

Those 48 stars were the chefs, largely unknown then, whom Gayot, Gault and Millau believed were in the process of transforming cuisine, and were being completely ignored by the Guide Michelin in the process. The Guide, respected and all powerful, was by its very nature a bastion of conservatism, rejecting anything that had become, in Gayot's words, "unruly." For Michelin, dishes such as the *filets de sole Brillat-Savarin* were the foundations of cuisine, and chefs such as Bocuse, Guérard, Louis Outhier and Alain Senderens who were shaking those foundations were firmly shut out of its pages.

Le Nouveau Guide, on the other hand, was purpose-built to embrace them. To that end, the three journalists not only extolled the new way of cooking but set down the rules which were to govern it, a list of ten principles published in 1972 which became the manifesto of *nouvelle cuisine*.

COLOURS AND FORMS

By that time the principles had already been disseminated. "We acted as the federators of these trends, introducing the pioneers to one another and publicising their concepts and compiling our discoveries." Those chefs who had before been unknown, and unknown to each other, began to all march to the same drum.

The soundness of their principles could not be faulted. They realised that modern life required fewer calories—the invention of elevators, cars and central heating saw to that. The development of food processors and other tools cried out for them to be used in new, sophisticated ways. And transport systems meant that anyone might have access to fresh produce, no matter how far from the countryside or the sea they might be.

Opposite: During the reign of *nouvelle cuisine*, portions grew smaller as plates grew larger.

Overleaf: According to Anton Mosimann, food is truly appetising when a meal is laid out artistically so that when guests look at the plate they cannot wait to eat.

And each chef brought something different to the movement. Guérard brought his health-consciousness. Outhier, who had worked at L'Oriental in Bangkok, was the one who introduced the Asian accent with spices and herbs. He knew how to use them: in minute quantities with subtle touches only. Bocuse bought charisma.

Before long *nouvelle cuisine* was popularised by journalists eager to discover the new thing. It became the rage, a new creed, and its intellectuals were Gault and Millau. "First, a dinner was an opportunity to satisfy all our senses," Gayot says, "beginning with sight. Food had to be presented in an artistic manner playing with colours and forms, and the plate had to be arranged as a work of art similar to a sculpture or a painting."

One can see already how this was going to lead to trouble. But wherever exaggerations, abuses or mistakes were committed in the name of *nouvelle cuisine* we must always remember

that the underlying principles were sound. Portions needed to be smaller, but when at the same time the plate got larger it was only natural for a diner to feel short-changed. And food has always needed to be attractively arranged. As Anton Mosimann has said, "We have all come to expect artistry in cooking as well as other aspects of life. When a meal is laid out artistically, when your guests look at the plate and cannot wait to eat, this is when food is truly appetising."

Nor is it surprising that presentation is so important to chefs. When cooking, they must be true to the food—as Point insisted, it must taste of what it is—but when plating they may give their personality free rein. To truly know a chef you cannot just taste his food, you must look at it, too. Yet even if a chef's food is beautiful, it might pay not to judge too hastily … such creations may still have been born in a crucible of overheated emotion and random acts of violence.

Raymond Blanc

THE GARDENER

"I feel privileged because I am self-taught. Completely. I never had one minute under a chef's guidance. Not one second."

Blanc

"I didn't want to upset him," Raymond Blanc says, "but I was just so excited." His hand goes unconsciously to his face. "I suggested that a sauce was too salty."

A solid copper pan can do a lot of damage: Blanc woke up in hospital. "Jaw, teeth. Smashed up." Yet it was not the chef that assaulted him who was fired.

The proprietor, after berating Blanc for upsetting his chef, offered to help him find another position. Nor did it hurt if that position was on the other side of the Channel. But France's loss, as they say, was England's gain. And what she gained was a conscience.

"At the age of seven my father had already taught me to hold earth in my hand, he'd say, 'taste it, look at it, and tell me if it's good earth or bad earth.'" He pauses. "Ask a chef that now! Ask a chef which fish is in season now, and they say, 'what bloody season, what are you talking about! I get oysters all year round,

I get sole all year round, seabass…'"

Not for much longer. Not if Raymond Blanc has anything to do with it. One day, a nation, indeed the world, may reap what he sows.

"We need to put our house back in order," he says, "in a big way."

THE GOOD EARTH

He remembers catching frogs for the table. "My father knew when to go, when the frogs would mate." His father, a watchmaker in a small village near Besançon, knew also where to find the secret troves of *petit gris*, the highly perfumed mushroom. They would gather wild asparagus, and sleep in the woods. Periodically they would 'rugby-tackle' a chicken for the pot. It taught him, as only childhood experience truly can, that food comes from the earth.

Fifty years later, at Le Manoir aux Quat' Saisons, his Michelin-starred country house hotel in Oxfordshire, that knowledge has not been forgotten. Food still comes from the earth—the 1½ acres that comprise his kitchen garden provide enough produce to cater to 80,000 guests per year—and Blanc remains as passionate, and as brutally frank (in 2001 he claimed that serving a child a microwaved meal was "an act of hate") as ever. He speaks plainly of the "misery and torture" involved in battery farming chickens, and how it reflects on his adopted land. "That is disgusting, disgraceful for a country," he says. "We should know better, we really should know better."

He is outspoken, too, on the culture of abuse and bullying within kitchens, particularly as it is represented in 'reality' television. "They do not reflect what is happening in our world today. These guys are dinosaurs who live in the Ice Age."

And with this delightfully mixed metaphor we are reminded that English is not Blanc's native language, nor England his native soil.

He came from a place, and a time, when one's vocation was decided by the schoolmaster. A career as a draughtsman was chosen for him, to which he was not at all suited. Briefly he was a nurse. He worked in a factory. Then, at 17, he had his life's great epiphany.

A JEWEL OF A RESTAURANT

He had begun to panic, because he could not find his 'gift'. Then on one warm August night he was in Besançon (the birthplace of Victor Hugo) and came upon a 'jewel' of a restaurant. He describes the scene with eyes shining: the terrace under moonlight, the lovers holding hands while tuxedoed waiters danced around them, flambéing, carving, in a kind of magical ballet. He knew. "Thank you," he whispered, "thank you, God." He was going to become a chef. Not a waiter. A chef.

He became a waiter. But even that took a while. He failed his first interview at that very same restaurant, Le Palais de la Bière, by telling the proprietor he must be hired, for "I will be a great chef one day." After a second interview he was taken on as a cleaner. He moved up the ladder, to dishwasher. Then, because of his

developing passion, he was made a *commis de salle*, carrying plates to the table. He dreamed about food, his whole life now devoted to this new passion; a passion that blinded him to the dangers of criticism.

"He was a great chef," Blanc says, "but he had a temper."

Blanc tells another story, too. He was carrying a tray of 20 drinks. A young woman ran into him. She apologised for smashing them in a delightful British accent; she was also very beautiful. He got carried away. "I thought, 'Oh my God, I have to go to England? Ha ha!" A seed, at the very least, was planted.

Either way, Blanc found himself in Oxford, at the Rose Revived Restaurant. He was still a waiter. But when the chef fell ill Blanc saw his chance and grabbed it with both hands. Two years later, with Blanc as chef, the restaurant had gained a Michelin star. He was completely self-taught. Also, he had met a girl. They married, and soon they had their own place, in the Summertown district of Oxford. "I started with nothing," Blanc says. "I mortgaged my own small house and put all my money into the business with my wife."

The called it Les Quat' Saisons, because "I have worshipped so much the seasons. They drive everything."

AN ENGLISH GARDEN

If you are to serve up to 200 covers a day from your own garden, it's not just the seasons. You're going to have to be organised.

The garden at Le Manoir aux Quat' Saisons, the country house hotel Blanc and his wife bought in 1984, is organised around two basic principles: productivity, and taste.

For example, rather than one large sowing, the gardeners sow small amounts of lettuce, green beans and peas every few weeks. This provides a succession of just-ripe produce; there is no surplus that must be used quickly or left to grow large and watery.

Taste, as we might imagine, is paramount. There is a constant search for the best varieties, and the decisions on which to grow and cook

Previous page: Chef Raymond Blanc at his restaurant at Le Manoir aux Quat' Saisons in Great Milton.

Opposite: The lavender path at at Le Manoir Aux Quat'Saisons

with are made by both chefs and gardeners. One year they tested 14 different varieties of cucumber.

Rotation, too, becomes essential. In an organic garden (it was certified in 2000) where there are no chemical controls, no crop may grow in the same place two years in a row, else soil-borne diseases and pests become entrenched. Crops are separated into four groups: roots and tubers; legumes (peas and beans); alliums (onions); and brassicas (cabbages), with a four-year rotation on each bed. And though imperfections must be tolerated in any organic garden, the encouragement of wildlife in the garden provides valuable pest relief. There are several ponds at Le Manoir that house toads, and ornamental plants are there to attract beneficial insects.

For the chef, however, it all comes down to one thing. "I want to know which is the best tasting spinach and I want to grow it."

THE YOUNG LION

Le Manoir was awarded two Michelin stars in 1986. It has been voted the UK restaurant the industry would most like to visit, and Blanc the most respected person in the industry. Like his fellow expatriates, the Roux brothers, he too has an OBE. But success took its toll on his first marriage, and on a second, and he freely acknowledges the relationship with his sons is troubled.

He has a surrogate family, though, in the number of chefs that have passed through his kitchen, and it is perhaps appropriate that his relationship with his greatest pupil, Marco Pierre White, should have been a volatile one.

White joined Blanc's brigade just as Le Manoir opened. "Raymond taught you to question things," he says. "Raymond is the most multidimensional chef this country has ever seen. No one has a palate like him. He is the only genius I ever met in the kitchen—the rest do it by numbers."

Doubtless Blanc, no more humble than any other great chef, would not disagree.

"I feel privileged because I am self-taught. Completely. I never had one minute under a chef's guidance. Not one second."

No, a greater hand seems to have guided Blanc to where he is now. He first talked of sustainability almost twenty years ago, long before such talk had become glib, or merely expedient. He had wanted to work with local farmers then, but they had already lost much of their craft. Only now are they getting it back. He had to change suppliers multiple times, because they were not prepared to provide him with true, written accountability for their produce. Now, he says, there are 150 items on his breakfast menu. "I know exactly where they come from. Every producer sent a complete technical sheet which tells me, exactly, the technique, any additives there would be, everything about that milk, about that cow."

He says that, when it comes to produce and the land, we have behaved like 'hooligans.' That things must change. And from his garden he is leading the charge.

"What you see … are the first signs of revolution."

This page: The quality of the produce at Le Manoir aux Quat' Saisons shines through in the vegetables accompanying a dish of hare fillets wrapped in bacon (far left); in a bowl of peaches poached in white wine (left); and in the preparation by Chef de Cuisine Gary Jones (below).

Overleaf: A selection of home-made breads at Le Manoir aux Quat' Saisons.

Sabayon with Asparagus

Trim two bunches of asparagus and cook in lightly salted water until just tender.

In a large bowl, whisk 4 medium egg whites with 50 ml of water until frothy. Place the bowl over a pan of boiling water and continue to whisk. When the eggs are at the consistency of mayonnaise, remove from the heat and continue whisking while adding 70 g of melted unsalted butter, some sea salt, a dash of cayenne pepper and a good squeeze of lemon juice.

Pass the sabayon through a muslin cloth and serve over the asparagus.

Personality

POTS, PAIN AND PRACTICAL JOKES

On the tables at Alain Chapel's restaurant you would find no salt: in Chapel's world, if you thought a dish should be saltier, you would be wrong.

He acknowledged that others might see him as difficult. "I am a Capricorn," he told Quentin Crewe, "a very difficult sign. Me and Stalin and Mao Tse Tung." But probably he was not smiling as he said it. In fact, he smiles in none of the photographs of him in *Great Chefs of France*.

The other chefs, by contrast, often seem to be grinning, and much is made of their sense of humour and love of practical jokes. Anecdotes abound: Point keeping visitors entranced at the serving hatch while a young commis would creep under the counter and paint their shoes; Bocuse switching tickets with Jean Troisgros as they drove to Paris so that Troisgros was forced to pay ten times the correct toll; Guérard on stage dressed as a woman singer at the launch of his second book, miming to pop songs, his colleagues in the audience none the

wiser; customers emerging from the Troisgros restaurant with corks trailing on strings tied to the back of their raincoat belt.

Yes, it is rare for anyone (save maybe Alain Chapel) to be wholly serious. It is also rare to find a profession outside the armed services where bullying and abuse, both verbal and physical, have long been accepted as just part of the working day.

ENLIGHTENED TIMES

No one would deny that things are much better than they were. We live in more enlightened times. Labour laws prevail. But it is the culture itself that has changed, and no doubt this is due to those who as apprentices had suffered the ministrations of bullying chefs, and vowed they would be different. Here Anton Mosimann describes the atmosphere in his kitchen:

"No shouting. No screaming. No swearing. It's not necessary. Do your homework, get organised, and get on with it. I don't lose my temper. I'm lucky, I suppose, to be good natured. Very often, if you shout, you show a weakness, because you haven't done your homework. I never criticise other chefs. They have their own styles. I have my own."

Indeed one reporter referred to his kitchen, somewhat facetiously, as like being inside 'a well-oiled cuckoo clock.' In reality, this is a compliment. But if we look at Mosimann's own words there is still an implicit criticism. Yes, he is saying, the culture has changed, but it has not changed completely. Raymond Blanc, whose face was so violently altered by an angry chef, has spoken out against bullying, particularly as exemplified by chefs on certain television programmes. He believes that violence, both verbal and physical, is still far too common in restaurant kitchens. He contends that there should be zero tolerance for this behaviour, and that offenders must be jailed.

Others, while not condoning violence, would say that those who cannot stand the heat should not be in the kitchen. It is a demanding, high-pressure environment, especially during service. It is hot, and expectations are high. No one should be surprised if tempers occasionally fray. Voices may be raised, things can be thrown. It is not necessary, but it happens.

THE WAY OF THE CHEF

There are some chefs who would never throw a plate even if their life depended on it, nor even raise their voice save to be heard. There are chefs whose kitchens work in silence, save for the calling out of orders and the response of *oui, chef,* from the brigade. There are kitchens that are rigidly hierarchical and there are those that seem to operate in a kind of controlled chaos. In the kitchen at restaurant Bras the team call the chef by his first name. Some chefs will not allow salt on their tables, serve a customer a Bloody Mary with their food, or cook a steak beyond medium-rare. Others will serve you whatever you ask for. They may be reverent or irreverent, surly, aloof, or jovial. But each chef will share some fundamental characteristics that seem innate to the profession.

In most there seems to be an overarching perfectionism which can never be put aside—a passion, almost a mania, for excellence. But the perfectionism is not for its own sake. Each chef understands that their job is first and foremost to please the customer. They know that the main act of a chef is that of *giving*. Without great generosity—of spirit, of time, and of effort—there can be no great chef.

There are other qualities, too. A steely determination, for example, is almost an entrance requirement. Mental and physical stamina and indeed a willingness to forebear pain are essential; the feet ache and the arms get burned with regularity. An eye, a nose and most of all a tongue which are finely attuned to the most subtle of sensations (in Bocuse's case he makes a show of being able to *see* that a sauce is too salty) are paramount. Finally, without the mental agility to know exactly where each dish is at at any given moment, and to ensure that everything goes out at the same time, perfectly, every time, a chef is lost.

IS IT WORTH IT?

Surely there must be easier trades to ply?

Yes, there are, so long as one remembers that being a chef is not really a trade, a job, or a profession. Alain Chapel (who referred to himself and Stalin in the same sentence) called being a chef an '*acte d'amour en permanence*,' which we might translate as an act of ongoing love. But if we are searching for a precise term the French word *metiér* is probably the best. It suggests something like a calling, something a person is drawn to, that they are chosen by, rather than necessarily choosing.

It is interesting that many chefs draw an analogy with music. Like music, theirs is an art of creation, and of joy. They may consider themselves conductors or soloists. They may prefer the structure of a classical score which they may imbue with their own emotion, or they might rather the freeform nature of modern jazz, with its emphasis on spontenaity and improvisation. Either way one gets the feeling that, despite the vagaries of style and temperament, the great chef at heart must consider himself as one thing: an artist.

Opposite Appreciating the art of the practical joke has always been a useful attribute for a trained chef.

Pierre Gagnaire

THE JAZZ MAN

"Before him, no one would have thought to season a grilled scallop with liquorice, to serve a pear dessert with lamb's lettuce, or fish with sweetbreads and foie gras."

Gagnaire

There is something of the beatnik in Pierre Gagnaire: with his mane of long, greying hair and air of Gallic hipster cool you might almost expect dim lights, the snapping of fingers and the low, sultry tones of a tenor sax to accompany him as he cooks. Perhaps some freeform jazz poetry.

This is not so facetious as it might sound. In the essay that accompanies the astonishingly beautiful photography in his 2003 book, *Pierre Gagnaire: Reflections on Culinary Artistry*, the writer speaks of a sense of 'energetic tension, motion, and rhyme.' Jazz, poetry and abstract art—particularly that of Kandinsky—are invoked as parallels to Gagnaire's cooking. The plate is likened to 'a blank white page.' And in the black and white photograph which accompanies his introduction Gagnaire is shown with both hands pressed to a furrowed forehead, eyes tightly closed, the very picture of an artist caught up in the agony of creation.

'I like,' he writes, 'the doubts of the musician, his awkwardness.'

Yet a few pages on he will write, 'I cannot conceive of a runny sauce; I immediately bind it. Or a sloppy ham and butter sandwich; I will assemble it into a neat cone.' Clearly, this man will not be so easily defined.

BORN INTO THE BUSINESS

Perhaps, had he been born into the America of Jack Kerouac and Charlie Parker and Jackson Pollock, he may have found his *metiér* as a poet, a musician, or a painter. But he was not. Instead he found himself born into a family who had opened a restaurant in post-war France, in Saint-Priest-in-Jarez, on the outskirts of Saint-Etienne. He was the eldest son, and that he would one day take over the business was a given.

It was not a profession he chose. For a long time it was not one he even enjoyed. Still, he attended a pastry course at 14, and was soon apprenticed to Jean Vignard, once chef at the Court of Sweden but now at a small restaurant in Lyon. Vignard's recipes were based on Lyon's simple bourgeois cuisine, but he had a profound knowledge of his ingredients and his tools. Most impressive was his command of the stove itself, how the arrangement of the coals would create areas of differing temperature, so that the pans danced a ballet across its surface as the cooking stages progressed, and it kept the young apprentice fascinated.

He moved on, to the kitchens of Bocuse and others, learning his craft in the crucibles of *nouvelle cuisine*. These were years of rebellion, of kicking against authority and constraint, and if it was here that Gagnaire learned technique, he learned also that technique was not all—that without *inspiration* a chef was merely a cook.

After his apprenticeship he returned to Le Clos Fleuri, the family restaurant. He claims that he was bored around the pots and pans.

"There was a point when I wasn't enjoying this *metiér*. One day I realized there is another way to approach cooking: that is to forget your apprenticeship and instead to find the heart, the spirit of the cuisine, to make it more than a *metiér*—[to make it] a means of expression. As I did that, I incorporated approaches that didn't exist up to then in French cuisine."

SAINT-ETIENNE

His early experiments were timid. But they grew bolder. More successful. He found an audience that began to respond. Yet with success came a feeling of restriction. Gagnaire felt bound to move on. He found an old photographer's studio in Saint-Etienne that had been converted to a cafeteria, and here, he claimed, he would banish 'routine' from the kitchen. He left behind technique. His cooking would be based on intuition now. Contrasts. Departures.

His problem was ingredients.

Actually, his problem was money. It is the same problem that countless young businessmen have encountered, but an undercapitalised restaurant suffers worse than

most, and a chef who is intent on creating a breakaway cuisine suffers most of all.

The pioneers of *nouvelle cuisine* had access to the finest, freshest and noblest of ingredients, and these were the bedrock of their cuisine. Indeed, their innovation was to deduct unnecessary technique from the equation, and to let what technique *was* necessary almost disappear behind the ingredients themselves.

Gagnaire chose another path. He would push his technique—his own innovative culinary approach—to the forefront, breaking from tradition as forcefully as Kandinsky breaking from figurative painting, or Charlie Parker inventing bebop. Yet he had neither access to, nor could he afford, the types of noble ingredients such an approach required.

Still, he persevered. His reputation grew, even on these meagre resources. And as he could afford better, more expensive ingredients, he began to seek them out, to use them with abandon. The painter who had for so long used watercolours was now painting in oils. He just forgot to count the cost, and by 1996 Gagnaire was bankrupt.

A 'BEAUTIFUL AND SAD ADVENTURE'

But before his fall, Gagnaire had flown awfully high. His first restaurant in Saint-Etienne was given 18/20 by Gault & Millau in 1984. His next venture, La Richelandiére, was awarded 19.5/20, along with three Michelin stars.

Gagnaire had done more than win accolades, however. And if the essayist in his book claims his cooking to be 'millions of light years' away from that of his old master, Vignard, such hyperbole is not altogether unwarranted. Gagnaire's journey has indeed been long, and his influence wide. The 'verticality' of food on the plate, for example, (even if it ultimately became a cliché) owes much to Gagnaire's original sense of architecture. Combinations of ingredients previously unthought of was also a hallmark of his development, not for the sake of novelty but because there was indeed some

Opposite: Chef Pierre Gagnaire and his team in the kitchen at his flagship Restaurant Pierre Gagnaire, Rue Balzac, Paris.

'gustatory arch' which connected them. It was just that no one else had seen it.

His cuisine in the early 1980s was truly a discovery of the unknown. And if it is true that all great art aspires to cliché, then we must remember that those clichés, frequently, began with Gagnaire. Before him, no one would have thought to season a grilled scallop with liquorice, to serve a pear dessert with lamb's lettuce, or fish with sweetbreads and foie gras. Gagnaire did, not due to some egregious desire for 'innovation', but because his talent told him it would work.

His talent for business was not yet so sure. "I had problems in Saint-Etienne," he says, simply. But those problems were considerable. La Richelandiére was forced to close, and Gagnaire was bankrupted. Yet he still had friends, and they rallied, buying the bulk of the restaurant's wine cellar so that Gagnaire was not to lose everything. His staff, too, stood by him. A beautiful and sad adventure, he calls it, and when it was over he was down, certainly. But he was not out.

PARIS

It is a bold man who, having presided over such a 'misfortune', decides to take himself to Paris and try again.

Gagnaire gives much credit to his wife, and to the loyalty of his team. With their help, he opened an eponymous restaurant in a small hotel on the Rue Balzac, and by 1998 he again had three stars. And though the experiences at Saint-Etienne had taken their toll, the struggle to reorganise his ideas would ultimately lead to another breakthrough.

It was from a suggestion by his wife, Chantal, that Gagnaire came upon his new idea. Like most great ideas it is both simple and obvious, and we are surprised that no one had thought of it before. His menus would be organised by ingredient, using each one as a theme around which to weave his variations. Langoustines, for example, might be served

four different ways: as a tartare, grilled, sautéed and made into a mousseline. Each presentation would have different, complementary, elements, different seasonings and garnishes. Like the jazzman, he would play each chorus a slightly different way. The menus might come with titles such as Catalan Landscape, The Orient or Deep Sea, and the 'theme' would be made explicit in some dishes, merely hinted at in others, as Gagnaire saw fit. He would even improvise, changing dishes on the spur of the moment—even during service—if he thought the menu would be better served by it.

This is not quite so radical as it might appear; in a way Gagnaire's approach can be seen to reflect the *Grand Service á la Francaise* so beloved of Câreme, in which dishes were presented all at the same time. For Gagnaire, his presentations are neither dishes nor full courses but rather a 'New Culinary Entity', by which multiple plates are presented to the diner simultaneously, positioned due to a defined plan, and to be eaten in a certain order. The diner is guided through the experience, and the revelations of taste and texture create movement and rhythm, melody and counterpoint.

It does not always succeed, and Gagnaire's work is not to everybody's taste. His food has been called 'precious', and his improvisations can prove too esoteric for some. Yet his status among chefs can never be overestimated. Nor can his influence. And the constant pilgrimage to his small, unfussy dining room on the Rue Balzac suggest that his admirers are many.

At the end of service he walks among them. He is as much ensuring their satisfaction as he is taking their (figurative) applause. Then he will depart, putting on his battered black leather coat and climbing aboard his motorcycle. It is late, and he may decide to hang his helmet in the crook of an elbow as he kicks the bike into life and roars off into the Paris night, hair streaming in the wind.

If you listen closely, on the breeze, you might hear the sound of a saxophone playing.

This page: Photographs by Peter Lippmann for the book, *Reinventing French Cuisine*, in which Gagnaire looks back at 40 years of his own culinary history. The innovative composition of many of the photographs reflects Gagnaire's culinary innovations.

Overleaf: Pierre Gagnaire in the dining room of his Paris restaurant, 1997.

John Dory with Sweet Peppers

Char 2 sweet red bell peppers over an open flame. When the skin is well blackened, enclose them into a plastic bag and let cool. Scrape the skin off the peppers and rinse under the tap. Drain well on paper towels, then slice into strips and set aside.

Chop 2 small onions into rings and skin and dice 1 European cucumber. Lay four strips of aluminium foil 30 cm long on a work surface. Divide the onion rings equally among the strips, along with the diced cucumber and sliced bell peppers. Lay a fillet of John Dory on the vegetables and top with a slice of lemon. Season with salt and pepper, then add a spoonful of white wine and a spoonful of oil to each. Seal as tightly as possible by folding and pinching the foil into a secure *papillote*.

Lay the *papillotes* carefully on a baking sheet and bake in an oven preheated to 200° C (400° F) for 7 minutes.

Remove the *papillotes* from the oven; they should be nicely puffed. Place them on hot dinner plates and bring them to the table as they are. The guests should open their *papillotes* simultaneously, so as to maximise the aroma when they are opened.

Critics

WRITERS, GOURMANDS AND THE *GUIDE MICHELIN*

If every chef is at heart an artist, then they must accept criticism as their lot, even if they do not like it. But they might take heart from the fact that the art of food criticism is a long and storied one, and at its root is that singular person, the gourmand.

Brillat-Savarin tells of a particularly witty woman of his acquaintance who was 'able to tell gourmands by their pronunciation of the word *good*, in such phrases as "That's good, that's very good," etc.; she declared that adepts instil into that one short monosyllable an accent of truth, tenderness, and enthusiasm such as ill-favoured palates can never attain.'

Jean Anthelme Brillat Savarin, one imagines, would have had just such a way with that short monosyllable.

He had a way with words in general. Even so, it is not by intention that he became the most famous of all writers on food. The book that made him so was written, almost as an afterthought, at the end of a busy life in which

he had been "gastrologue, gastronome, musician, jurist, philosopher," and much of it was more than a little tongue-in-cheek. Its full title gives us some idea: *Physiology of Taste: or, Meditations on Transcendental Gastronomy: A Theoretical, Historical and Up-to-Date Work Dedicated to the Gastronomes of Paris, by a Professor and Member of Several Literary and Learned Societies.*

Those were more leisurely times. Brillat-Savarin was born before the Revolution, he had lived Talleyrand's 'sweet' life, and after the vicissitudes of 1789 and Napoleon he spent his later years in some measure of comfort again. There he wrote a masterpiece, invented the phrase "you are what you eat," among many others, and shortly thereafter died as he had lived, a happy, good-humoured fellow.

THE CRITIC

Brillat-Savarin was not a critic; no doubt he had dined at many a restaurant, including Beauvilliers', though he never tells us so, much less makes comment on the food; he is much happier with an anecdote about how in America he beat two Englishmen in a drinking contest.

But another Frenchman, born three years after Brillat-Savarin in 1758, certainly *was* a critic—almost certainly the very first—and a much less pleasant character to boot.

Alexandre Balthasar Laurent Grimod de la Reynière was born with deformed hands, rejected by his aristocratic mother, and after studying and then giving up the law became a professional gourmet—it was printed on his business card—and writer. For this he required prosthetic fingers, which he covered with white gloves. He hosted an infamous dinner at which he mocked the social aspirations of his parents by naming the humble suppliers of the food served as his relatives, and was banished to the provinces. He returned after his father's death to find the family fortune gone, and turned to writing to support himself, inventing the restaurant guide in the process.

The first annual *Almanach des Gourmands*, published in 1803, was an anecdotal and practical guide to Paris, with particular reference to its eating-houses. It was wildly successful, walking its readers through the city, neighbourhood by neighbourhood, evaluating shops and restaurants for quality. Essentially, here the modern guidebook was born.

But Grimod did not stop there. In a further burst of inspiration, described in the second volume, he created a *Jurie des Gourmands*, who at regular dinners tested the produce of caterers and suppliers and then awarded a *légitimation*, a kind of certificate of merit, to those of which they approved. Of course, they approved of almost everything they were given, which meant they were given even more food to approve!

The *Almanach* continued until 1812, the guide-book section shortened in later editions and relegated to the back, because for a 'real' writer such as Grimod the task of keeping a guide current was boring and repetitive; he was much happier writing essays on the history of tablecloths or the cannibalistic symbolism of Louis XVI's decapitation a decade earlier. By

then he was under pressure from Napoleon's censors and faced lawsuits for corrupt practices. He retired to the country, where he lived another 25 years. His writings have proved less lasting than those of Brillat-Savarin, but one aphorism, 'Cheese is the biscuit of drunkards', certainly deserves to be remembered.

THE PRINCE

The gastronomic publishing industry Grimod had single-handedly invented continued to expand. At the same time the gourmet, that particularly French invention, flourished. The rise of Escoffier, combined with the thirty years of peace in Europe before World War I, saw a surge of interest in everything to do with food: societies, academies, brotherhoods, institutes, gourmet circles and clubs fostered discussion, debate, conversation and consumption. Especially consumption.

And if there was ever a man who embodied consumption, that man was Curnonsky. The name was an affectation (his real name was Maurice Edmund Sailland) but there was no pretence in his passion for food. Fifty or more clubs and academies sought him for their president and solicited his presence at their feasts. Certainly he embodied the popular image of the gastronome; large, fleshy, and of prodigious appetite, crowds would literally gather to watch him eat.

Curnonsky's great test of any restaurant was how well they cooked lamb: here one observer gives a delightful description of the tasting process.

"His whole face would be impassive, but when the first slice went in his mouth, a muscle would twitch. Then another slice from the pinker part. Another muscle twitched. He seemed to have muscles all over his vast face, which twitched according to what he was eating. One here for chicken legs, one above the eyebrow for asparagus, and so on. The crowd waited to see the judgement spread over his face. When it came it was final."

If Curnonsky's verdict was final, his influence was also vast—if a restaurant found favour with him then it was assured of success—nor was it merely confined to Paris. He undertook what amounted to a tourist crusade, embarking on a project to catalogue all the regions of France, their produce, specialities, local menus, wines, cheeses, herbs and game. He thought of regional cooking as the 'ideal marriage of gastronomy and tourism', and his *La France gastronomique* was intended to run to 32 volumes. It was interrupted by the death of his collaborator, though they had completed 28 of them, and these were condensed into a single edition, published in 1933.

By then Curnonsky had already been officially crowned the Prince of Gastronomes by public referendum, and wherever he went there was a table laid ready for him, and the finest of wines placed at his disposal. The good life was obviously good for him; Curnonsky (literally *why-not-sky*?) the Prince of Gastronomes died in an accident in 1956 at the ripe old age of 84.

THE STARS

The most influential of modern critics, however, are anonymous. What's more, they write nothing so fancy as a 'review'. They simply assign stars, giving or taking away according to their own particular criteria, in a manner which in Quentin Crewe's words is 'aloof, cool—and supremely powerful'.

They are the Guide Michelin and its inspectors, the offspring of a strange, uniquely French, marriage between the gourmet-writer and a tyre company.

The owner of that tyre company, André Michelin, seemed to know what he was doing. "This Guide appears with the century" he wrote in 1900, "it will last as long as the century." And longer, we can now say. It seems unlikely, too, that Monsieur Michelin imagined his Guide would cover not just France but eventually Europe, Tokyo and New York as well.

But Michelin's first guide, authored by the man himself, was published in an age when the private motor vehicle was still a novelty, and people still needed encouragement to take up driving. Michelin's genius was to recognised

that what they needed were *destinations*. And for a quarter of a century it was just that—a guide to cities, towns and places of interest. Then in 1926 a single-star rating for restaurants was introduced. Two- and three-star ratings were added in 1931, and the gold standard by which restaurants worldwide would come to be judged was now in place.

The Michelin system is deceptively simple. At a one-star establishment you would expect to find 'good cooking in its class'. If a restaurant offers 'excellent cooking, worthy of a detour', then it merits two stars. Three stars and one should experience the 'best cooking in France, worthy of a special journey'. There is also a system of crossed forks and spoons to rate the amenities, one being 'plain but good' up to five for 'luxury'.

But it is the stars that count. One of the main reasons for this is that chefs and restaurateurs trust Michelin to be impartial, and consequently just. The inspector is always incognito, so he or she receives no special attention. The meal is always paid for. Only after the meal does he or she identify themself, and request to see the kitchen, the cellar and other facilities. The inspector is judging the establishment on criteria which any discriminating customer would use—the quality and imagination of the food, the service, the wine list—and starred restaurants are visited several times a year, to ensure standards are consistently maintained.

Of course the Guide Michelin, like any institution of long standing, has had its share of criticism. Assertions have been made by insiders that the Guide does not even visit all the establishments it recommends, and that the reputations of some chefs have been enough for them to keep their rating, despite parlous drops in standards.

Nor is the Michelin the only game in town. In France *Le Nouveau Guide*—set up to challenge directly the Michelin's hegemony— evolved from a monthly publication to become the Gault & Millau, which rates restaurants according to its own 20 point scale (19.5 being the maximum ever awarded, because 20 would represent perfection). In Britain the Automobile Association has its own guide, which awards rosettes; indeed most countries have some variation of the Michelin concept, anonymous inspectors judging restaurants according to specific criteria.

Still it is the Guide Michelin—the little red book—that continues to set the standard, and broaden its reach. Its influence can bring a restaurant fame, or drive a chef to despair, even suicide. It has the power not just to award stars. Indeed, it can make them.

Left: A photograph of the late Michelin Star Chef Jacques Pic, in a cabinet at the restaurant he founded Maison Pic in Valence, France.

Joël Robuchon

THE SUPERSTAR

" At a time when French chefs barely deigned to serve the humble tuber Robuchon's *pommes purée* were a revelation, if not a revolution. "

Robuchon

This from the advertising that heralded his arrival in Las Vegas: 'Every meal in your life has prepared you for this moment. Joël Robuchon, Chef of the Century.'

One can forgive the excesses of advertising copywriters—it's their job, after all. The fact remains; this 'beaky, tightly-wound little guy' has been called chef of the century so often, by so many, that it has begun to stick.

So Robuchon won his first Michelin star just three months after taking on his first restaurant, Jamin, in 1981. So he got his third star three years later. So it was the fastest rise in the guide's history. We're still talking about a century that contained Point, Bocuse, Guérard *et al*.

So why Robuchon? Why a man whose worldwide reputation is based, as he freely acknowledges, on mashed potatoes?

Robuchon himself credits Jean Delaveyne, the unsung hero of French cooking. A largely self-taught cook, Delaveyne, as much as anyone, challenged the way Escoffier's method had straightjacketed French chefs, and in doing so paved the way for *nouvelle cuisine*. Michel Guérard considers him his 'spiritual father.' Robuchon feels the same; Delaveyne taught him that cooking was "more than just technique—it was reflection."

APPRENTICESHIP

He had been intended for the priesthood. Then at the age of fifteen he was taken from the seminary and put to work in the Hotel Relais in Poitiers, his home town. The official reason was his family's financial woes. But in an interview marking his arrival in New York he made this telling comment as to why boys of his generation entered the kitchen. "You're not doing so well at school at 15 or 16, so why don't you go peel potatoes, at least you won't be hungry."

He stayed three years (one might imagine a lot of potatoes were peeled) before becoming a Compagnon du Tour de France, the travelling apprenticeship that dates back to the Middle Ages. In moving around the French countryside for up to five years, a young apprentice could experience regional techniques and ingredients under a variety of master chefs. It would be the making of the young Robuchon. In just over twenty years he would be universally acclaimed as a culinary genius.

"It may take seven years to be a doctor," Jean Delaveyne had said, "but fifty years to be a chef."

Joël Robuchon, chef of the century, retired at fifty-one.

BACK TO THE FUTURE

At Jamin he was renowned for the orderliness and cleanliness of his kitchen, and for the relentless perfectionism of his cuisine. His focus was always on making each ingredient taste of itself, creating in his prime such sublime dishes as *gelée de caviar a la crème de chou-fleur* and *galette de truffles aux oignons et lard fume*. But his food—always profoundly modern in its presentation—is nevertheless seen as instrumental in leading French cooking away from the excessive reductionism of *nouvelle cuisine*, and over time came to harken back to a more authentic, even bourgeois, French cuisine; long-braised leg of lamb from his Poitiers childhood, slow-roasted goat showered with fresh spring garlic and parsley, a simple roasted pigeon served with shoestring potatoes. They all appeared on his menu.

And when it came to potatoes, there was only one sort that mattered. At a time when French chefs barely deigned to serve the humble tuber Robuchon's *pommes purée* were a revelation, if not a revolution. "Give me butter and more butter," Point had exclaimed, and Robuchon had heard the cry. His mashed potatoes seemed to be as much butter as potato, and it was this unctuous, creamy, irresistible combination that people could not get enough of. A superstar, truly, was here.

He just wasn't here to stay. He had been awarded the *Meilleur Ouvrier de France* in 1976.

He had taken Jamin to three stars in three years and kept it that way for a decade. He had then moved to a larger premises, named it for himself, and taken that to three stars, all the while telling people that he would retire at 50.

He was only off by one year. In July 1996 he handed the keys to his restaurant to Alain Ducasse and walked away. Ducasse was Robuchon's heir-apparent, with three stars of his own, and it was he who was expected to take cuisine into the next century. Robuchon, it seems, had done all he wanted to do.

"I started working at the age of 15 and worked all my life. It wasn't until I was 50 years old that I saw the snow in the mountains."

THE GREATEST

At the end of the millennium the Gault-Millau guide named Robuchon as one of *three* chefs of the century, along with Frécy Girardet and Paul Bocuse (a fact frequently overlooked in much of his subsequent press). And he had never really gone away—he had regular television shows in France, and a recent tally suggests there are some 45 books with his name on them somewhere. True, he no longer had his own kitchen, but it was hardly 'retirement.'

A man with such drive does not simply retire. A man who has spent every day for 35 years thinking about food does not suddenly stop thinking. He had previously travelled to Japan with Paul Bocuse and come away impressed. He had a holiday home in Alicante in Spain. He had been a Michelin-starred chef.

Japan. Spain. France. Hmm. Sushi. Tapas. *Haute cuisine*. Hmmm. One can just imagine the wheels spinning.

One can imagine that seeing the heir to his throne amassing so much new territory might also have had an effect. Alain Ducasse was soon to become the first chef to have three stars in three different countries—Monaco, France, the USA—and his bistro-style Spoon outlets were proliferating. Seeing all this, it seems unlikely such a man as Joël Robuchon would go gently into that good night.

C'EST UNE REVOLUTION!

So exclaimed *Le Figaro* upon the opening of L'Atelier de Joël Robuchon in 2005, and for a Paris that remembered the glories of Jamin it most certainly was. But Robuchon had already developed and refined his revolutionary concept in Tokyo, and more perceptive commentators came to see that, as with all great ideas, it had a stunning simplicity. It's a wonder no-one thought of it sooner.

They had, of course. But it took the chef of the century to create a Michelin-starred restaurant in the style of a tapas or sushi bar, standardise its menu, decor and presentation, then roll that concept out across the world.

And remember that Robuchon's *ateliers* (the word means workshop or studio) are not the sole vehicle for his culinary comeback. There are stand-alone restaurants in Tokyo, Monaco and elsewhere, and on top of everything there is his fine-dining venture, The Mansion at the MGM Grand casino in Las Vegas, which also opened in 2005 and continues to garner gushing praise from every comer. Truly, they say, the superstar has returned, better than ever.

But it is L'Atelier de Joël Robuchon, whether that workshop be in Paris, London, New York or Tel Aviv, that remains the most interesting manifestation of his return, and the French press was right to proclaim it a revolution. Not because the chefs wore black instead of white, or because they did not take bookings (they do, now, for the first sitting). Not because the restaurant was arranged with a counter and stools (not designed for lingering on) around an open kitchen, so that diners could watch and even interact with the chefs as they prepared appetizer-sized, tapas-style dishes. And not even because there would soon be identical such restaurants (don't even think it) dotting the globe, something that not long ago would have been anathema to the very *idea* of *haute cuisine*.

What is interesting is that the dish no-one ever leaves without ordering is—you guessed it—mashed potatoes.

WOULD YOU LIKE FRIES WITH THAT?

Sam Phillips famously claimed that if he could find a white boy who could sing like a negro, he would make a billion dollars. Just as famously, he found that boy, though he was to sell Elvis Presley's contract for somewhat less. Elvis went on to sell over a billion records.

Around the same time as Phillips was selling himself short another American, Ray Kroc, was starting to get frustrated with his business partners, the McDonald brothers, for not recognising the potential that *he* saw in their small chain of hamburger restaurants.

And in the years since he came out of retirement Joël Robuchon has amassed 17 Michelin stars, more than any other chef on the planet. If he has learned his lessons as well as he seems to have, there'll be no stopping him. He'll be bigger than Elvis.

This page: A selection of dishes by Joël Robuchon, including *L'oeuf de poule* (far left); *Caviar Oscètre dans une délicate gelée* (left); and *Sphère de sucre à la violette et litchi glace au lait* below.

Overleaf: The signature red and black colour scheme of Robuchon's L'Atelier branch is seen here in L'Atelier Las Vegas (above); starring Château Restaurant Joël Robuchon, Tokyo (below which is located in a faithful architectural reproduction of a Loire Château.

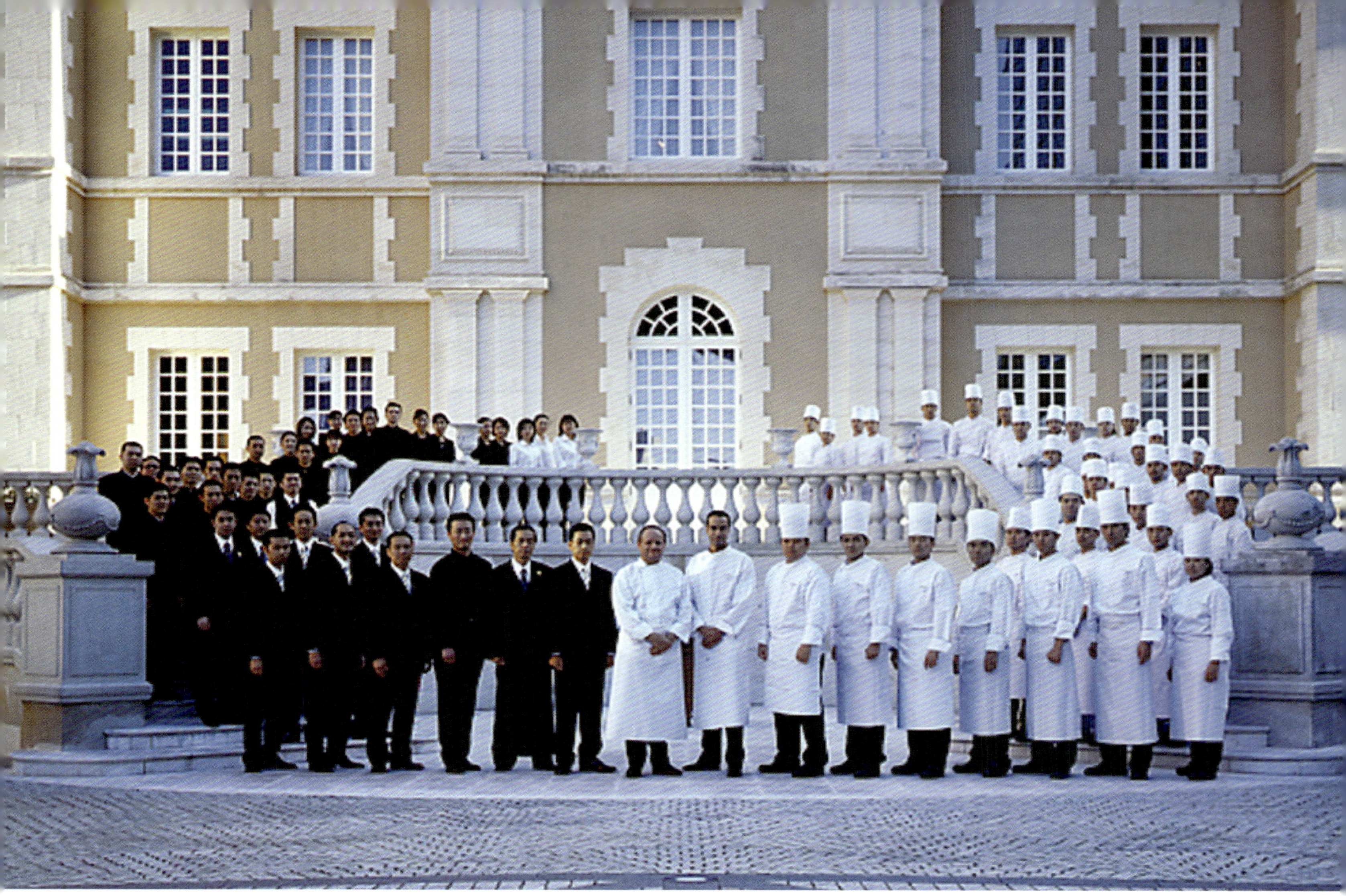

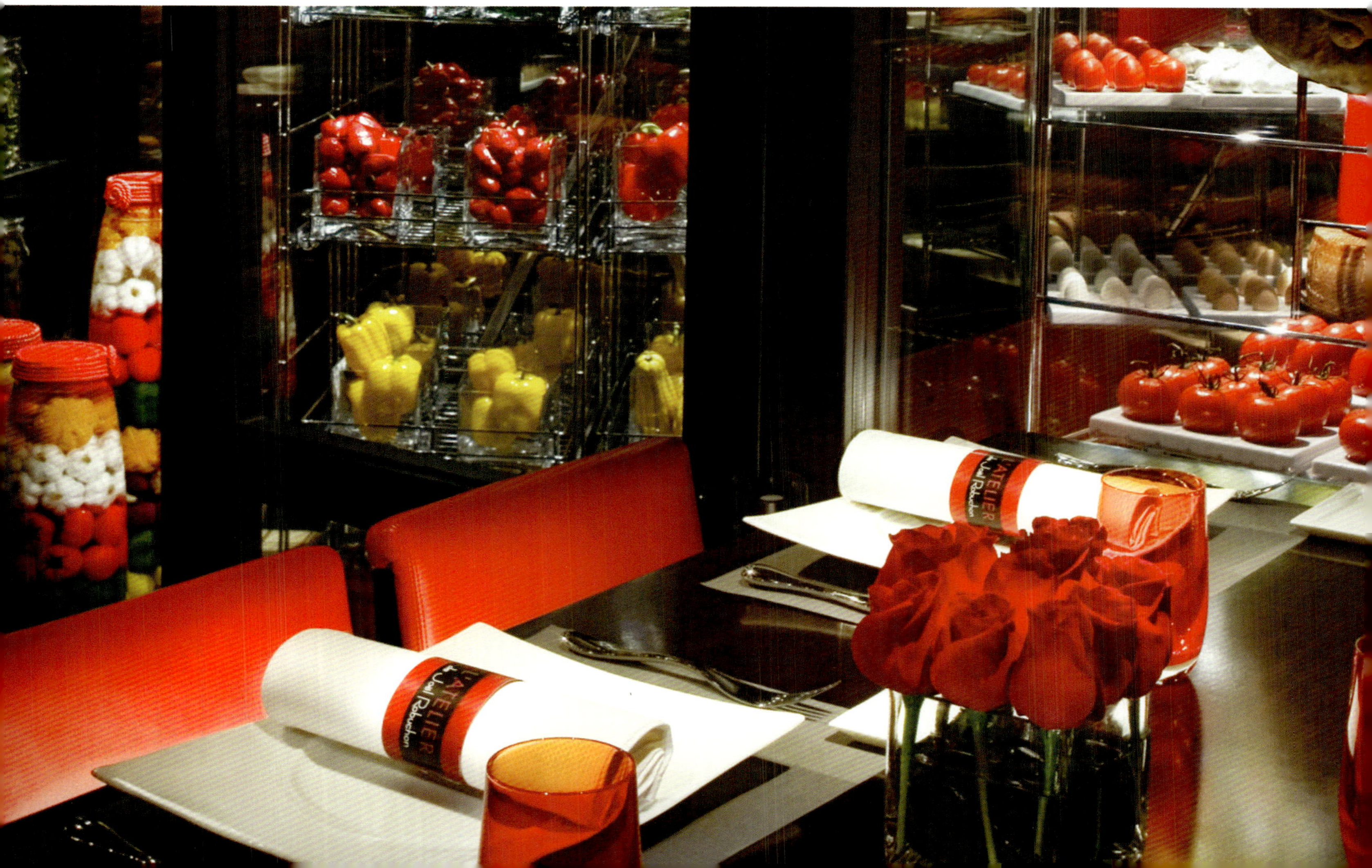
L'ATELIER

Pommes Purée

Scrub 1 kg of baking potatoes, but do not peel them. Cook the potatoes uncovered over moderate heat until a knife inserted into a potato comes away easily, about 20 to 30 minutes. Drain immediately.

In a large saucepan, bring 1 cup of whole milk just to a boil, then set aside.

Peel the potatoes as soon as they are cool enough to handle. Pass the potatoes through the finest grid of a food mill into a large heavy-bottomed saucepan set over a low heat. With a wooden spatula, stir the potatoes vigorously for 5 minutes to dry them

Begin adding about 12 tablespoons of butter, little by little, stirring vigorously until each batch of butter is thoroughly incorporated. The mixture should be fluffy and light.

Slowly add the hot milk in a thin stream, stirring vigorously until the milk is thoroughly incorporated. Pass the mixture through a flat fine mesh sieve, into another heavy-bottomed saucepan. Stir vigorously. If the puree seems heavy or stiff, add additional butter and milk, stirring all the while. Add sea salt to taste.

The puree may be made up to 1 hour in advance: to keep warm, place in the top of a double boiler, uncovered, over simmering water, and stir occasionally to keep smooth.

Fame

THE RISE OF THE SUPERSTAR CHEF

There is celebrity. Then fame. Then there is *standing*. Carême had the first two, but in the rigid social world of 19th century Paris he could never have the third.

To put it this way, James de Rothschild, Carême's last employer, was at that time the richest man in France—ten times richer than even the King—and even *he* had to buy his way into post-Napoleonic high society. To do that he threw parties, dinners and extravagant balls, all of them catered by Carême. And he did not just invite society; artists, writers, even architects were cultivated; Victor Hugo, Balzac, Ingres, Chopin, Liszt and Paganini all dined *chez* Rothschild. By then Carême was as much an artist, and as well-known, as any of them. Still, he stayed in his kitchen.

This was long the way of the chef. They might have celebrity, and status, but they could never attend their own party. The Aga Khan might dine *chez* Point (and consume eight portions of his *gratin de queues d'ecrevisses*

at a sitting), but Point would never eat with him. Yet twenty years later Bocuse was dining with presidents.

What had changed?

We might be tempted to answer with just one word: television, a medium that has given celebrity to many a mediocre talent in many an arena. But much as it may have helped, television was not responsible for the rise of the superstar chef. Food has to be *tasted*, and if in the final third of the 20th century chefs *en masse* grew famous it was mainly because more and more people were able to eat their food. Where once you had to be a Prince or a Rothschild to sample Carême's cuisine, now anyone could experience what the great chefs had to offer. Urged on by the restaurant guides and the popular press, the public went out to dine, and it was the public who made stars of the great chefs, just as they had made stars of Elvis and Marilyn Monroe.

Put simply, chefs now had standing. More, that standing now had value. It was something they could sell.

THE CULT OF PERSONALITY

Bocuse had to wait before he could sell himself. First, he needed his third star. Then he needed to know that if he was away from the restaurant the food would taste just as it would if he were there. So he spent years training his *chef-de-cuisine*, Roger Jaloux, to ensure that his kitchen would be in capable hands—that no one could ever claim they had had a bad meal at restaurant Paul Bocuse. Only then could he sell Bocuse to the world.

There was much to sell. Wine. Books. Utensils. A chef's name may be attached to many things, and one with a talent for self-promotion can spread their net very wide indeed. Bocuse did, and for a time he was the most famous chef in the world, with the endorsements to prove it.

Obviously not every chef took that route. Some, the ones that had fame thrust upon them, chose to stay in their kitchens and cook, simply letting their notoriety draw customers to them; if those customers were occasionally the Queen of England or the Shah of Iran, that for them was enough. But it must be said that these were the exception. What was it that Bocuse said? "If the tap is running, I may as well sit under it." Well, the tap was indeed running, and there was room enough under it for everybody.

But it was here that some small, subtle shift seemed to occur. Point, it has been said, was a purveyor of happiness—his interest lay solely in giving pleasure—and La Pyramide was known for its friendliness as much as for its food. But as chefs grew more famous, so a sort of reverse expectation arose; it was not that the meal would be worthy of the diner, but whether the diner would be worthy of the meal. You are entering the temple of a great man, the restaurant's atmosphere would whisper, be sure that you enjoy it. And if you are fortunate, you may even have your menu signed by the man himself, to take home as a souvenir.

NO EASY LIFE

But if chefs chose to sit under fame's tap awhile, it is difficult to blame them—it is only human nature, after all. For many of them a working life of sixteen-hour days had been the norm, particularly as apprentices, and if the workload became slightly less onerous once they became their own masters, still, it is no easy life. A restaurant is a complex thing, and the physical, financial and emotional pressures involved in its day-to-day running can be immense. So if someone wishes to hail you as a genius, and fly you to Bahrain to cook a one-off meal, you would be foolish to say no.

But even those who chose to spend most of their time in their kitchens could still capitalise on their growing reknown. Few would resist the temptation to see their recipes in print, or indeed their names on royalty cheques. Many could find it within themselves to append their name to some product or another—Bras with his knives, Guérard with a range of frozen foods—so long as quality and utility were assured. Some, like the Roux brothers, set up shops in which to sell their own products, and there were those who set up cooking schools, which gave back to their profession even as they gave revenue to the chef.

And of course there were others who had no qualm whatsoever about appearing on television. Anton Mosimann's journey to Sheffield proved that a great chef could also be good talent, just as in France Bocuse's overwhelming personality proved to be undimmed even by the small screen. There was no such thing as bad publicity, for the more people who knew your name, the more people who might come to your restaurant.

Which meant that you could not be gone too long. Most, as we have seen, had little desire to be. Their kitchen, their restaurant—this was where a chef felt at home. Most had followed a familiar path. They had dreamed in childhood of being a chef. They had trained in great kitchens, often with iconic chefs. Then they had found a kitchen to call their own and spent years building their reputations in the

only possible way—through sheer hard work. They had built a loyal *brigade* who made their creations possible. And when fame knocked on their door it was often after a decade or more in the same place, doing the same thing. If the restaurant now became a temple to themselves and their cuisine, so be it. It was not as if they had removed themselves to some Olympus. They could still meet their customers, still walk through their dining rooms and sign their menus. Take them from their restaurants and where would they be?

Exchange of gastronomic culture
in the Orient and the West

Above: Chefs (left
to right) Nobuyuki
Matsuhisa, Ferran Adrià,
Joël Robuchon and
Heston Blumenthal,
seen here with Yukio
Hattori (center),
contribute global
culinary understanding
at the World Summit
of Gastronomy 2009 in
Tokyo, Japan.

Opposite and below:
Charlie Trotter
(opposite), Gordon
Ramsay (bottom left)
and Marco Pierre White
(bottom right) take time
out from the kitchen to
promote their books.

Alain Ducasse

THE SURVIVOR

"I continued to think, continued my projects, continued to manage my restaurant. Intellectually, I never left the kitchen. I began to understand that I could have a restaurant without being obligated to be there physically."

Things change. For example, in a 1998 *New York Times* article marking his acquisition of six Michelin stars, the aeroplane from which Alain Ducasse survived his famous air crash was a humble Piper Aztec. Ten years (and 15 stars) later, when reporting on the opening of his new New York restaurant, Adour, the same newspaper noted that it was a Lear jet he was travelling in on that fateful day.

No matter. The essential facts remain. In August 1984 Ducasse and four colleagues took off from Saint Tropez. They were going to open a hotel restaurant in Courchevel, in the French Alps. The weather was bad. "I was in a hurry, which is why we decided to fly." The plane struck the side of a mountain: only Ducasse survived. He was thrown clear of the wreckage and lay in the snow, fully conscious, for almost seven hours before being rescued. Doctors considered amputating his leg; for a year he could not stand at all. His right arm was

so badly injured that he could not lift even a paring knife.

It seems almost redundant to note that such things will change a man. At the very least, they will give him time to think.

"I continued making menus," he says of his time in hospital. "I continued to think, continued my projects, continued to manage my restaurant. Intellectually, I never left the kitchen. I began to understand that I could have a restaurant without being obligated to be there physically."

Time, indeed, to change the very notion of what it is to be a chef.

THE MERCHANT OF HAPPINESS

He calls himself a 'merchant of happiness'. Still, he notes, "it's a serious business, pleasure." A business that, at time of writing, runs to 24 restaurants, four inns, four bakeries, two cooking schools, a hotel consortium, and a publishing house. Which would leave little time, it seems, for the plain business of cooking.

Ducasse's response lies in a quote that has taken on a life of its own. Do we, he asks, expect Yves Saint Laurent to stitch every item of clothing? No, we do not. "The role of the chef is to train people to take care of the clients, who live in the spirit which he develops over the years. The walls of the restaurant sweat his philosophy."

And what *is* his philosophy? In short, success, predicated on attention to detail. "I am obsessed with details," he often says. "If we make sure of every one of the details, it will not change … like a Swiss clock." Nor does he mean just in the kitchen; the font for the menus, the butter dishes, the curtain rods; everything passes through Ducasse.

It is in all of his kitchens, though, where his touch must be most sure. He follows the career of younger chefs, often for years, before personally seeking them out. They are then inducted into what has been called 'a culinary boot camp' in Monaco. Ducasse happily likens it to a sect. "When I tell someone, 'The venison sauce isn't robust enough,' he immediately knows what I mean because he's been formatted, conditioned in Monaco." They are not tortured, he says, but they work hard. And if they succeed, they become part of the circle.

"He's closer to me," one of his executive chefs says, "than my own father."

THE PRICE IS RIGHT

His own mentor was Alain Chapel. He became an apprentice at age 16, despite his parents' objections. Raised on a farm in the Landes district of southwestern France, where the family grew vegetables and raised geese, ducks and turkeys, they wanted him to continue his schooling. He, on the other hand, was sure of what he wanted to do—the smells of his grandmother's cooking had seen to that.

Six years later he was in Chapel's kitchen, once memorably described as 'like one of those beautiful nineteenth-century pumping-engines, moving majestically and silently, seemingly without effort, yet delivering immense power.'

That power was imparted to the food, and Ducasse recalls happily paying three weeks wages for the privilege of experiencing it from the other side. "Magical," he says. "The excellence of the table, the beauty of the cutlery, *le service*, *le luxe*…".

Such plaudits, and more, would be his in little less than a decade, becoming at 34 the youngest chef in France to be awarded three Michelin stars, at the Hotel de Paris in Monte Carlo.

He took the hotel's restaurant, Louis XV, in 1987, only three years after the accident. He could still not walk unaided. But the stars were destined to come—he had insisted in his contract that if he did not deliver them in four years he could be dismissed. What was to come next was not so much destined as it was truly historical.

UNREASONABLE MEN

It was the first time a hotel restaurant had won three stars; both Ducasse and restaurant Louis XV were famous. But in France in the early 1990s there was famous, and then there was Robuchon. Not since the heyday of Bocuse had one man so dominated the culinary landscape. And now he claimed he was going to retire.

Ducasse makes it sound perfectly reasonable. "Everybody knew Joël Robuchon was going to retire, but nobody called him." The Louis XV was closed at midweek, and Robuchon's Paris restaurant was closed at weekends. "So I said, 'All right, to keep myself busy … I'll do it'" He had already opened a country inn in Provence… where was the problem?

History, it has been said, is not made by reasonable men.

It is now so commonplace for a Michelin-starred chef to have multiple establishments that we might wonder what is wrong with those who choose not to. Before Ducasse, however, it was almost inconceivable. Yes, Paul Bocuse had half shares in restaurants in Osaka and Tokyo and yes, he travelled often, but he had only one *kitchen*, and he was criticized frequently for spending so much time away from it.

Even Robuchon had only had one restaurant at a time. The notion that a true chef might preside over multiple establishments was a truly radical departure.

Certainly it was to prove too radical for the Guide Michelin. Only Eugenie Brazier in the 1930's held six stars at once; for La Mere Brazier in Lyons and Le Col de la Luere in the countryside nearby. Ducasse intended to shuttle between Paris and Monaco.

Ducasse puts it plainly. "Everybody thought I was crazy."

STARS WON AND LOST

The year after he had taken over from Robuchon he retained—or re-earned—the restaurant's three stars. It was a remarkable feat. Only it was not to be a triumph. The Michelin judges had seen fit to take a star from the Louis XV, as if unwilling to imagine that a single chef, however brilliant, could be capable of such achievement.

Ducasse was. The downgrading was seen merely as a sanction, and it was not to last. Not least, it had to be acknowledged that for a man nearly killed in an air crash, flying weekly between Monaco and Paris required a dramatic strength of will. And from then on, Ducasse was virtually unstoppable. He opened another restaurant in Paris. One in Tokyo. Another in Paris. As his wife, more than twenty years his junior, says: "That's how he works. If he has a passion, if he wants something, he will not give up."

He, like everyone, wanted New York. "I have Paris, Monaco, Tokyo," he says, "but New York … gives you global legitimacy. One can live without New York, but it's better not to."

Don't let it be said he failed. He opened Alain Ducasse at Essex House in 2000, and for a while possessed an unprecedented nine Michelin stars. New Yorkers, however, proved to be a tough crowd, and after the initial success criticisms soon appeared. The prices were too high! The food pretentious! They gave you a choice of ten pens with which to sign the bill! Even his other restaurants were not immune: one reviewer travelled to Paris and Monaco to make comparisons. "We have gone from Robuchon," she wrote, "to Robo-chef." The Essex House restaurant closed in 2007.

WHAT NEXT?

His mentor, Alain Chapel once claimed that if his restaurant were to turn over twenty million francs a year "I would sell it and go and start another little restaurant." He refused to serve more than seventy covers at any meal.

We could not begin to calculate how many meals Alain Ducasse serves: every night food is presented in his name on three continents (as well as in space: in 2003 he devised the menu for the international space station) by chefs whose names will never rank alongside his. This is no doubt as it should be. His restaurants are no mere conveyor-belts for standardised food—there is no central warehouse, no dishes on multiple menus, no knives or plates or glasses that are shared. Yet each of the dishes comes from the mind of just one man. Alain Ducasse. A man whose grandmother was so annoyed by his constant questions that she refused to teach him. Instead, she would send him to the garden to pick vegetables.

"I now have in my head the original memory of the taste of a tomato, a cucumber, an onion, lettuce," he explains. "My grandmother would wash them, and exactly ten minutes after they'd been growing, we would eat. Feeding yourself from nature, that's true luxury, absolute and elemental. It cannot be bought. It must be cultivated." This from a man who now makes his ice cream with milk from the Prince of Monaco's cows.

This page: Ducasse's food, such as the appetizer of duck foie gras (far left) and a classic vol-au-vent (below) represents perfection in the Classical French style. Ducasse himself, seen here tasting a dish at the Louis XV (left), is not often in the kitchen, relying instead on his well-trained staff.

Overleaf: The dining room of the Louis XV restaurant is decorated in the style of 17th century Versailles.

Baba au Rhum

In a large stainless steel bowl, dissolve 1 sachet of dried
yeast in 1/3 cup of milk. Stir over a medium heat until warm.
Remove from the heat and stir in 1/4 cup of sifted flour,
cover and set in a warm place for 20 minutes.

Beat 7 tablespoons of softened unsalted butter with
2 tablespoons of sugar and 2 tablespoons of flour. Add
4 eggs, one at a time, and beat well. When the yeast dough
has risen and become spongy, whisk in this mixture, plus a
further 1 1/4 cups of flour, to make a thick, doughlike batter.
Spoon the batter into eight greased dariole moulds. Bake in
a 180° C (350° F) oven for 20 minutes.

Stir 1 cup of sugar into 2 cups of water in a saucepan and
bring to the boil. Remove from the heat and stir in the zest
of 1 orange, in strips. When cool, add 1/2 a cup of rum.

When the babas are risen and golden, remove from the
oven and unmold. Dip them into the syrup to saturate and
then leave on a wire rack to cool. When cool, brush with
warmed, strained apricot jam.

To serve, split the babas lengthwise and spoon over more
rum, then top with vanilla whipped cream.

Empires

HOW TO BE IN TWO PLACES AT ONCE

Ducasse prefers Yves Saint Laurent, because he is French, but most commonly it is Armani that chefs use as their example. Do you expect, they will say, that Armani sews every one of the jackets himself? The answer, of course, is no: we do not expect the designer to also be the seamstress. Yet we expect that the chef whose name is above the door is the one who has cooked our steak. At the very least we imagine him to have been in the kitchen whilst it was being cooked.

When Ducasse, lying in his hospital bed, saw that this need not be so, he was not imagining any fundamental shift in the *way* things were done. He was simply realising that it was all a matter of perception. Since Escoffier, the kitchen had become an assembly line. The dish is constructed by multiple hands, and the chef is merely the foreman, overseeing the process.

The great chefs, however, were conductors —their art was to bring together the elements in a way that created something greater than the sum of its parts. Just as a piece of music depends on the interplay between each instrument, the finished dish requires something which is to a certain degree improvised, a kind of magic which happens when the *brigade* is working as one. Ducasse saw that if the score was right, the orchestra well rehearsed, and the stage set, the audience would not realise that the conductor had left the building. Indeed, the conductor might be in another city, conducting an entirely different orchestra, and hence be getting paid twice for one night's work.

Possibly we are impugning Mr Ducasse's motives here. Few of us survive plane crashes, and we should not presume to know what goes on in the minds of those that do. We can only know that, after his hiccup with the Guide Michelin, Ducasse made it possible for a chef to preside over multiple three-star restaurants. The question is, why should they wish to?

LOVE, OR MONEY?

Could it really be only about the money? As we have seen, Ducasse's great mentor, Alain Chapel, professed to care nothing about money: in 1977 the closing of his restaurant one day per week reportedly cost him two million francs a year in lost revenue. But every hour of every day a Ducasse restaurant somewhere is open, making money. That's what businesses do, and a businessman must be allowed to expand as he sees fit, or at least as the market allows. If ultimately the market did not allow Ducasse's first venture into New York, for example, it permitted him to open twice in Tokyo in one year. The market showed Joël Robuchon that a single concept might be successfully rolled out across the globe. It proved that London and Tokyo were more conducive for Pierre Gagnaire than regional France had been. He would not put it that way, though. As to why he went to Tokyo, he says: "I am not a businessman. I am someone who creates cuisine. For me, that's the most important thing. If someone comes to me and makes a proposition, then I will say 'yes' or 'no.'"

Perhaps it was Gagnaire's bankruptcy which prompts him to say he is not a businessman. Either way, the statement is disingenuous; a chef with only one restaurant might make that claim, but a chef with four or five may not; by that stage, he is in business, well and truly. So why does this sound like criticism? Is the nature of the chef such that the normal rules do not apply?

THE 'TOUCH'

"Each restaurant must have a personality," Ducasse says, "the sentiment of the man or woman who made it, who gave their touch, their ideas." That may be it, the word 'touch.' The restaurant is not a bank, not a hardware store or a supermarket. It is a place where, on any given evening, magic may happen. The great restaurateurs, whether they are chefs or not, have long recognised this—Beauvilliers' sword was as much for his customers aggrandisement as it was for his own.

A great restaurant must have the touch, and if it does, we are then sceptical that this touch can be reproduced over and over again. Could Point have replicated La Pyramide anywhere else? We have to believe not.

Yet Madame Point carried on, and for seven years under Paul Mercier, La Pyramide retained its three stars. It may no longer have had Point, but it still had his food. For all that his was *la cuisine du moment*, many of his dishes had taken years to create, test and perfect before they ever went on the menu. The *gratin de queues d'ecrevisses* was such a dish, and only once Point and his wife, who tested all his creations, believed that it could be improved no further did they offer it to their customers.

This, then, is the 'touch.' The chef who spends years perfecting his recipes, who selects the fittings and the drapes, who chooses the menu covers; it is this personality which permeates the restaurant, and all who work there labour in support of his or her vision.

Obviously, it is a labour of love—and a question of loyalty. A *chef-de-cuisine* may stay with his chef for most of his working life, even though his abilities mean he might easily be more prosperous in his own establishment. Often it is a matter of temperament or ambition—some have their eye less firmly fixed on greatness than others—and such chefs are happy to be the support players, even the soloists. They just don't wish to be the conductor, and it is on the shoulders of such men and women that culinary empires are built.

EMPIRE BUILDING

But empires need an emperor. Bocuse, who was such a man himself, has said that a great chef is one who finds two new dishes in a lifetime, and that in his opinion there are but a limited number of chefs who will leave any lasting mark in the history of cuisine. Yet there are a number who have already left an indelible mark on the restaurant business. Bocuse was the first to leave his kitchen for any length of time, and Ducasse the first to hold multiple stars. Joël Robuchon was the first to realise that standardisation and *haute cuisine* are not necessarily antithetical. Pierre Gagnaire recognised that an idiosyncratic, freeform style

Opposite: Alain Ducasse outside Spoon Tokyo. The Spoon franchise began with Spoon Paris, a fusion bistro famous for its bubblegum ice cream. There are Spoon branches in Mauritius and at London Sanderson hotel.

is still no impediment to expansion. Thomas Keller saw that if you had a video hook-up between your kitchens in California and New York then you could effectively be in two places at once.

That is the thing: a chef still has to *be* there, even if only occasionally. Touch cannot be achieved remotely. Pierre Gagnaire, speaking to the Japan *Times* on the subject of his Tokyo restaurant gaining its second star, said "I'm in contact [with the restaurant] daily, and I come over to Tokyo every two to three months and I stay eight days. I stay in the kitchen; I don't go sightseeing."

Currently Gagnaire has fewer than half a dozen restaurants. Ducasse has 24 and counting, and each of them receives his touch—for his recent New York opening it was Ducasse that decided that the American beef was superior to the Australian, for example, so that was the one they would use. For *Le Jules Verne*, the iconic restaurant on the second level of the Eiffel Tower he had won the right to re-open, it was Ducasse who chose each specific fabric that would be used: for uniforms, napkins, even for tying up menus. Ducasse who chooses the serving dishes. Ducasse who picks the artworks. Ducasse who only sleeps four hours a night.

But does Ducasse still cook, that is the question. To which the answer is, of course he does. Because a chef who no longer cooks is one who is in very real danger of losing his touch.

Left: A view of Paris from Alain Ducasse's newest restaurant, situated on the second level of the Eiffel Tower.

Thomas Keller

THE AMERICAN

" For all the lessons Fernand Point's heirs have learnt, very few have remembered that for Point one restaurant was enough, and Keller soon cast his bread upon the waters; his food was too good, and he too driven. "

Keller

Nobody—nobody—is suggesting he is the master incarnate. And should the man himself let slip that he was born in 1955, the year that Fernand Point died, Thomas Keller is not for a moment suggesting anything along the lines of transmigrating souls. Think of him rather as a pearl grown from Point's oyster. Or, more precisely, from Point's *Ma Gastronomie*, the great man's unique *mélange* of maxims, philosophy and technique. Before reading that, Keller has said, cooking was just a job. After Point, it became a calling. Then an obsession. And before too long he was the best chef in America.

GRIT + TIME

Without the speck of grit the pearl will never grow. For Keller it was an unnamed cook in the Florida restaurant his mother managed who, in deciding to quit without notice, provided that speck. His mother was desperate; Keller's career was born.

We do not know exactly when he encountered Point's book. We do know that on another auspicious date, America's 200th birthday, he was in Rhode Island to watch the tall ships pass by. He got a job as a fish cook, even though he knew nothing about cooking fish. That was 1976. The next year he was back in Florida with his own restaurant, but that failed after a year and a half. Still, we suspect by then he had heard the call. A few summers spent in casual cooking jobs, a stint in a French bistro in New York, and then… Paris. He was obsessed with French technique by now, and worked at such famed restaurants as Guy Savoy, Taillevent and Pré Catelan, following a tradition as old as the cuisine he was learning.

But he was no Joël Robuchon, blazing across the firmament. He did his time in France, then returned to America and further served in New York. Again he opened his own restaurant

GREAT, GRAND & FAMOUS CHEFS AND THEIR SIGNATURE DISHES

that again failed. He moved on, to Los Angeles this time, cowed but not beaten.

"In cooking," he says, "it's a lot of repetition … you have to make croissants ten thousand times to really understand the process. Then when you can do it without thinking about the process, you're liberated, free…"

It was 1994 by the time Keller freed his pearl from the shell.

THE PEARL

Yountville is a small town in California's Napa Valley, 150 miles (240 km) north of San Francisco. On its main street, barely a mile long, there is a restaurant that diners often drive past once or even twice before recognising it as their destination. It is The French Laundry, once hailed 'the most exciting place to eat in the United States.' And no, even after a decade and a half you still can't get a table.

From the restaurant's very beginnings, working within the boundaries of a rigorous classical technique, Keller strove always towards perfection; if the produce he had to work with was imperfect he suffered enormously, and let those around him know it; for he is "a very driven individual." So says a chef who spent two years in his kitchen. Indeed his passion for improvement is the stuff of legend.

"If I sauté [a] fish, I want to do it again, only find better, fresher fish, a different sauté pan and perfect what I am doing." But in the introduction to his French Laundry Cookbook he acknowledges the true reason behind such a pursuit. "When you acknowledge, as you must, that there is no such thing as perfect food, only the ideal of it, then the real purpose of striving toward perfection becomes clear: to make people happy. That's what cooking is all about."

The French Laundry certainly serves that purpose: despite the fact that the cost of the experience can rise to four figures, the only universal complaint is that it is so difficult to secure a booking. Which is good for some—Keller jokes that the woman who supplies the restaurant's butter, from a farm in Vermont with

a herd of only six, named a newly acquired cow after him. She called it 'Cash.'

By then *Time* magazine had named him the best chef in America, and he had been described as the near-perfect embodiment of the 21st-century American chef, combining culinary, entrepreneurial and business personas, seamlessly and elegantly, into an exquisitely rendered portrait of success.

THE OYSTER

Think of them as the milk-fed veal or the foie gras of the sea, these humble bivalves. Known to humans since the earliest times and prized almost universally—the Greeks farmed them, the Romans went all the way to Britain for them—they remain the sea's tenderest morsels.

Of course, anything that popular is unlikely to prosper. As early as the 17th century oysters were becoming scarce, and through necessity (a world without oysters!) cultivation became the norm.

It really couldn't be easier. Seed oysters are affixed to tiles, and the tiles are then tethered some way out to sea. There they stay for a period of years until, at the point they are deemed large enough, they are transferred to inshore beds for fattening. They don't need to be force-fed like geese or massaged like Kobe beef. They just sit there, feeding and growing fat. All they need is water.

But, just as in real estate, it's *location* that counts. This is why oysters are generally identified by geography rather than species, for it is the quality of the water that is all-important. Fattening beds are situated at or near a rivermouth, because the overgrowth of the liver is stimulated by the mix of fresh and sea water. The oyster's flavour, on the other hand, is governed by the salinity of its home waters, and by the mineral traces it absorbs. The water's temperature determines how rapidly the oyster grows, and even defines its sex.

It's a simple equation: a surfeit of warmth and food will usually result in female oysters that are plump, creamy and rich with eggs; cold water can delay sexual maturity almost

Opposite: In the kitchen at the French Laundry. By all accounts this is a calm, quiet kitchen with an impeccably drilled *brigade de cuisine*.

indefinitely and gives the oyster's flesh a crisp, lean, ozone-like tang. This means a Pacific oyster is unlike an Atlantic oyster which bears little resemblance to a Southern Ocean oyster. It's *all* about location.

THE PROMISED LAND

America. The continent which, as F. Scott Fitzgerald wrote, was the last place in history to be truly commensurate with man's capacity for wonder. Its vastness, its riches, served for two centuries to grow an empire unequalled in the modern world.

For the people of that empire, it must have seemed that they need only sit and wait, for all things would eventually come to them. Many did just that, feeling that if it wasn't to be found in this great expanse of land, between sea and shining sea, then it was probably of little value anyway.

But there has always been another type of American, the seeker after truth, or beauty, or perfection, who long since realised that you have to go away before you can come back again, and that what you bring back might just be the making of you. These were the men and women who brought the news from foreign lands. They carried with them other traditions, other techniques, and when they anchored these amidst America's impossibly fertile currents, well, all they needed to do then was sit back and watch them grow.

OYSTERS AND PEARLS

For all the lessons Fernand Point's heirs *have* learnt, very few have remembered that for Point one restaurant was enough, and Keller soon cast his bread upon the waters; his food was too good, and he too driven. The French Laundry was followed by a bistro, Bouchon, and then Bouchon Bakery. In 2003 the The French Laundry was named at number one of the London-based Restaurant magazine's inaugural list of 'The World's 50 Best Restaurants.'

Then, in 2004, Keller opened Per Se in New York. In two years it had three Michelin stars, and a year later The French Laundry was awarded the same, and Keller became the first American chef to oversee two three-star establishments. He opened a Bouchon and Bouchon Bakery in Las Vegas, and another restaurant in Yountville, Ad Hoc, a casual dining emporium serving the comfort food Keller remembered from his childhood. He also produced a range of designer tableware named, in honour of his inspiration, Point. There are cookbooks, too (the French Laundry cookbook has gone at least 17 editions), and his own wine.

An 'exquisitely rendered portrait of success' indeed.

At a gala dinner, where patrons lined up for an autograph, the president of the Culinary Institute of America introduced Keller as 'this generation's Paul Bocuse.' That he is not. Just as Bocuse could have sprung from nowhere but France, Keller's story is uniquely American.

Because he was thinking of a popular ice-cream chain when he created his signature starter: a miniature hand-rolled ice cream cone filled with red onion creme fraiche and topped with a scoop of tuna tartare.

Because his New York restaurant cost US$12 million, yet resides in a shopping mall.

Because to improve his business skills he created an advisory board that includes a psychologist and 'executive coach.'

And because when this son of a military man and a working mother was asked why he was returning New York, a city where more than 15 years ago he opened a critically acclaimed restaurant that nevertheless failed, he laughed. "The challenge, I guess," he said, "to see if I can be everything I can be." Because that's the American way.

This page: Precision, presentation, playfulness. Thomas Keller deftly filets a salmon (left) wooden clothes pegs accompany a selection of petit fours (right); Keller's signature Oysters and Pearls, an elegant dish and a visual and verbal pun.

Overleaf: The French Laundry (above); Cornet of Atlantic Salmon (below) served al fresco.

Oysters and Pearls

Soak 1/3 cup small pearl tapioca in 1 cup of milk for 1 hour.

Shuck 16 oysters. Trim away the muscle and the outer ruffled edge of each oyster and place the trimmings in a saucepan. Reserve the whole trimmed oysters and strain the oyster juice into a separate bowl.

Whip 1/2 cup of cream just until it holds its shape and store in the refrigerator.

Drain the softened tapioca in a strainer and discard the milk. Rinse the tapioca under cold running water, then place it in a small heavy pot.

Pour 3/4 cup milk and 3/4 cup cream over the oyster trimmings. Bring to a simmer, then strain the infused liquid onto the tapioca. Cook the tapioca over medium heat, stirring constantly with a wooden spoon, until it has thickened and the spoon leaves a trail when it is pulled through, 7 to 8 minutes. Continue to cook for another 5 to 7 minutes, until the tapioca has no resistance in the centre and is translucent. Remove the pot from the heat and set aside in a warm place.

Place 4 large egg yolks and half the oyster juice in a metal bowl set over a pan of hot water. Whisk vigorously over medium heat for 2 to 3 minutes to incorporate as much air as possible. The finished sabayon will have thickened and lightened, the foam will have subsided, and the sabayon will hold a ribbon when it falls from the whisk. If the mixture begins to break, remove it from the heat and whisk quickly off the heat for a moment to recombine, then return to the heat.

Stir the hot sabayon into the tapioca, along with a generous amount of black pepper. Mix in 1/4 cup of crème fraîche and the whipped cream. The tapioca will be a creamy pale yellow with the tapioca pearls suspended in the mixture. Season lightly with salt, remembering that the oysters and the caviar garnish will both be salty. Immediately spoon 1/4 cup tapioca into eight gratin dishes. Tap the gratin dishes on the counter so that the tapioca forms an even layer. Cover and refrigerate until ready to use, or for up to a day.

Preheat the oven to 180° C (350° F).

Combine 3 tbsp vermouth, the remaining reserved oyster juice, 1½ tbsp minced shallots and 1½ tbsp vinegar in a small saucepan. Simmer until most of the liquid has evaporated. Whisk 8 tbsp chilled butter piece by piece.

Meanwhile, place the dishes of tapioca on a baking sheet and heat in the oven for 4 to 5 minutes, or until they just begin to puff up. Add the oysters and some chopped chives to the sauce to warm through.

Spoon 2 oysters and some of the sauce over each gratin and garnish with caviar. Serve immediately.

Location

YOU CAN PUT A GREAT RESTAURANT ANYWHERE

Here are some names which go together: New York, Paris, London, Tokyo, Yountville, Great Milton, Roses, Bray.

Why? Because you are as likely to eat the meal of your life in a small town in Northern California or a quaint English village as you are in New York, Paris or London. And in Tokyo you will find restaurants with a total of 191 Michelin stars—more than any other city.

Put simply, the old adage of 'location, location, location' no longer applies. The world's most famous restaurant is in a seaside town on Spain's Mediterranean coast, where it started life as a minigolf course. Two of England's three three-star restaurants are in the same small village an hour out of London. Both are housed in what used to be pubs. The French Laundry was previously … a laundry.

Many a great restaurant has sprung from humble origins. Often the great *chefs-patron* began at the family *auberge*, or inn, cooking for the local villagers and those travellers who might stop by on their way to somewhere else. Nor were locations always particularly favourable. Restaurant Paul Bocuse, situated in what was originally a village, Collonges-au-Mont-d'Or, that has now been swallowed by Lyon's sprawl, is located right beside the railway tracks—the building shakes whenever a train goes by—and on the other side runs a busy road. Indeed, Bocuse in the 1970s, when he was the most famous chef in the world and his restaurant a place of gastronomic pilgrimage, still considered it a *restaurant de route*, whose role was to feed the people who might be driving north or south.

Or so he claimed: we have already observed that great chefs have a tendency to be disingenuous when it comes to talking about their achievements. The fact remains—a restaurant needs customers. Nor does it pay to be picky about where those customers come from. Locals and the odd tourist or travelling salesman have been enough to sustain many a humble restaurant.

But it goes without saying that a three-star restaurant is no longer humble. It cannot afford to be. Your customers are as likely to be travelling diplomats as travelling salesmen, movie stars more often than locals.

The provincial three-star chefs took this in their stride, yet ensured there was a place for locals should they still wish to come. The next generation, many of whom came from a different tradition (and indeed were often not even French) had no family *auberge* waiting for them when they had finished their training. Their aspirations, too, were different. Bright lights and big cities have long held the greatest attraction for the ambitious, and the lure of streets filled with sophisticated diners with money to spend proved irresistible to many chefs.

PARIS

Paris requires no explanation. It was home to the first restaurant. It was the place Carême was born, and the city where he died. It is the City of Light, the epicentre of European sophistication, and the gustatory capital of the world. Quite simply, it is Paris.

Its restaurants are the stuff of legend—Maxim's, Taillevent, La Tour d'Argent (over a million servings of pressed duck!), the Lucas-Carton, The Ritz—to the point that Paris is synonymous with *haute cuisine*. Even if in 1977 there were twice as many three-star restaurants in the provinces, Paris still had six, and no

other city in the world could boast that. For Robuchon, Ducasse and Gagnaire, Paris was the ultimate proving ground. Sure, Ducasse may have had three stars in Monte Carlo, but if he had not got them in Paris, too, his empire would never have been founded. Gagnaire had had three stars in St. Etienne, but look where that had got him—bankrupt.

Michel Bras on the other hand evinced no desire to conquer Paris: he was too rooted in his native soil, just as the provincial *chefs-patron* had been. When finally one single restaurant was not enough, it was to Japan that he gravitated. Even here, Bras found himself in Toya, on the island of Hokkaido, rather than the bustle of Tokyo, where he would have been in the company of, and in competition with, the three other members of that quartet of modern French greats, Robuchon, Ducasse and Gagnaire.

But even should those three vacate the city tomorrow, the world of Paris dining would be only a little troubled. It is too great a city, its eating houses too many and varied—from *haute cuisine* temples to historic *belle-epoque* brasseries down to neighbourhood bistros whose food in any other country might qualify as fine dining—to leave anyone wanting for too long. That is its great joy; that one can enter any establishment, grand or humble, and know that chances are one will leave it a little happier. Because, after all, this *is* Paris.

Opposite: Michel Bras surveys the landscape around his restaurant in Laguiole, South Western France.

Above: The landscape of Yountville in the Napa Valley, Northern California — home to vineyards, farms and the French Laundry.

AH ROUX & S GIRALDIN, LICENSED TO SELL INTOXICATING LIQUOR FOR CONSUMPTION ON PREMISES W

LONDON

London is not Paris. But thanks to the efforts of Anton Mossiman, Raymond Blanc and the brothers Roux, it's no longer a century behind it, either.

London is perhaps the most cosmopolitan of all the world's great cities, its population the most varied. Because that is the case, the range of food on offer is dizzying. From Bengal to Burundi, Japan to Jamaica, Mexico to Madagascar and New Zealand to Norway, in London you can find food from all of them.

At the pinnacles of fine dining one is a little less spoiled for choice—but only a little—and what one loses in choice one makes up for in atmosphere. If it's true that if you sit in one place long enough the whole world will pass you by, then if you sit anywhere in London the world will pass by in half the time; in places like Nobu or The Ivy celebrities both major and minor populate half the tables, while the other half are filled with a mixture of stylish but blasé locals and enthusiastic tourists. A supermodel, or Madonna, might walk in at any moment, but it is only the tourists who will raise their heads.

NEW YORK

New York is the *toughest* restaurant scene in the world; unless you are a native you have to have made it somewhere else before you can make it here, and even then there are no guarantees. No less a chef than Ducasse found that out, to his cost.

New York, more than anywhere else, is the province of restaurateurs, of location, of *hip*. In many instances the food is a long way down the list of a restaurant's requirements. The address, the name of the decorator, or whether you can get Donald Trump on your guest list for opening night may account for your success far more than the quality of your cooking.

This is an an exaggeration, though not much of one. As Ducasse said before his second attempt at conquering New York, "When you open a restaurant, it's not the same in London, in Paris, in Tokyo or New York. You always have to understand the men and women who live in that town." He realised that it was about 'clarity'. "That's our philosophy. Everyone in New York is so rushed, so stressed, you have to give them easy pleasure."

Would that it were so simple. For New York, *everything* has to be right. The food. The service. The décor. The location. The price. The clientele. The reviews. Everything. And if it's not, you will find yourself in Yountville.

YOUNTVILLE

Which might give the impression that Yountville is somehow a bad place to be. Assuredly, it is not. Indeed, if you have failed once in New York it is the perfect place to take stock, to regroup, and to slowly rebuild your reputation until it becomes unassailable. In a small town such as Yountville you have time to perfect your cuisine; the locals will be forgiving; if the tourists come once but do not return it doesn't really matter, for there will always be more tourists.

But the location cannot be too obscure, or no one will ever 'discover' your restaurant. And your food must be truly exceptional. People will not travel for the merely excellent. Fulfil those two requirements, however, and the simple fact is that people *will* come, whether it is to Yountville, Laguiole, Great Milton or Bray. And if you can make it there, well…

Daniel Boulud

THE FARM BOY

" Before Ducasse, before Keller, before Robuchon, Daniel Boulud had taken Manhattan. But New York is not a prize you can keep without a fight. "

Boulud

"If it's meat, it needs to rest—we fire it when we get the order so they have time to cook it. The fish, we know, is up to a seven-minute cooking time, so the fish will be based on what the meat guy says. At the end, the saucier will say how many minutes away he is based on what he has to fire. They work a lot together because we have a central stove. But, it's like every restaurant, when you get a rush, you get a rush, and you get … slammed…"

It is in this period of exquisitely controlled chaos when everything has to happen at once ('slammed' is by far the politest term for it) that a chef will show his true colours. And when you hear Daniel Boloud, once of St. Pierre de Chandieu, about twenty miles outside Lyon, and now at the beating heart of American cooking, you *know* what his colours are. But we should let him tell it, motivating his team as they cater a fundraising dinner for then-president Clinton.

"Let's kick ass!" he says.

HANGING OUT

Once upon a time he was a simple French farm boy. The Boulud family were smallholders— they raised whatever would grow—and every market day they would take their produce to sell in Lyon. They also ran a café on the first floor of the family home, where six generations of Boulud women had cooked. In the backyard was huge electric pylon; in the 1960s the local nobleman paid the valley's farmers to locate the powerlines that fed the area on their land, where they would not spoil his view. Now there is a swimming pool and a tennis court, too, a testament to the success of the Boulud's favoured son.

He was 14 when he went to work at Nandron, a two-starred restaurant only metres away from Lyon's central market. A greater fortune could not have befallen him.

"Since I was a teenager, I had chefs like Paul Bocuse kicking my butt," he says.

It may be literally true: if the seismic shift that Lyonnais gastronomy represented had a ground zero, then a café in the square beside the market at Lyons is probably it. Bocuse, the Troisgrois brothers, George Blanc and Alain Chapel would place their orders at the market and, while their trucks were being loaded, retire to the café for a breakfast of tripe, sausages, fresh bread and butter, and coffee. The young Boulud would hang around, eager to be accepted by these great men of gastronomy. And if in time he was, we might imagine his 'butt' being once or twice kicked in the process.

Whatever. His apprenticeship had begun, and it was to be from a dream team of master chefs that Boulud would learn his trade; first Gerard Nandron and then Georges Blanc, Roger Vergé and finally Michel Guérard. Even an average student could not help but learn. Boulud was a cut above.

Roger Vergé still recalls how impressed he was by Boulud's affinity for sauces. "A good chef has to be a good saucier first," he explains. "You must understand their complexity, balance, and seasonings, and to know how to associate them with fish, meat, or vegetables. It requires a perfectionist drive for the composition of flavors and ingredients, the impeccable cooking of each vegetable to achieve its full flavour potential. What Daniel first indicated to me in my kitchen is a mastery of the simplest ingredients."

BREAKFAST IN AMERICA

It was from Michel Guérard that Boulud learned how to put it all together. "It's not even so much about technique … it is about understanding the connecting wire of the recipe and being sensitive to how each ingredient hangs off that wire." And then he was done; the apprenticeship was over.

He was now a small fish in a very big pond. But it is at such moments that fate steps into a young man's life, and for Boulud fate came in the shape of America. In 1981, at the age of 26, he became chef to the European Commission's ambassador in Washington, D.C.

It was, in the words of one reporter, 'a good gig.' Diplomatic dinner parties required excellence, certainly, but they did not demand the hours that a restaurant would. Boulud had the time to get to know his surroundings, and to decide that he liked them. When the ambassador was re-posted back to Europe, Boulud did not go with him. Instead he jumped in his car and drove north, to New York. He had an audition to go to, and he knew if he could make it there…

"I made a fifteen-course lunch to blow them away. I wanted it, so I threw everything I knew at them." He got the job. For the first time, Boulud was serving his farm-inspired *haute cuisine* recipes to the world's most demanding diners. The critics soon took notice, and the notices were good.

START SPREADIN' THE NEWS…

It was Boulud's command of technique which set him apart. It was his singular apprenticeship which had taught him to look to local tradition and ingredients as a basis for invention. It was a legendary New York restaurant that gave him a stage.

Sirio Maccioni has been called the 'greatest restaurateur since Prohibition.' That claim is perhaps exaggerated. Even so, from a humble village in Tuscany Maccioni had risen to the top: his restaurant, Le Cirque, was playing host to the cream of New York society, both high and low. The decadent years of disco and cocaine were giving way to a new hedonism based on money, expensive wine and *haute cuisine*, and Le Cirque was its Studio 54; a glittering den of celebrity where no request was too outrageous. But suddenly Maccioni found himself without a chef.

Boulud's reputation was already made. He had other offers to consider, but Maccioni was the kind of man you don't refuse. "It's hard to have a dialogue with Sirio," Boulud says. "Basically, you listen."

Still it was a genuine collaboration, in that some of the food was Italian, some of it was French. They were both still country boys at heart, and their great innovation was in offering peasant food to high society—on Le Cirque's menu pot-au-feu, bollito misto, lard and focaccia and pigs' feet and lentils vied with the most refined sauces and labor-intensive *haute cuisine*. There Boulud invented his signature scallops black tie (scallops and black truffles) and paupiette of sea bass, and there he was inspired to pair white truffles and baked potato, lots of butter and grainy sea salt. "Baked potatoes," he says, a trifle disingenuously, "always move well on an American menu." And move they did—at $35 per serve.

MOVING ON UP

After six years Boulud had outgrown Le Cirque. He wanted his own name above the door.

He chose to use his Christian name. The first version of Restaurant Daniel suffered a shaky start, but it was not long before Boulud got the New York Times' maximum four stars. Soon he was about the biggest fish in the pond—reservations were 'by recommendation only'—but the restaurant was too small. As his business adviser says, "Daniel's ambition was not satisfied simply having a society place."

Maccioni had since closed Le Cirque, in part due to a 'pugnacious' hotel union. The building was now being redeveloped into condominiums, and the space was again available. Ironically, given their parting had not been without rancour, Boulud's new Restaurant Daniel would reside where he had previously come to fame. The alterations to the landmarked interior, which was a 1925 version of a Venetian palazzo, would come in at $10 million.

This was 1998. A reporter on hand for the opening gives us the flavour of the kitchen.

"'Let's get everyone in here. I want 60 out … *tout de suite* … move it!" Five chefs in white tunics race up from the prep kitchen downstairs. "What time is it? How do I know if we are on time! *Merde!*'"

THE BIG POND

Boulud's timing was pretty good. Before Ducasse, before Keller, before Robuchon, Daniel Boulud had taken Manhattan. But New York is not a prize you can keep without a fight.

In 2006 seven current or former workers at Restaurant Daniel filed a lawsuit claiming they were denied promotions to higher-paying and more visible positions. The lawsuit also claimed that the restaurant discriminated against the workers, immigrants from Latin America and Bangladesh, because of their ethnicity, race and national origin. Demonstrations outside the restaurant had been going on for two years, organised by what might be called a 'pugnacious' workers' rights centre. Sirio Maccioni may perhaps have chuckled. Eventually the case was settled out of court.

Boulud's empire had expanded comfortably by then, with eight restaurants to his name, including the more-casual DB Bistro Moderne, immediately famous for serving what was then, at $27, the most expensive hamburger in New York.

But it pays to remember just where such empires spring from. As an apprentice at Nandron, Boulud worked 13-hour days for five French francs a month. "No one asked if you were happy with the arrangement," he says. At Le Cirque he may have supplied the food for Manhattan's most glamorous dining room, but that makes the kitchen no more glamorous. Because no matter how big a fish you are, it's the same in every restaurant. Sometimes you just get … slammed.

This page: Chef Daniel Boulud working in the kitchen at Lumiere in Vancouver (far left); Maine peekytoe crab as served at Restaurant Daniel (left); black sea bass with syrah sauce, also from Restaurant Daniel (below).

Overleaf: Restaurant Daniel's grand neo-classical entrance on East 65th Street, New York.

Paupiettes of Sea Bass

Cut 4 fillets of sea bass as rectangular as possible by trimming off uneven edges with a sharp knife. Salt and pepper the fillets and sprinkle them with chopped thyme.

Peel 2 very large baking potatoes. Cut each potato lengthwise into very thin, long slices with a vegetable slicer or mandolin. Each potato should yield about 16 slices. Do not rinse the potato slices as their starch will help the wrapped slices stick together. Toss the potato slices in 1 tablespoon of melted butter and a pinch of salt.

Working on parchment paper, choose 8 potato slices of approximately the same length. Place a fillet of fish horizontally at the top of the parchment paper so you can match the length of the potato wrap to the length of the fish. Place the first slice of potato perpendicular to the fish starting on the left side. Place a second slice overlapping the first one by about 1/2 cm from the left edge. Continue overlapping the potato slices until you have covered an area equal to the length of the fillet of fish. Centre the fish horizontally in the middle of the potato wrap and fold the edges of the potatoes over the fish to enclose it entirely. Repeat the same process for the remaining fillets and refrigerate.

Slice the white part of 2 leeks very finely. Sweat the leeks in butter until soft, about 4 minutes. Salt and pepper to taste and keep warm.

Heat olive oil in a pot over high heat. Add reserved sea bass bones, chopped shallots, mushrooms, and a sprig of thyme sprig. Cook for 8–10 minutes, stirring often. Add 1 cup of chicken stock, bring to a boil, and cook until completely reduced. Add one bottle of good red wine, bring to a boil and reduce by half. Remove and discard the fish bones. Reduce the sauce by half again. Add 1 tablespoon of double cream, stir, and bring to a boil over low heat. Whip in 1 tablespoon of butter, a pinch of sugar, and salt and pepper to taste. Strain the sauce with a fine strainer and keep warm.

Saute the paupiettes of sea bass in butter until golden brown, about 3–5 minutes on each side. If the fish is very thick, finish cooking in the oven for 4–5 minutes.

Place a bed of leeks in the middle of 4 warm serving plates and ladle the sauce around the leeks—about 2 tablespoons per plate. Place a paupiette of sea bass on top of the leeks and garnish thyme. Sprinkle the plate with minced chives.

Fusion

FRENCH TECHNIQUE, OTHER CUISINES

aniel Boulud went to America, but Bocuse went to Japan.

The year he won his third Michelin star, Bocuse travelled to Osaka to study with Shizuo Tsuji, a great master of the traditional style. Bocuse marvelled at Japanese techniques, the ingredients and the insistence on seasonality. "I never expected the influence of Japan to be as great as it is," he said.

Anton Mosimann, too, went to Osaka, in 1970. "We western cooks can learn so much from the Japanese with regard to their desire for perfection and beauty in culinary art." And in the late 1970s a young Japanese chef named Nobu Matsuhisa arrived in Los Angeles via Lima, Peru and Anchorage, Alaska. He did not bring sushi with him— the sushi revolution had already begun in America. What he carried with him instead was an idea, born of the comida china (Chinese food) he had experienced in Peru. That idea was fusion.

Fusion. If there is one word that the modern chef has come to revile above all others, it is that one. Even Tetsuya, whose cuisine in fact bears many of fusion's supposed hallmarks, says "I don't know what it means, fusion. There is not really such a thing, such a word in cooking; it's more like to confuse people, a confusion."

But fusion does not quite deserve the bad reputation it seems to have acquired. Nor can Nobu be entirely blamed—it was in the 1960s that a chef named Richard Wing combined French and Chinese cooking at his family's Imperial Dynasty restaurant in Hanford, California, and so creating a cuisine that came to be called 'chinois'. It was fusion; it just didn't know it yet.

Surprisingly, no one had really thought of it before. In the South of France, Louis Outhier had incorporated Asian spices into nouvelle cuisine, though in a most subtle and discreet fashion— his cooking was never anything but French. Still, a young Austrian chef, Wolfgang Puck, who was completing his training at a three-

star restaurant in nearby Provence, was paying attention. He, like Nobu, would soon end up in Los Angeles. There he would help pioneer fusion cuisine (one of his restaurants was named "Chinois"), invent the 'designer pizza' and become one of America's greatest celebrity chefs.

THE MELTING POT

If America has long been a place of reinvention, where people might remake their old selves and become something new, something different, then truly Los Angeles is its capital. Here a waitress might become a movie star, an Austrian chef (or indeed an Austrian bodybuilder) might become a superstar, and a Japanese sushi chef might become a global restaurant brand.

First, he would have to go to Chinatown.

Nobu's inspiration came from Lima, Peru, where he had been persuaded that the large Japanese population meant that a sushi restaurant there would be a goldmine. That turned out to be not quite the case. But before

he left Nobu became entranced by the local Chinese restaurants, run by descendants of the coolies brought over to build the ill-fated and never completed railroad over the Andes. The strange thing was, the Chinese food they served did not taste like Chinese food. The predominant local ingredients—coriander, chilis, avocados and oils—had caused it to evolve into something regional and unique. And if Chinese food could be altered with radical, hitherto unthought of combinations, he reasoned, why not Japanese?

It turned out that it could. The subtle, delicate food of Japan could be enlivened with peppers, chili and garlic, South-American style. It could be enriched with butter and cream, and therefore French-ified, as it were. Instead of making sushi from tuna it might just as easily be presented as 'tartare.' Halibut cheeks could be fried and served with a spicy sauce made from wasabi, cream and garlic. Black cod could have a sweet miso sauce, which in turn might inspire Robert De Niro to nickname you 'the Codfather.'

Opposite: A selection of modern Indonesian appetisers.

This page: Nobu Matsuhisa, chef of Nobu Restaurant in the Metropolitan Hotel in London holds up a plate of sushi.

Overleaf: A single serving of Asian scallop tapa with chopsticks

Truly, in America, anything is possible.

In this land of opportunity, for example, a French-trained Austrian chef might invent the "Jewish pizza," topping it with smoked salmon, creme fraîche and caviar, and so become one of the world's most successful restaurateurs. For it was Wolfgang Puck who realised that a pizza need not be traditional, that it could be topped with prawns, perhaps, or goats cheese, or duck sausage, and that people would still lap it up. And it was Wolfgang Puck who also realised that it was not necessarily the food which was the most important element for success; stars in a guidebook mattered much less than stars sitting at table. Cruise, Stallone, Gibson, Schwarzenegger: these were the stars Puck attracted, and Spago, his world-famous Beverly Hills restaurant, became the epicentre of Hollywood celebrity culture. And where the stars gather, the public are never far behind.

INFLUENCE AND INTERPRETATION

Of course, Puck did not 'invent' either the designer pizza or the celebrity restaurant—few successful people have actually had to invent anything. Reputedly his model for Spago was a place called Le Pizza in the old port at Cannes. Serving salads, grilled fish, simple pasta and pizza from a wood-burning oven, it had long been patronised by the glamorous set, because it offered a breathtaking view of the bay, and was mere steps away from their moored yachts. Puck simply transposed the concept to Hollywood.

Indeed, 'California cuisine', the logical precursor to fusion, which was typified by the food of chefs like Puck and Alice Waters' protegée Jeremiah Tower, looked a lot like the food of Puck's Provençal training. Nor was Nobu's Japanese-Peruvian fare so radical as it might actually appear. The borders of cuisine have always been porous, and cultures have absorbed influences one from another for as long as there have been cultures to interact.

As Bocuse has said, rarely is there anything new under the sun. "I believe that in cooking like in music," he says. "One doesn't invent much. One makes interpretations, but the word "invention"

for me is a bit pretentious. To mix chocolate with tomatoes or tomatoes with jam—that's not an invention. A sole with chocolate? The sole is a good product, chocolate is a good product; the two mixed together … give you shit."

Fortunately the most egregious of these sorts of culinary mismatches are long gone. Chefs such as Nobu and Tetsuya, who combine with Western traditions the techniques and ingredients from their Asian heritage, are sensitive to the requirements of both. But neither are they precious. "I don't mind Greek or Chinese or Japanese or French or Italian," says Tetsuya, "I use that. So it looks absolutely like European food but when you taste it, it tastes more like Asian or whatever."

And it is interesting that what we may still call fusion cuisine exists mainly in the United States and Australia, where it once went under the almost proprietary name of 'Pacific-Rim' cuisine. This is because the two countries share a relatively short history compared to the rest of the world; they each have unique immigration histories; and most importantly, they lack any long, defined culinary tradition.

Yet even countries with a long and defined culinary tradition have not influenced cooking in quite the way that French and Japanese cuisine have. For a start, other cuisines have never benefited from a Carême, or an Escoffier; men with a genius not just for cooking but also for writing, who were obsessed with codifying cooking in a way that was almost scientific in its exactitude. Nor was it just cooking they attended to. Their reach extended to all aspects of kitchen practice. As Alain Ducasse says, "The real 'French touch' is method, professionalism, rigour and organisation."

But even a French chef may admit that there is still a little something lacking. "There is no philosophy in French cuisine," according to Pierre Gagnaire, "but in Japan you find cuisine alongside gardens, floral art, pottery: there is a very philosophical connection." And then Ducasse puts the two together. "With a code and a feeling," he says, "there's alchemy." Just so long as you don't call it fusion.

Tetsuya Wakuda

THE QUIET MAN

" Few places other than Australia, he believes, would have allowed his cuisine to develop in the way it has. In Australia, he says quite simply, he has been free to do as he will. "

Tetsuya

eanwhile, on the other side of the world, a young man arrived in a foreign land. He knew nothing of the language, little of the culture. He did know a bit about cooking. He worked with those who could teach him. He learned. He opened a small restaurant. Then a bigger one.

Pretty soon that restaurant was one of the best in the world. Even so, he didn't care to talk about it much. But if you pressed him about it he would say, with the humility that is so prized in his adopted land, "I'm just a cook. It's only food. Yes. In the end, it's just food."

Tetsuya Wakuda, the accidental chef. "I am very lucky, I think."

Australia is lucky, too. Tets, as he is universally known, was not intending to stay—he was just planning to earn some money before embarking for America. Famously, he knew only that in Australia kangaroos and koalas were 'everywhere' (he soon learned differently) but he knew enough of the language to tell a Greek real estate

agent that he needed three things—a room, a job, and English lessons! The real estate agent had a suggestion. He said, "Tetsuya, the best school is in the kitchen. They feed you, teach you English then they pay you at the end of the week. What other school does that?"

TRUST YOUR INSTINCTS

If this suggests that Tets found both his home and his vocation completely by accident, then that is not strictly true. For three years he had worked in a large Tokyo hotel, learning western food as well as Japanese. "All the basic techniques." But as training was entirely dependent on the whim of the chef for whom one worked, Tets was not convinced that cooking was really for him. Indeed, he had an idea that he might become a gunsmith.

But when he arrived in Australia at the age of 22 he found himself, thanks to the good advice he had received from his real estate agent, again in a kitchen. Washing dishes. It was a start. And a little later on, when a chef named Tony Bilson needed a sushi chef for his restaurant, Kinselas, Tets stepped up. In return, Bilson taught him to cook.

"I started by doing some Japanese food … and then he gave me the chance to do other things and he basically told me to trust my instincts and to try mixtures."

The kitchen at Kinselas was set up like a Japanese kitchen, "with a lot of Japanese knives," and Tets began to feel more confident there, not least due to Bilson's encouragement. He had the opportunity to test a lot of his 'mixtures'. But he was also learning that first of all cooking about technique, about precision and attention to detail. "Then you bring it to the next level; you work on taste and textures."

Tets worked. And learned. Then he moved on. Six months here, a year there, working with others from whom he could learn. He helped start a few places: Roses, Kytes, Ultimo's, which he could have taken over "but the rent was very high and the position not so good … and then this place came available." A tiny shopfront in suburban Rozelle that he called simply Tetsuya's. And tiny it truly was (the downstairs dining room sat around 20) but from little things big things can grow.

ROZELLE

By then Tets had married. Which was lucky, because that meant he had someone to help him in the kitchen, and as the kitchen was just about big enough for two it worked out fine. His wife, whom he taught, did cold larder and presentation. The restaurant sat 44 people, and the menu was four courses. Between them Tets and his wife served nearly 200 dishes every day. He didn't pre-cook anything, and he changed the menu every three to four weeks. Cooking was his life.

But Tets did not cook for himself—he cooked for his customers. Having a restaurant is "about making people feel comfortable, about recognising your customers, and remembering what they like," he says. And what they liked

was Tets' food. As one critic noted, his dishes, "conjured up in a kitchen roughly the size of the passenger section of a stretch limo, are subtle, elegant, exquisitely balanced and in no way designed to draw attention to their creator."

Yet they could not help but do so. Though there has been much talk of 'fusion', of 'Pacific-Rim cuisine', these were not the dishes that Tets presented. His 'mixtures' were a combination of the Japanese tastes of his homeland and the French technique he had learned from Bilson, always exquisitely presented and guided by an extraordinarily sure hand.

Or mouth. Because for Tets, there is only one real secret to cooking. You must like to eat. "If you eat, you taste, so you know." He pats his stomach. "You have to be a good eater."

But simply being 'a good eater' does not account for Tets' success. His luck in finding himself in a country which boasted no great culinary history cannot be underestimated. Few places other than Australia, he believes, would have allowed his cuisine to develop in the way it has. In Australia, he says quite simply, has has been free to do as he will.

This is due in part to the wave of immigration that followed World War II. Europeans, particularly Greeks and Italians, arrived in the tens of thousands. Asians, too, and those from the Middle East found homes from home in Australian cities, and their influence permeated the culture, and the food. In a way, Australian cuisine was but a blank slate, to be written on in a dozen languages or more.

"Australia is a young country … we don't have centuries of food history," he says. "Each cuisine has certain things you can do, you cannot do. And we don't have that."

GROWING

Because no one told Tets what he couldn't do, he just went on and did it. His passion was all-consuming. He had little in the way of family life. He had only Tetsuya's, his customers, and his staff.

Which kept on growing. Though Tets' success had been virtually instantaneous, it was nearly four years before he was able to expand both kitchen and dining rooms. And even though there were now eight in the kitchen, if Tets was not there the restaurant did not open. To all intents and purposes, for Tets the restaurant was home.

He never returned to Japan. But nor did he forget where he had come from. In his expanded kitchen he continued to marry the flavours and techniques of east and west. He used no dairy products, because "people seem to expect that in a Japanese-style restaurant." He served a lot of seafood, and in dishes such as his confit of ocean trout with unpasteurised roe Tets managed to create dishes that would long stand the test of time.

KENT STREET

He stayed in Rozelle for ten years. The restaurant was full almost constantly. It won three hats in the *Sydney Morning Herald Good Food Guide*, Australia's equivalent of the Michelin. Tets was recognised (along with Rockpool's Neil Perry) as the country's greatest culinary asset.

Though it would be a stretch to claim that he did not even notice, Tets' focus was always on the food. He no longer cooked everything himself—he had staff now—but he could not help touching, tasting and testing everything in the kitchen. And still, if he was not in the kitchen the restaurant was closed.

But in 1998 he was asked by the James Beard Foundation if he would go to New York and cook. He said yes. He closed the restaurant for a month, taking his staff with him. And it may have been then that he realised that one day he would be able to let go.

In 2000 Tets let go of Rozelle, moving Tetsuya's to a heritage building in Sydney's CBD. The space was much larger, requiring even more people to realise his vision. He had always claimed that "my staff are my family and it's wonderful to see them grow." Here he would have to let them grow further. In a way it was almost humbling. Yet he had no choice but to learn to delegate.

He learned. He taught. Then he delegated. He found that it was the palate which it took longest to train, but eventually he could say, 'it's not like I would do, it's not the same, but it's very good.' And one day, after 14 years, he might even sit down at a table in his own restaurant and enjoy food not cooked by him.

He did. And then he promptly fell asleep.

MONACO

It is fortunate that Tets *did* learn to delegate, because quietly, humbly, he had become a chef of international standing. He had always stated that he would not travel beyond his restaurant save for charity or for friends. But his status amongst his peers was such that there were many invitations he could not refuse. He was invited, for example, alongside such luminaries as Albert Roux, Ferran Adria, Daniel Boulud and Juan Mari Arzak, to attend the 81st birthday celebration of Paul Bocuse in Monaco. More, he was asked to cook for it.

He could not say no. Bocuse first visited Japan in 1965, and Tets acknowledges his influence in imbuing Japanese chefs with French technique. "I will always be grateful to Bocuse," he says, because he "had an enormous impact on chefs in my native country … a profound effect on chefs and restaurantgoers everywhere."

Even those in Sydney, Australia who had once dreamed of going to America, but have instead found themselves at the very peak of their profession. As friend and equal Charlie Trotter has said, "His amazing technique, Asian heritage, sincere humility, and insatiable curiosity combine to create incredible, soulful dishes that exude passion in every bite."

Tets, if pressed, would doubtless put it differently.

"I am not precious about it. Food is food. In the end, you have to eat."

This page: Examples of Tetsuya's blend of Japanese and French cuisine can be seen in his saikyo yaki of ocean perch (far left); terrine of Queensland spanner-crab with buckwheat, and smoked ocean trout with Osetra caviar (below).

Overleaf: Tetsuya's occupies a heritage-listed site, with the main dining room overlooking a Japanese-style garden.

Confit of Ocean Trout

Skin a 350 g fillet of ocean trout and cut crosswise into 70–80 g pieces—they should weigh no more than 100 g.

In a small tray, immerse the ocean trout in a mixture of grapeseed oil and olive oil, coriander, pepper, basil, thyme and garlic. Cover and allow to marinate for a few hours in the fridge.

Preheat the oven to its lowest possible setting. Take the fish out of the oil and allow to come to room temperature. Cover the base of a baking tray with chopped celery and carrot. Put the ocean trout on top and place in the oven. Cook with the door open so that the fish cooks gently, painting the surface every few minutes with the marinade. This should take no more than 10 minutes: the flesh should not have changed colour at all, and feel lukewarm to the touch.

Remove the fish from the oven and allow to cool to room temperature.

Puree 1/4 bunch of Italian parsley with 100 ml of olive oil in a blender. Add 1/2 tablespoon of capers and blend.

Finely slice 1/4 of a bulb of fennel on a mandolin. Toss with lemon juice, salt and pepper to taste, and some lemon-scented oil or lemon zest.

Sprinkle the top of the fish with finely chopped chives, konbu and a little sea salt. Place some fennel salad on the base of the plate. Put the ocean trout on top and drizzle a little parsley oil all around. Dot the ocean trout with caviar at regular intervals.

Borders

THE TASTE OF INTERNATIONALISM

Tetsuya Wakuda has no Michelin stars: he is the only one of our chefs not to. But we must assume this fact is of little concern to him. It is simply an accident of geography, and perhaps fate, that he should have arrived in Australia and stayed. Had he set up his restaurant in any of the 21 countries—including his native Japan—which Michelin inspectors now visit there is no doubt that he too would have his stars.

Which is not to say he will not get them. In 2007 Michelin published its first guide to Tokyo, and in 2008 the Michelin Guide's director, Jean-Luc Naret, stated that the company was considering their options "from India to Australia." Because cuisine, just like publishing and tires, is global.

That Michelin should be looking east is hardly surprising. As Jean-Luc Naret says, "Japan—and Tokyo in particular—seemed the natural gateway to Asia, which is so rich in gourmet food and cooking traditions."

But what was surprising was that Tokyo restaurants were awarded a total of 191 stars, more than triple the number of Paris. Eight of those restaurants were given three stars (Paris has but 10 three-star establishments) and it confirmed Tokyo as prime contender for the title of dining capital of the world. In 2008, when the star count rose to 227, with another three-star restaurant added, Naret told a press conference that "Tokyo is, and remains, the most starred city in the world. Japanese cuisine is dynamic, diverse, rich and interesting."

The rest of the world, it seemed, was lacking something. But what?

Perhaps a scientific paper published in 1909 by a Japanese chemist named Kikunae Ikeda is the first place to look. There one will find, extracted from seaweed, the ionic form of monovalent glutamate, or glutamic acid. Ikeda named it umami, and it has become known, after sweet, salty, sour and bitter, as the fifth taste.

Umami is a Japanese word meaning savoury, and it is this 'meaty' flavour particular to dashi stock, made from kelp (kombu) and bonito flakes (katsuobushi) which Ikeda successfully isolated. The flavour it describes is common to such savoury products as meat, cheese, and mushrooms; in fact, nearly a century earlier, Brillat-Savarin's had described it as *osmazome*, which was his early attempt to encapsulate the main flavoring component of meat as extracted in the stock-making process.

But it is in Asian cuisines such as Japan's, where meat and meaty flavours play a much smaller part, that the understanding of umami as a taste with its own specific receptors—and hence the necessity of catering specifically to them—has become integral.

EAST MEETS WEST

Of course there is much more to it than seaweed and fish flakes. We have seen that the integration of Japanese flavours and techniques with those of the west have proved remarkably successful for chefs like Nobu Matsuhisa and Tetsuya Wakuda. But these both ply their trade away from their native land. What is it that accounts for the Tokyo chefs' new-found success?

For an answer to that we might look to Kiyomi Mikuni, regarded by diners, critics and fellow chefs alike as perhaps the most innovative and talented non-traditional Japanese chef currently at work.

Born in Hokkaido, the son of a fisherman, Mikuni set out at a young age, going first to Sapporo and then to the Imperial Hotel in Tokyo. Later he made his way to Geneva to take a job at the Japanese Embassy, and it was in Geneva that he encountered French cuisine.

He was hooked, and spent the next eight years working under some of the greatest French chefs; like Ducasse, Mikuni found himself a disciple of Alain Chapel whom, like Ducasse, he still considers his true master. But he was not destined to remain in France, and in1985 Mikuni returned to Japan and opened his own restaurant, incorporating elements from both French and Japanese traditions. "As a chef, I specialise in French cuisine," Mikuni says, "but I am also Japanese and a native of Hokkaido, which is an area famous for its kombu. The basis of my cuisine is French, but, in adding my Japanese sense of taste with umami, I have developed and original cuisine style. Umami, continuing from the four tastes of the west—sweet, salty, bitter, sour—makes a fifth, Japanese-born taste."

To accompany grilled fish, for example, Mikuni might serve a risotto of made with green peas and traditional dashi stock, or blend the flavours of rosemary and chervil with maitake (a perfumed mushroom) and a Japanese herb called kaiware. In fact, he owes his fame to the skillful mingling of two very different cuisines.

It would be a mistake, however, to imagine that all or even many of Tokyo's great chefs have French cuisine as the basis of their cooking. Michelin's Jean-Luc Naret has spoken of "a tradition passed on from generation to generation and refined by today's chefs," and of the nine three-star restaurants, four serve traditional Japanese cuisine and two are sushi bars.

Nor are Michelin fastidious about applying standards of decor, ambiance or even facilities. Located near a subway exit in the basement of an office building, the three-star Sukiyabashi Jiro does not even have its own bathroom. The restaurant is tiny, seating only about 20 people at its counter and tables; still, it is the stuff of sushi legend. Chef Jiro Ono is considered a national treasure, and his chefs make their way each day to the huge Tsukiji fish market, a short walk away, and return with only the best and freshest. In stark contrast, Hamadaya is located in a former geisha house in an older Tokyo neighbourhood, and the services of geisha are still offered as part of the dining experience. The food is elegant classical Japanese cuisine, with a strong emphasis on seasonal elements, the finest ingredients and service on beautiful dishes. Such are the choices available in the world's new culinary capital, and with an estimated 160,000 restaurants in the city, it is possible for the committed diner to find anything and everything inbetween.

Opposite: Jiro Ono, 81-year-old master sushi chef, shows off his famously soft hands, one of the secrets to his renowned sushi, in front of Ono's sushi restaurant, Sukiyabashi Jiro, in Tokyo, Japan. Sukiyabashi Jiro was awarded three Michelin stars in 2007.

THE NEXT BIG THING

The first Michelin guide to Tokyo sold over 300,000 copies, and must be accounted a phenomenal success. But with success often comes criticism, and Michelin is still accused of having a French bias: there are three French restaurants at the top of the Tokyo list, but no Chinese, no Italian, no tofu restaurants.

Jean-Luc Naret disagrees. "There are 40 types of cuisine in the London guide," he counters. "We are giving stars to Indian, Chinese and Japanese restaurants…" And if it is true that the company is seriously considering devoting a guide to Shanghai, as has been claimed, then certainly the tally of starred Chinese restaurants will grow accordingly. Or perhaps Australia might be next. Or Hong Kong. Or Macau.

Yet wherever Michelin goes, it must be remembered that it is chefs who make cuisine, not critics. Chefs such as René Redzepi of Copenhagen's Noma, whose regeneration of lost Nordic traditions, cutting-edge techniques and assiduous sourcing of native Scandinavian ingredients have become the hallmarks of a new Danish cooking. So intent is Redzepi on authentic ingredients that Noma employs up to five foragers, whose sole job is to gather up wild produce, and his menu changes monthly to reflect the seasonality of his produce—horseradish 'snow' with razor clams wrapped in parsley jelly with clam juice, dill and parsley being just one example of this dynamic Scandinavian cuisine.

Another Scandinavian chef who is refining and personalising Nordic traditions is Magnus Ek, whose Swedish restaurant, Oaxen Skärgårdskrog, is located on an island accessible only by ferry, and even then only in summer. "A true modernist, Ek creates dishes that are pared down but complex," says *Food & Wine* magazine, "as with his lobster carpaccio on herb ice accompanied by green-tea jelly."

Or his king crab porridge in red wine and basil vierge with caramelized emulsion of pig's blood and shellfish butter, lardo in crispy pastry and salt-baked celeriac, flavoured with some of the 15 or more types of wild local herbs Ek and his wife gather whilst out walking their dogs.

Nor is the combination of innovation and tradition confined to northern Europe. After learning his skills at various Michelin starred establishments, chef Alex Atala returned to his native Brazil to open D.O.M. in 1999. Here he applies French techniques to Brazilian ingredients, creating tasting menus that might include a codfish brandade in a black bean reduction, or filhote—a type of catfish—in a manioc crust, or a salad of pumpkin, crayfish and squid with Amazonian flowers.

And in Sydney, Peter Gilmour at Quay complements the restaurant's unrivalled views of the harbour, Bridge and Opera House with innovative modern Australian cuisine such as his signature 'sea pearls', individual balls of smoked eel brandade encased with slow braised octopus tentacle and egg white pearls, tartare of sea scallop with horseradish créme fraiche coated with tapioca pearls, silver leaf and rosemary flowers, and pearl meat and abalone encased in dashi jelly.

Each of these chefs is engaged in taking cuisine in new and exciting directions. And there are countless others, in Argentina and in Africa, the West Indies and the South Pacific, combining new ingredients with traditional techniques, foreign flavours with local styles. Their efforts are impossible to catalogue, because only the very best and most passionate of them will rise to the level of a Ducasse or a Guérard. But if they are true chefs, in the purest sense of the word, then even if they do not go to Michelin, it is possible that Michelin might one day come to them.

Left: Chef Pierre Gagnaire of France gives a demonstration during the World Summit of Gastronomy 2009 held in Tokyo, Japan. The three-day summit was a culinary cultural exchange which examined global culinary issues while promoting awareness of Japanese food culture.

Marco Pierre White

THE ROCK STAR

" He taught by example about passion, drive, and commitment. He taught them that a chef could look like a junkie and live like a rock star, if he chose, because none of that mattered so long as he could cook. "

In the early editions of his groundbreaking cookbook, *White Heat*, there is a photograph of a young, blonde commis with his face buried in his hands. That young chef is Gordon Ramsay. He may or may not be crying.

Marco Pierre White did that to people. He himself says his kitchen was 'the hardest in Britain.' And if it was the Roux brothers that taught the British how to cook, it was White who taught them how to be chefs. That is he taught by example about passion, drive, and commitment. He taught them that a chef could look like a junkie and live like a rock star, if he chose, because none of that mattered so long as he could cook.

Marco Pierre White. That boy could *cook*.

A MOTHER'S SON

His mother died when he was six. As we might imagine, it affected him quite strongly.

She was Italian; it was she who named him (his brothers names are Graham, Clive, and Craig), and it was with her, in Italy, that he recalls the happiest moments of his life, eating vegetable ravioli and fruit from the tree.

His father was from Yorkshire, and from him he learned to polish his shoes.

After his mother died, life at home was 'very strict and severe, very Victorian.' His headmaster told him when he left school that he would be nothing in life. As it turned out, he was wrong. White would become the second-youngest chef ever to gain three Michelin stars.

"I wanted that first Michelin star so much," White says. "That star was all I could think of."

FIRST STEPS

He claims he was not interested in cooking, only that when he left school he wanted freedom, a good time. But his father was a chef in a Leeds hotel, and for White to take a job in a North Yorkshire hotel seems more than coincidental.

Food quickly became an obsession. It was nurtured at The Box Tree in nearby Ilkley by a chef who, though not classically trained, had dined at all the two- and three-star restaurants, and thereby taught himself to cook. The cuisine was classical, and White had found a calling: he would sit and polish the silverware and the copper pans after everyone else had gone home.

He learned French cuisine. He did not learn the language, and when two years later he applied to La Gavroche, he could not understand the application form, which was all in French, and gave up. But after missing a train back to Yorkshire and wandering the London streets all night, he showed up again at La Gavroche's door. "He had no appointment," Albert Roux recalls, "and only £5 in his pocket." In *White Heat*, White recalls, more accurately, that it was £7.36. Either way, Roux was struck by the 19 year-old White's passion. He offered him an apprenticeship, so long as he cut his hair.

EDUCATION

It's possible that White could not have had a better training in classical technique had he spent his entire apprenticeship in France, given that his teachers were the Roux brothers, Pierre Koffmann, Nico Ladenis and Raymond Blanc.

From each he learned something different. From Albert Roux he learned 'the proper use of extravagance.' From Ladenis at Chez Nico that perfection is necessarily a slow pursuit.

Koffmann offered him rehabilitation. White had burned some culinary bridges by then, gone off to be a 'gastro-punk,' cooking just enough to finance another round of decadence in a world of alcohol and drugs. Realising he needed to return to cooking he turned up at Koffmann's La Tante Claire and offered to work one day for nothing. He did the same the next day, and the next. Soon he had worked a month for no pay, and a place was found for him. From this, White learned commitment, and (some) humility.

THE YOUNG LION

White was only a year at Le Manoir aux Quat'Saisons, joining Blanc's brigade in 1984, the year it opened. He was 23. Blanc, he says, taught him the most important thing of all— that food should taste of what it is—but by now White was not to be easily told. "Raymond couldn't hold the reins on me," he says. He was too hungry, too talented. And it was not long before they were locked in mortal combat.

It began late one night: White had argued a technical point with Blanc during service. Blanc berated him. White told him to fuck off. The confrontation escalated, and a challenge was laid down. They would each cook a terrine of rabbit and langoustines: the staff would judge the winner.

They worked in silence, the young lion and the old campaigner. "If I'd lost the challenge," Blanc says, "I'd have lost the business. Marco knew, too. We were fighting to the death."

Blanc won. But only just. White left soon after. Twenty years on, though, they remain friends. "There's an element of madness in us both," White says.

After leaving Blanc, White was out on his own. First, he ran the kitchen at the Six Bells public house in the Kings Road, Chelsea. Then he went supernova.

"Any chef who says he does it for love is a liar," he claims in *White Heat*. "At the end of the day it's all about money." But for a while, first at Harveys and then at the Oak Room at Le Meridien Picadilly, White's incandescent personality and sublime food gave lie to that statement. It wasn't about love. Nor was it about money. It was about beautiful food on a plate. It was, in a way, about life itself.

HARVEYS

He has called the kitchens at Harveys 'the SAS' of kitchens. "I became driven, totally driven, totally critical of myself, wanting every dish to be three-star, and that … changes you, and changes the way you behave to people."

The kitchen was small, the team was young—White himself was only 26—and the food sublime. But it came at a cost that could be counted in the lines on his face. People assumed he was on drugs. The kitchen during service could be a brutal place. Even the dining room saw its share of drama. White ejected a critic who was foolish enough to wear bicycle clips to dinner. He threw out customers who he considered rude. Someone asked for chips, which weren't on the menu: he hand cut them himself, served them on a silver platter, and charged the customer £25 for the privilege.

Mainly, though, he served the food of the gods. A tagliatelle of oysters with caviar, a dish he dedicated to his mother. Hot foie gras with lentils du pays and sherry vinegar sauce. A fricasee of sea scallops and calamari with ginger and sauce Nero. Braised pig's trotters and mashed potatoes. Simple dishes, with a minimum of tastes, yet elevated to the sublime. "His genius is reflected on the plate," said Albert Roux. And it was true.

He had his three stars at 33, yet he still wore the same blue apron as his staff, "because we're all *commis*, we're all still learning."

WHITE HEAT

He did not wear his name on his jacket, either, and in *White Heat* disparaged any chef that did. It was just one of the the things that made the book so unlike any other. Half the photographs were in black and white. Some showed him being tackled by his brigade; in those pictures in which White is not cooking he is invariably smoking a cigarette. Often he looks dissolute, close to collapse.

It is in the text, however, that the difference is most pronounced. He calls most other British chefs 'a joke', likening them to labourers whose brains wouldn't fill a square inch of his kitchen. He also claims that he wishes he wasn't a cook, that he doesn't enjoy what he does. "It's all sweat and toil and dirt," he says, "it's misery." Not exactly what one would expect from a Michelin-starred chef, it's true.

Looking back, however, he acknowledges that he had … issues. "I was so unhappy in my twenties, desperately unhappy. There was an awful lot of … stuff … I hadn't dealt with."

GIVING UP

It couldn't last, and it didn't; White gave up cooking at 38, "because it was at the age my mother died." He even gave Michelin back its stars. He claims he resented being judged by people who knew less than he did, and that spending 16 hours in a kitchen every day was stunting his growth. He had developed a taste for fishing, and for hunting. His womanising (by 2007 he'd had three marriages fail) was the stuff of legend.

But whatever the cost, cooking had been good to Marco Pierre White. He had parlayed his success, along with his celebrity, into an empire comprised of a dozen or more of London's top restaurants, along with an upmarket pizza chain. In 2007 he followed in the footsteps of the man he had once reduced to tears by hosting a season of Hell's Kitchen, in which unwitting celebrities are—in theory—taught to cook. He could afford to spend £2,500 on wine when taking a journalist to lunch. And he could afford to be sanguine about his former self.

'I was terrible. I didn't like myself. No one could.'

But it doesn't really matter, because that boy could *cook*.

This page: Marco Pierre White in action (left); with his executive head chef Calum Watson during the launch of his cookware collection at Harrods (right); a dessert of summer fruits in wine jelly with coulis served at the White's Oak Room at Le Meridien Piccadilly hotel, London, in the late 1990s

Overleaf: Marco Pierre White sitting in the Oak Room.

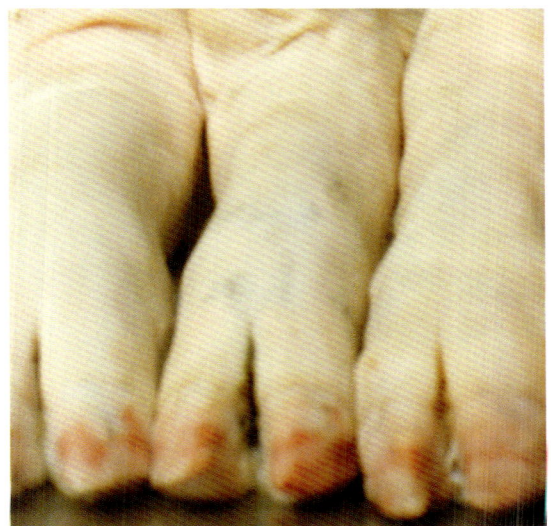

Pig's Trotter Pierre Koffman

Cook 6 boned pig's trotters in a hot oven with carrots, celery, onion, white wine, veal stock and thyme for about 3 hours, until they are a rich dark brown.

For the stuffing, soak 40 g of dried morels in cold water for 10 minutes, then drain, rinse and repeat. Remove the sinew and membranes from 650 g of sweetbreads. Cut the sweetbreads into cubes and fry over a high heat until they are golden brown. Add the soaked morels and half a finely diced onion and cook for one minute more. Season with salt and pepper, drain the mixture through a colander and leave to cool. When cool, bind the mixture with a small amount of chicken mousse made by processing chicken, tarragon, an egg and some double cream in a blender.

Fry two chicken legs, the sweetbread trimmings, sliced mushrooms, shallots, garlic, thyme and a bay leaf. When these are cooked, deglaze the pan with a splash of sherry vinegar, and again with an equal amount of cognac. Add 400 ml of Madeira and reduce the mixture until it has a caramelised appearance. Then add a combination of chicken and veal stock to cover the bones and the vegetables, drop in 4 dried morels and simmer for 20 minutes. Pass the sauce several times through a sieve and keep warm.

Butter one side of 6 large squares of foil. Stuff each trotter carefully so that the skin forms its original shape. Roll the foil tightly around the trotter and twist at either end to seal securely. Put these parcels in the refrigerator for about 15 minutes to set. Then in a large pan of boiling water, poach the trotters for about 12 minutes.

Just before serving, reduce the sauce a little and season with salt and pepper. Add a few drops of lemon juice, one or two drops of cream and a knob of butter.

Serve each pig's trotter with some mashed potato, fried wild mushrooms, roast button onions and a generous amount of sauce.

Texts

THE PASSING ON OF KNOWLEDGE

Anton Mosimann takes a 400-year-old cookbook down from the shelf, leather bound, handwritten, the ink faded by the centuries. Bookmarked is a recipe for chocolate sorbet. "Chocolate sorbet," he says, "can you imagine? Four hundred years ago, they were making chocolate sorbet. Today, we will make that, and people will think wow! This is modern food."

Mosimann's ancient cookbook goes unnamed. We do know that at only four centuries old it is by no means the earliest titled cookbook—in the late fourteenth century two such works, *The Forme of Cury* ('the art of cooking') compiled by the cooks of England's Richard II, and *Le Viander*, by the Frenchman known as Taillevent, provide evidence of Medieval cooking that was little changed from Roman times. Yet in both books there are recipes which are virtually identical, and both use similar terms—'*galantine*' and 'galyntyne' for

example— to describe techniques familiar to modern chefs.

Food, then, was something the French and the English had in common, particularly in the Middle Ages. But it was the Italians who had the edge; centuries of trade by the great city-states had resulted in great wealth and its corollaries, elegant living and refined eating. And, as in so much of modern Western culture, it was the transmission of Renaissance ideas—in art, architecture, and politics as well as cooking—that spread this refinement to the less civilised north. Indeed, the first printed cookbook was published in Venice in 1475, and translated into French in 1505. Catherine de Medici bought her Florentine chefs with her when she married the Duc d'Orléans in 1533, and her favourite dish, cockerel's crests and kidneys, survived into the twentieth century to appear on the menus of Michel Guérard and Alain Chapel.

The spread of the Italian merchant class north resulted in Lyons becoming an important hub for trade and diplomacy. The merchants brought their chefs, and the chefs bought copies of an even more influential Italian cookbook, Bartolomeo Scappi's *Cuoco Secreto di Papa Pio Quinto*, published in 1570. In it can be found the first printed picture of a fork. Scappi discusses place settings, now with all three utensils, and how waiters should change the plates during the meal. The dishes he gives recipes for are ones we would be happy eating; puff pastries filled with sweetbreads and *prosciutto*, pigeons stewed with mortadella sausages and onions.

THE RIVER

Compare Marco Pierre White's *White Heat*, published in 1990 and, in that it inspired a fresh new generation of young people to become chefs, one of the most influential of modern cookbooks. In it he features such dishes as rabbit served in a puff pastry case with onions, braised pig's trotters and woodcock served with lentils. Dishes that could easily travel back in time 400 years, to Scappi's Italy, just as Mosimann's chocolate sorbet has travelled forward.

"Everyone else looks to France for their inspiration," White wrote, "or maybe China or Thailand nowadays, but I look to Italy. The Italians are great cooks."

White's influences are freely acknowledged in his book. Of the braised pig's trotter with mashed potato, which came to be his signature dish, he states quite plainly that it's "Pierre Koffmann's dish, that's his perfection." And the nature of influence is such that the dish is no longer solely White's; since his retirement from the kitchen the Frenchman Jean-Christophe Novelli has adopted it for his own. Influence flows, like time or a river, never ceasing or stopping in one place for too long.

"Marco only came to steal my recipes," Koffmann himself says. "But he's one of the best chefs I ever had in my kitchen—always looking, always listening, wanting to absorb as much as possible."

Great chefs learn. Then they cook. And finally they teach. Bocuse has already stated that he thinks great chefs are rare, and that it is not in inventing dishes that they leave their mark, but rather in inspiring a new generation of pupils. Obviously Fernand Point provides his model here, and it is not too fanciful to consider Point's humble little notebook, *Ma Gastronomie*, as being the source of a mighty torrent of influence.

Point's little book is more of a philosophical tract than a cookbook, a collection of the aphorisms he loved so much rather than a collection of recipes, and it is perhaps this which accounts for its status among chefs. It embodies the nature of cooking, rather than trying to explain it, and it seems to have acted on a certain generation of chefs as a kind of Zen and the Art of Cooking, so that the kitchen became a calling, rather than a job.

For a subsequent generation, *White Heat* accomplished much the same thing, in that the photographs appeared to portray a kind of debauched, Byronic glamour, which was in reality something quite different. White's single-mindedness, obsession even, came out only through a reading of the text—the casual disparaging of other chefs done not for effect but because they did not share his unwavering commitment; the comment that a lobster was "more beautiful to me than most women."

Here, obviously, was a young man with genuine, all-consuming passion. It struck a chord with other young men and women, many of whom would claim *White Heat* as the main inspiration for choosing cooking as a career.

THE LINE OF SUCCESSION

In 1651, François Pierre de La Varenne published *Le Cuisinier François*. More than a century before Carême, Varenne was the first truly modern chef. In working for a cousin of Catherine de Medici, who too had imported Florentine chefs to France, had learned from their more refined style of cooking—the delicate flavours of mushrooms and truffles

replacing heavy spices, sauces made from just lemon or vinegar added to the pan juices. An accomplished writer as well as a great cook, he wrote down these advances in a beautiful style, recording not just recipes but overseeing the entire field of cooking, in a fashion that paved the way for Carême and Escoffier. And by including his name in the title of his work he presaged the modern celebrity chef.

No doubt Anton Mosimann has a copy of *Le Cuisinier François* among his collection of cookbooks, just as he would have the works of Carême and Escoffier and Point's *Ma Gastronomie*. Doubtless the works of

his contemporaries feature in his library, too. Bocuse's works alone would take up a whole shelf, though Guérard's single volume *Cuisine Minceur* might rival them all in influence. Thomas Keller's books would be there, acknowledging their debt to Point, while Michel Bras' *Essential Cuisine* and Pierre Gagnaire's *Reflections on Culinary Artistry* would tell the story of the individualist chef, ploughing his own furrow. Mosimann's own books would probably be represented. And if one took down a copy of his *The Art of Anton Mosimann*, and read through his introduction, this phrase might stand out.

marco pierre white

WHITE HEAT

MITCHELL BEAZLEY   PHOTOGRAPHS BY BOB CARLOS CLARKE

"At The Dorchester I set up weekly training courses and actively encouraged everyone to participate. In the kitchen with my staff, I have always seen my own role as leading, guiding and advising."

It is perhaps asking too much that a person both teach *and* inspire. Probably they cannot be achieved both at the same time. "In our profession," Mosimann says, "it is vital to learn the basics: how to poach, how to grill, how to braise." Which is simply an extension of Point's maxim that success is but a lot of little things done perfectly. And these things one *can* learn from a book. But a book cannot give you everything. Marco Pierre White tells of his very first day on the job; he was given a chinois and a small ladle and told to sieve an enormous stockpot. "The stock was a thick glutinous jelly and it took me three hours to force it through the sieve—no one told me to warm it first and then pour it through."

Maybe he was remembering that morning when he wrote the introduction to *White Heat*. You're buying this book because you want to cook well, he asks, because you want to cook Michelin stars? Forget it, he says, save your money. Go buy a saucepan.

Opposite: Front spiece of Antonin Carême's *Le Pâtissier Royal Parisier ou Traité Elementaire et Pratique de la Pâtisserie Ancienne et Moderne*, published in 1815. The book contained not only recipes, but also architectural designs for sugar confectionery.

This page: The cover of the groundbreaking and hugely influential *White Heat*, first published in 1990

Gordon Ramsay

THE PERFECTIONIST

" He swore that he would never fail at anything again. "If I can't have an FA cup medal," he would later say, "I want a third Michelin star." "

Ramsay

There are certain statements one never expects to hear. 'My name is Gordon Ramsay, and I am addicted to perfection,' is probably one of them. No, what one expects to hear from the mouth of Gordon Ramsay is the 'f-word.' And hear it one did.

In the 50 minutes of his debut television show, *Ramsay's Kitchen Nightmares*, Gordon Ramsay said the f-word 111 times. He was, at 37 years old, already a multimillionaire. He employed 850 people. He had gained more Michelin stars in less time than any other British chef. Still it was the f-word, far more than his cooking ever could, that made him truly famous.

'Ramsay swears four or five times a minute,' said Britain's normally staid *Times*. 'It is a joy to watch.' A columnist from London's *Evening Standard* concurred. 'Gordon is a natural on television because he is so compelling,' she enthused, 'so passionate and so unbelievably rude.'

Indeed.

Compelling. Passionate. Rude. Helpful as these three adjectives are in understanding Gordon Ramsay, ultimately they do not suffice. As he himself has said, it is this pursuit of *perfection* that defines him, as a cook and as a man.

FATHERS AND SONS

If it is not simplistic to say that we are all what our parents made us, more or less, then we might say that Gordon Ramsay's father made him into the most famous chef of his generation.

He did that by taking the seven year old Ramsay to his first football game.

Ramsay recalls in his biography that it was 'an ugly, dirty match played in front of a frightening, threatening and sporadically violent crowd.' "And I loved everything about it."

The team was Glasgow Rangers, his father's

team. A hard-drinking Scotsman, also called Gordon, Ramsay senior was also an abusive man who had been a successful swimmer in his teens and saw life as a brutal competition. He had two interests: music and football, and he pursued a musical career at which he would ultimately fail. Ramsay claims that he could 'smell' that failure, and he hated it. He hated more the way his father treated his mother.

What he loved was football. And by the strange logic of children in abusive homes, he reasoned that if he could make his father proud enough then he might leave his mother alone. So he vowed that he would one day play for Glasgow Rangers.

He very nearly did. Grim determination and a certain natural ability meant that he was selected for the reserve team. The whole family moved back to Scotland to support him. After two years he was ready for the first team. He played two games, and in the third it was all over. He suffered a knee injury from which he never fully recovered, and at 19 years old he walked in to a meeting to be told that he was being let go from the club.

"Every dream I'd ever had had been taken away."

He swore that he would never fail at anything again. "If I can't have an FA cup medal," he would later say, "I want a third Michelin star."

IN THE KITCHEN

His father thought cooking was for 'poofs'. Ramsay saw it differently. His mother had worked in an upscale tea-rooms, and in their kitchens he had sensed a certain energy, a teamwork, that he found exciting. He had enrolled at a catering college before being accepted for Rangers, and now that football was closed to him he tried it again: the day a lecturer began screaming at the class for their lack of interest he was hooked.

He was driven to succeed. He knew that to do that he had to learn from the best, and he chose Marco Pierre White. He thrived on the aggression prevalent in White's kitchen. "The

most important thing for a chef is that you've got to be able to take a bollocking." But he never told anyone about his past, terrified that White might say, 'you were a failed footballer, now you're a failed chef'. He could take the 17-hour days. He could accept the abuse. He could not, would not, accept the idea of failure.

White saw how hard Ramsay was prepared to work, and after pushing him as far and as hard as he could, sent him to those who could push him further. The Roux brothers, Guy Savoy, Joël Robuchon and Reg Grundy, the Australian creator of *Neighbours*. He learned from all of them, even if, from Grundy, it was only how the other half lived. From Robuchon he learned to duck: the chef of the century once threw a plate of langoustines at Ramsay's head because his presentation was not up to scratch. (Compared to him, Ramsay says, Marco Pierre White is a 'f**king pussycat'.) Guy Savoy taught him that four hours sleep should be enough for a chef. Of the Roux brothers and La Gavroche he simply says, "there was no better or more exciting place in the business to be."

THE COLOUR PURPLE

Fulham, in west London, was not the best or most exciting place to open a restaurant. The site, just off the traffic-heavy main road, had a long history of failed ventures. Yet Ramsay, after six years tutelage from the masters, was desperate. He wanted his own place.

He called it Aubergine.

It, and Ramsay, became overnight sensations. The 45 seats were filled every evening. Sometimes the waiting list was 75 strong, and Saturday night reservations were sold off to the highest bidder. Ramsay had arrived. And with his own place came his own style. "That's me on the plate," he could say of his roast seabass with braised salsify and jus vanilla. He was 26 years old.

Of the 282 pages in Ramsay's biography, it takes only seven to cover the years of his training. The opening of his first restaurant needs just four more. Published in 2006, it ends with Ramsay taking helicopter lessons and scouting around Scotland for a football team to buy, and you don't get *there* with just one 45-seat restaurant.

FAME

You do need stars, however. Aubergine gained its first in 1995. Ramsay was still in his kitchen then, working 18 hour days with a team of just seven, inspecting each plate as it went out and as it came back in again, to see what had and hadn't been eaten. Celebrity diners were abundant. A second star came in 1997.

The story may have ended there. Yes, for a man so driven that third star was inevitable. Even so, it was a confluence of other factors which turned a foul-mouthed young Scottish chef in to a business mogul and media star.

The first, ironically, was that Ramsay's financial backers were intent on expanding—they planned on replicating the Aubergine formula across the globe, including a chain of Aubergine pizza houses. Ramsay was appalled. His idea was that restaurants were personal, and he had no interest whatsoever in 'clones'.

The second, of course, was television. As Ramsay was in the process of extricating himself from his partners, running Aubergine and preparing to open his new restaurant, Gordon Ramsay, on the site La Tante Clare, a film crew was following his every move. Shown over two months, the television series that came of it, *Boiling Point*, made not just headlines. It made Ramsay.

BOILING POINT

The explosion of interest in chefs and cooking had begun: the producers wanted to follow a personable, charismatic, 'possibly even volatile chef', so that the world could see what really went on behind the kitchen doors.

'Possibly even volatile.' Well, they certainly got what they wanted. 'The man is clearly an ogre, and rarely has television witnessed anybody being so vile to their staff', wrote one reviewer. And it was true. Ramsay's pathological need for perfection manifested itself in wholesale abuse of anyone, be they staff, supplier or critic, who could not fulfil that demand. Food, and the plates it was on, was regularly dumped in the bin, or flung at errant chefs. The invective was vicious. He called a Michelin reviewer something rarely heard on television. As an ex-employee cycled away in tears Ramsay muttered "I don't give a shit." He cared for only one thing.

"Every dish, every meal, every day has to be perfection."

His estranged father—they met once in more than ten years—never got to taste his elder son's success, or see his younger, more favoured son spiral into addiction. But Ramsay's success has been phenomenal. Along with Ducasse and Robuchon he has become one of the great empire builders of cooking, yet he generates almost as much revenue from his media enterprise. He is a devoted family man himself, yet appears to spend every waking moment attending to his business. A man whose constant verbal abuse of his staff made him famous, yet when he walked away from Aubergine 46 of those staff chose to follow him.

But most of all, he is really just someone addicted to pleasing people. Desperate to make his father happy as a child, psychologists will say, as an adult he *still* needs to be liked by everyone. The greater his food, the more people will compliment him. The more he shouts and swears on television, the more likely those who meet him in real life will realise he is really 'a decent bloke'.

"I readily admit," he says, "[it] is my own serious addiction."

Suffice to say, if a psychologist were to analyse his signature dish, a subtle, pale and delicate soup of mushrooms and white beans that has been whipped into a froth at the last moment, she might have something to say about that, too.

This page: Lime parfait with melon sorbet and honeycomb at Cerise, Conrad Hotel, Tokyo (far left); a fish dish at Gordon Ramsay at Claridges (left); crab mayonnaise with avocado and sweetcorn, tomato gazpacho, as served at Cerise.

Overleaf: Chef Ramsay at his Chelsea restaurant in 2001 (top); Ramsay's Trianon palace restaurant, Versailles, west of Paris.

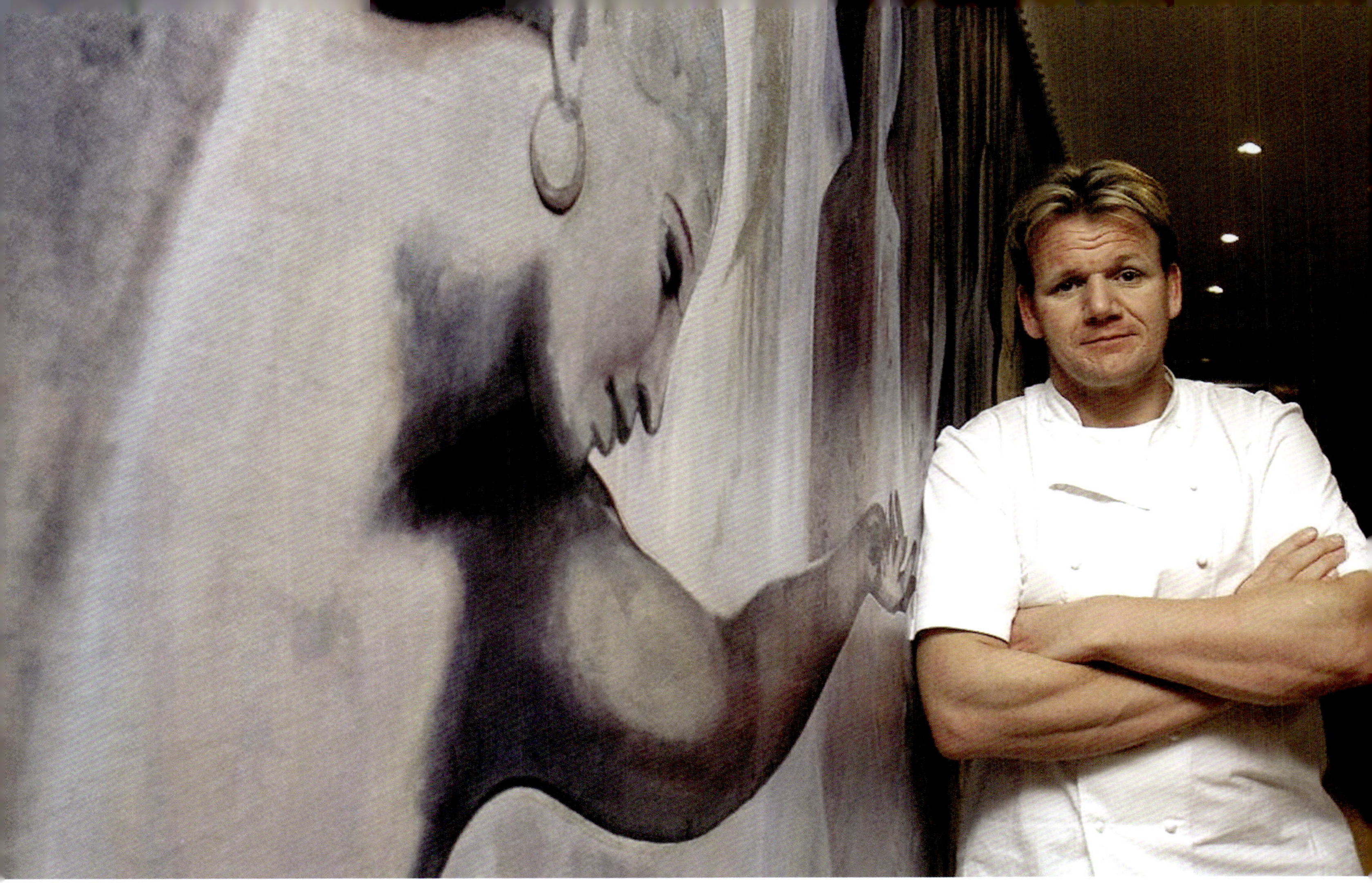

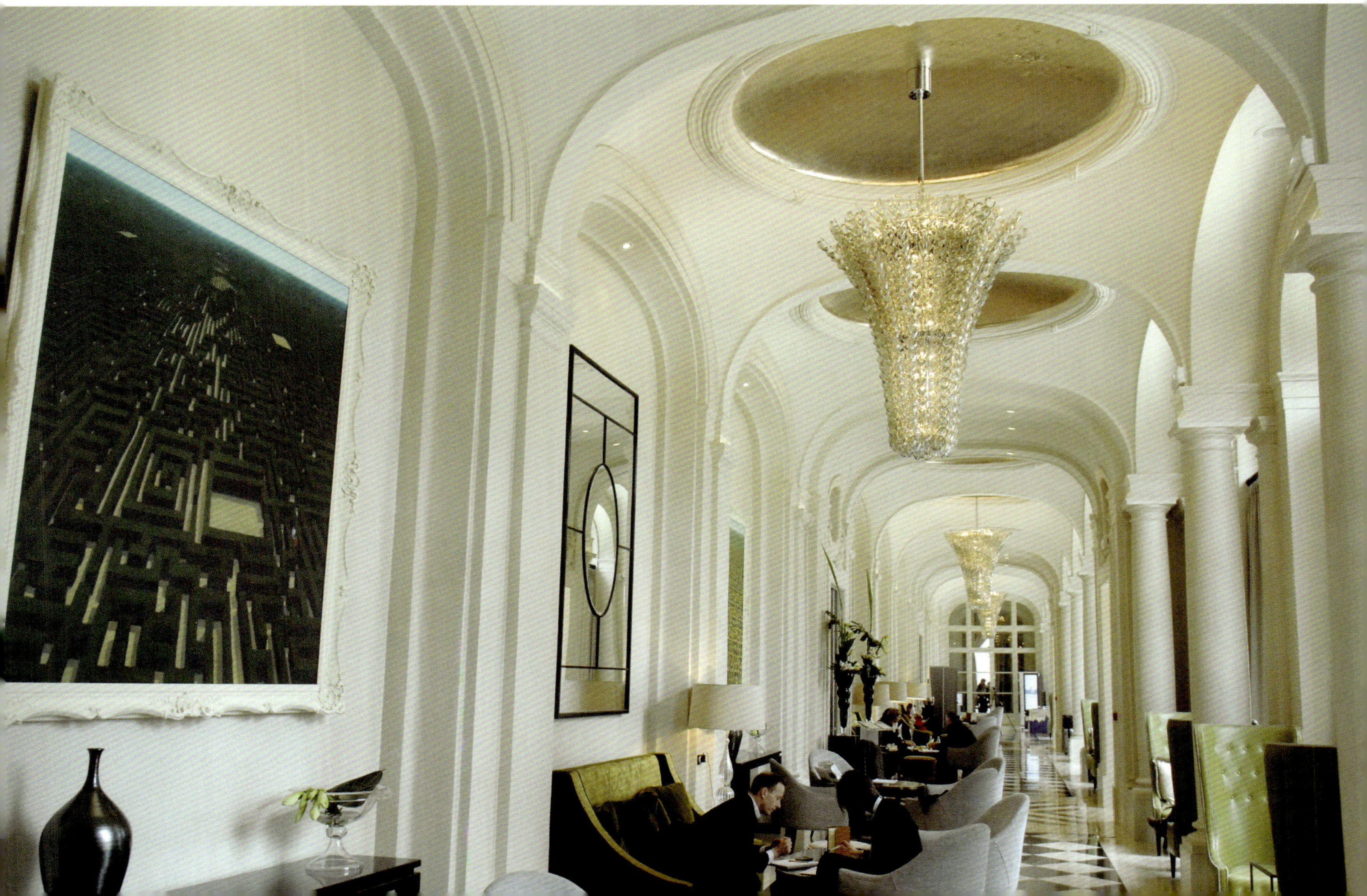

Cappuccino of White Beans

Soak 250 g of dried white haricot beans overnight and then transfer them to a large pan. Cover with lightly salted cold water. Put in 1 small peeled onion, 2 small peeled carrots and a bouquet garni. Boil vigorously for 10 minutes, then simmer for a further 1–1½ hours until the beans are tender.

Remove about 4–5 tablespoons of the beans and reserve for the garnish. Continue simmering the remaining beans for a further 10–15 minutes until they are very soft. Drain the beans, discarding the onion, carrot and bouquet garni, but reserving a few tablespoons of the cooking liquid.

Put the beans into a blender and whiz to a fine purée, adding some of the cooking liquid if necessary. Pass the purée through a fine sieve pressing the pulp with the back of a ladle.

Boil 800 ml of vegetable stock for about 5 minutes until slightly reduced. Mix the reduced stock with the bean purée in a large pan. Simmer for 5 minutes. Whisk in 150 ml of double cream and season well. Add 1 1/2 tsp of truffle oil, according to taste.

Just before serving, whisk in a few knobs of ice-cold butter, using an electric hand blender to froth up the soup. Divide the reserved beans between warmed cappuccino cups or wide tea cups. Spoon the frothy soup over the beans and serve immediately, garnished with truffle slices.

TAKING STOCK

We might consider Escoffier the first truly 'modern' chef. Certainly he was the one who modernised the restaurant kitchen, its practices, and its food. And it is often forgotten that it was Escoffier who collaborated with one Julius Maggi in the development of the famous Maggi bouillon Kub, as it was originally known, a process of 'deconstructing' food as dramatic then as anything done in the kitchens of elBulli, The Fat Duck or Restaurant Arzak today.

By the time that the books of the Old Testament came to be written it was already being said that there is nothing new under the sun. Early in the 21st century, a number of chefs are proving that this is not necessarily true by pushing the boundaries of what food should look, feel and taste like and incorporating into their work ideas that come from the worlds of science, art and philosophy. And it is important to remember that, new and radical as their creations may be, they result from a tradition of innovation that is as old as cooking itself.

We have already seen that Escoffier was not a tall man: when he played billiards against his friend Paul Daffis (incidentally the father of Escoffier's future wife), Daffis complained that Escoffier had the advantage because he did not have to bend over to sight the cue! But as Isaac Newtown famously said of his own achievements, 'If we see further, it is because we are standing on the shoulders of giants.' It is equally true the achievements of today's chefs may come about only because they stand on the shoulders of Auguste Escoffier.

A. Escoffier

Opposite: A late
nineteenth century
advertisement for
Maggi stock cubes,
c. 1890. Escoffier
collaborated on
the development of this
store-cupboard staple.

Left: A portrait of
Auguste Escoffier, the
'king of kitchens

Ferran Adrià

THE ALCHEMIST

"One of elBulli's rules," he says, "is not to know what you are going to dine on. Creativity and surprise go hand in hand. There is no room for repetition."

Adrià

hat more, really, needs to be said about Ferran Adrià, that chef turned writer Anthony Bourdain has not so neatly encapsulated—in just three words—when he calls him 'the foam dude.'

Quite a lot, obviously.

For a start, he's not just the foam dude; he's the foam phenomenon. When bookings for the coming six month season at elBulli open, over two million people apply for the privilege of dining there. That takes a little more than just foam. That takes alchemy. Magic. He says so himself.

'Cooking is a language through which all the following properties can be expressed: harmony, creativity, beauty, poetry, complexity, magic, humour, provocation, culture.'

This is point 1 of the 23-point Philosophical Synthesis of elBulli. Point 21 declares that 'Decontextualisation, irony, performance, spectacle are completely legitimate, providing they are not superficial but are closely bound up with the process of gastronomic reflection.'

And you thought it was just dinner.

One critic has claimed that Adrià's food moves 'inexorably towards disembodiment.' He presents food as gel, foam, smoke. Even 'air'. Some have asked if this is in fact a good thing.

The answer can only be, yes. Two million Adrià fans can't be wrong, nor does Michelin give out their three stars lightly. To cap it off, elBulli has topped Restaurant magazines World's 50 Best Restaurants poll for the past two years, and has never fallen out of the top three.

CREATIVITY MEANS NOT COPYING

Physically, though, Ferran Adrià Acosta has not gone very far at all. Born in Catalonia's second largest city he is, like all Catalans, fiercely wedded to his native region. As a 16-year-old his travels took him just as far as Ibiza, where he worked in a kitchen. His national service saw him serve in the navy as a cook. A fellow Catalan suggested he spend his month's leave working at elBulli, in the town of Roses, two hours drive north of Barcelona. He did, and liked it. He arranged to join the staff the following year.

That was 1984. Adrià was *chef de partie*. After the chef announced his departure, manager Juli Soler convinced Adrià and Christian Lutaud to share duties as chef de cuisine. Adrià was 22 years old. The pair learned their trade in their own kitchen. They also went to France, studying under Georges Blanc, Jaques Pic and the Troisgros brothers. Their food embraced the heritage of classical cooking and the advances of *nouvelle cuisine*, with a smattering of local influences. But essentially they were followers.

Lutaud departed in 1987, leaving Adrià in charge of the team. Then, on a visit to the Côte d'Azur to visit some of the prestigious restaurants of the area, they attended a demonstration by the distinguished chef at the Hotel Negresco. During a discussion, someone asked him to define creativity.

"Creativity is not copying," he said.

This simple sentence held the key. As Adrià notes on the elBulli website, 'This was the start of our plunge into creativity.' And note that he says *our*; for Adrià, it is never 'I'. It is always 'we.'

They began closing for the winter—ironically, because it was a financial necessity —just as their outlook on cooking was profoundly changing.

Through the *Gault & Millau* guide they had become aware of the names of two men who were to influence them most, Pierre Gagnaire and Michel Bras. Geographically, either of them were very far away, Gagnaire in St. Etienne and Bras in Aubrac, and Adrià and his collaborators could experience their cuisine *in situ*. From Gagnaire (and his association with Hervé This) they learned that 'everything is possible.' From Bras they discovered sensitivity, nature, and a cooking 'based on purity.' They had set their compass. Now it was time to enter unknown territory.

THE WORKSHOP

In 1990 the owners of elBulli retired and the restaurant was sold to Adrià and his team. At the same time, a sculptor who was both friend and customer invited Adrià to his workshop in Barcelona. He cooked, the sculptor sculpted, and they engaged in a series of conversations on the nature of creativity. Adrià got to know 'how a creative mind works,' something he says he had never before seen up close. More, Adrià was in a kitchen creating, *without* having to cook for the restaurant. Here the concept of elBulli workshop was born.

Their platform for greatness would require three more legs. First, they would require a dedicated creative team, a 'development squad' as they termed it, to carry the torch of creativity forward. Then, they would have to define just what that creativity was.

Not copying was simply the beginning. They would need to completely redefine the terms of their search: they were not interested in merely creating new recipes from products, concepts or techniques already in existence. No. They wanted *new* concepts, *new* techniques.

They termed this search, appropriately enough, technique-concept creativity, an approach exemplified in dishes such as their 'textured vegetable panaché,' an otherworldly creation in which the vegetables are removed from their original form, their shape, colour and texture all converted so that only the essential taste remains familiar. It looked, on the plate, very little like food. But it worked. At least Joël Robuchon thought so.

In 1992 the chef of the century had booked to dine at elBulli. To the team's disappointment, he told them on arriving that he had only time for a quick meal, as he had a train to catch back to Paris. Of course, they had planned on presenting their full menu. Robuchon was half way through. He looked at his watch. Oh well, he said, there will always be another train.

STRANGE FRUIT

Their watershed came in 1994. Robuchon was already hinting that he considered Adrià heir to his title of world's greatest chef. Adrià, on the other hand, was becoming an artist. Technique-concept creativity was bearing strange and wonderful fruit: foams, new pastas and raviolis, new forms of caramelisation. They dined—for the first time—at their own restaurant. "This gave us a completely new perspective," Adrià says impishly. At the same time, Robuchon

Previous spread: The terrace at ElBulli, in Roses, Girona, Spain.

Opposite: Chef Ferran Adrià at elBulli, with the kitchen visible behind him.

advised them to separate their creative work from the restaurant service. It was good advice.

So had begun the period that mapped their future. They took the first tentative steps towards the creation of their permanent Workshop. The 1995 *Gault & Millau* guide awarded them its highest score. And in 1997 they gained their third Michelin star, only the third Spanish restaurant to do so.

THE FUTURE IS BORN

Olive and sour cream 'Oreos'. Popcorn foam. Butter ravioli. Melon caviar. Parmesan foam with raspberry muesli. Green tea air. Praline frost. Olive oil gnocchi. Pea jelly.

This was elBulli in 2005. And it must be remembered that, in Adrià's world, the words frost, foam and air are not mere adjectives: they are nouns. The popcorn foam is literally foam that tastes like popcorn. The caviar of melon is not merely tiny balls of melon cut with a super-small melon baller. No, it is melon that has been treated to elBulli's (still secret) technique of spherification, so that each sphere has both a shell and an interior, exploding between the teeth just as fine caviar would. The pea jelly is similar, but on a larger scale: the ball of jelly, to be eaten in one mouthful, contains a centre of hot pea soup. The green tea air that accompanies a smoked scampi is like the previous foams yet somehow lighter still, the most nebulous possible substance to which flavour might still be attached.

The elBulli menu offers more prosaic dishes, too: a seaweed tempura with saffron, a delicate Thai soup with coconut tofu, or slices of truffle over brioche. But they will be followed by a ravioli that is in fact truffles suspended in anchovy jelly and decorated with green olive air. Or slices of raw monkfish liver that the diner 'cooks' for themselves in a bowl of hot consommé. Or oysters that are really sea slugs. With Adrià, you just don't know.

"One of elBulli's rules," he says, "is not to know what you are going to dine on. Creativity and surprise go hand in hand. There is no room for repetition."

THE GENERAL CATALOGUE

By 1999 the team knew that they were going where none had gone before. They began to document each of their dishes, in what was to become known as the General Catalogue. "They do that for Picasso," Adrià says, in a rare usage of the first person singular, "why not for me?"

In truth, their efforts were not so self-serving: in the beginning they wanted simply to conduct an analysis of their cuisine, to draw an 'evolutionary map' by which they could chart it's progress, and numbering, dating and photographing each dish was the obvious place to start. From there they could define the parameters of change in their cuisine. That it provided in retrospect a 'history' was largely secondary to that purpose.

At the same time, a permanent site for the elBulli taller (workshop) was established in Barcelona, and the creative team was split. Now, the technique-concept creativity had no more boundaries to constrain it, expecially when in 2001 lunchtime service was discontinued. The team could take flight. They had to. For in any enterprise which is built on constant innovation, there is no time for rest.

"People who come to elBulli come to eat creativity. Because this is the most important fact about elBulli."

"WAS IT GOOD?"

This is the question Anthony Bourdain asks himself after dining with Adrià at the chef's table in elBulli's kitchen, in his 2004 documentary, *Decoding Ferran Adrià*.

"I don't know if that's a word one should use when describing the elBulli experience," he decides.

What words *should* one use, then? In truth, unless one has *had* the elBulli experience, it's hard to know. So, if we are to get any idea, we must rely on the reports of those who have been, and tasted. Bourdain likens the experience to both an amusement park ride and a work of art, "in every sense of that word." Then he pauses for a moment, as if he knows these words do not quite suffice.

"Adrià likes the word 'magic'," he says, "and that's exactly what it felt like." Magic.

This page: A selection
of dishes from elBulli,
including deconstructed
pina colada (far left);
jellied false *pousse-pieds*
(left) and a dessert of
passionfruit with whisky
(below).

Overleaf: The dining room
of elBulli in 2003 (above) a
selection of memorabilia
relating to the restaurant's
name, *el bulli*, a small
bulldog (below).

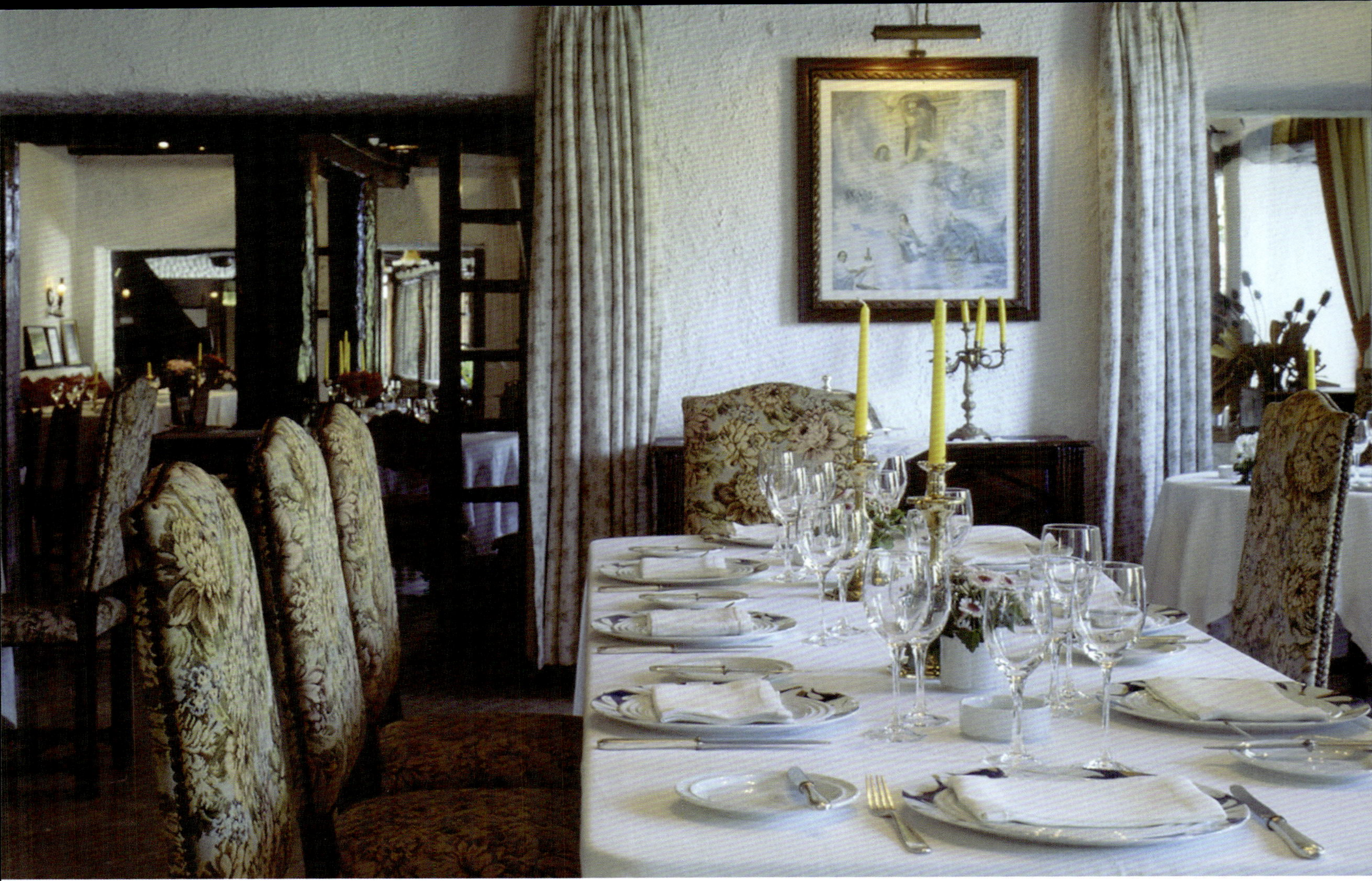

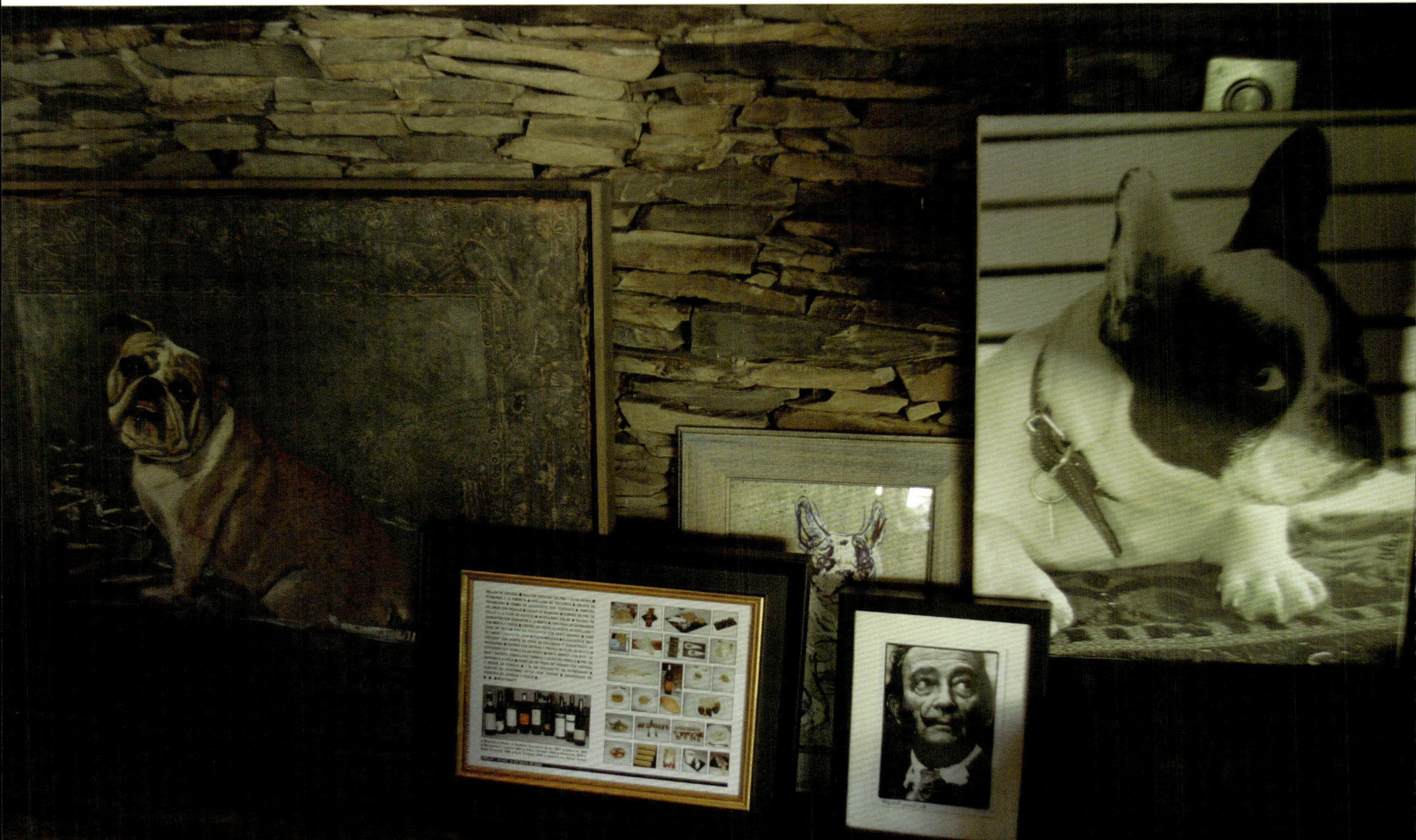

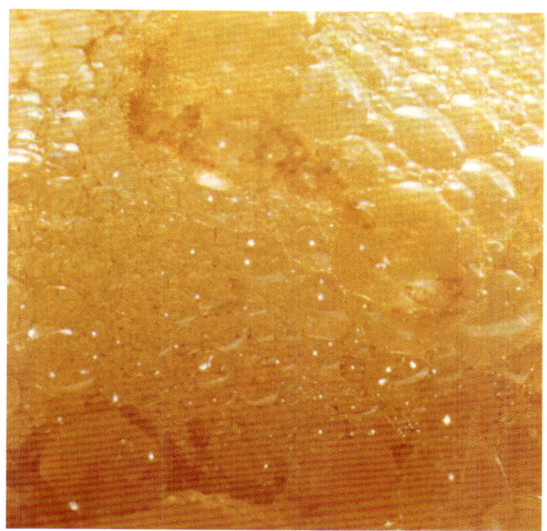

Cloud of Carrot

Peel 2 kgs of carrots and cut off the ends. Blend, reserving the juice.

Let 500 g of Simone Gatto tangerine juice stand, undisturbed, for 24 hours so pulp separates and settles to the bottom. Remove liquid from top with a syringe until only the pulp remains, taking care not to disturb and re-mix the liquid and pulp. Freeze the pulp.

Dilute 60 g of soluble powdered coconut in 150 g of water. Add a few drops of bitter almond flavoring and place in the freezer to obtain an iced texture.

Emulsify the carrot juice in blender on highest setting until "cloud" consistency is achieved.

Spoon tangerine pulp and coconut ice on centre of a plate. Place carrot clouds around pulp and ice, and garnish with a dot of curry powder.

molecules

"WHAT WILL YOU MAKE OF THIS MYRIAD OF NEW TASTES?"

There are no two ways around it: cooking *is* science. Even the simplest of culinary transactions—say, boiling an egg—involve a complex set of processes which, though they may easily be described in lay terms, can only be fully explained using the language of chemistry. The changing of molecules from one state to another via the application of heat? That's science. The use of salt to preserve food? That's also science. The conversion of milk into cheese? Science.

Oh, and should you wish to then un-boil that egg? *Only* science can help you there. Here's how. When an egg is cooked, the protein molecules unroll themselves, link up and enclose the water molecules. In order to 'uncook' the egg, you need to detach the protein molecules from each other. By adding a product like sodium borohydride, the egg becomes liquid within three hours. For those who wish to try this at home, vitamin C also does the trick.

MOLECULAR GASTRONOMY

Like fusion before it, the term 'molecular gastronomy' is not to every chef's taste. Raymond Blanc goes so far as to call it 'intellectual masturbation', saying, "I do not want to be titillated by a piece of food with bicarbonate inside which explodes in my mouth. That doesn't excite me."

Anton Mosimann has a more pragmatic take. "It's a good thing," he says. "Chemistry is important in the mix of ingredients. Take a soufflé. If you take certain ingredients together to make a sweet dessert, put it in oven, the soufflé rises. Why? Ninety-nine percent of people never talk about it, never think about it. You have to explain the ifs and buts. Then cooking becomes much easier. You understand much more about it."

Understanding is the key. For many, the words 'molecular gastronomy' still conjure up a vision of scientists in laboratories concocting weird, experimental foodstuffs that few in their right mind would wish to eat. This is in marked contrast with Harold McGee's definition of molecular gastronomy as 'the scientific study of deliciousness' which makes it an infinitely more appetising proposition.

In many ways, the term is an unnecessary complication of this simple pursuit. It is also no new thing. In the introduction to his *On Food and Cooking*, the book to which most chefs look for their understanding of the science of food, McGee quotes Brillat-Savarin lecturing his own cook:

"You are a little opinionated, and I have had some trouble in making you understand that the phenomena which take place in your laboratory are nothing other than the execution of the eternal laws of nature, and that certain things which you do without thinking, and only because you have seen others do them, derive nonetheless from the highest scientific principles."

The scientific investigation of those principles has long been ongoing. The creative use of the fruits of these investigations, along with new technology and ingredients, has allowed chefs to produce ground-breaking dishes in non-traditional forms, textures and combinations of flavour. But whether these enterprises are undertaken together or apart, the process has come to be known by the catch-all term: whenever a chemist discovers how to double the number of known tastes, or a chef turns an avocado into foam, molecular gastronomy it is. What's more, it is here to stay.

A QUESTION OF SOUFFLÉ

The term was, of course, coined by scientists. French chemist Hervé This (pronounced Tees) and retired Oxford physicist the late Nicholas Kurti had come together through a shared interest in food. Hungarian born Kurti had been one of the first television cooks in Britain: in 1969 he presented a show called 'The Physicist in the Kitchen', in which he would do such things as make meringue in a vacuum chamber, or cook sausages by connecting them across a car battery.

Food was his passion, reflected in the fact that he once said, "I think it is a sad reflection on our civilisation that while we can and do measure the temperature in the atmosphere of Venus we do not know what goes on inside our soufflés," and he was an early advocate of applying scientific knowledge to culinary questions.

It was exactly this that bought about This' culinary career. Soon after he completed his *Grandes Écoles* diploma in physical chemistry he invited friends to dinner. He made a cheese soufflé; the recipe that said to add the egg yolks two at a time. "Because I was a rational man," he says, "I decided to put in all of the yolks together. It was a failure." And being a scientist, he wanted to know why.

This began collecting what he calls "precisions," pieces of cooking lore gleaned from all manner of sources, from 19th century cookbooks, old wives' tales or the practices of modern chefs, and then testing their validity. Soon this mutual interest led him to encounter Kurti, and together they conducted experiments in their spare time, and in 1988 the pair coined a term to describe the field of their endeavour.

But This and Kurti were not the sole avatars of molecular gastronomy. Its unsung heroine is an American woman named Elizabeth Cawdry Thomas. She had studied at the Cordon Bleu school in London, ran a cooking school in Berkeley, California, and her first husband had been a physicist. She counted many physicists as friends.

In 1988, just as This and Kurti were informally christening a brand-new discipline, Thomas attended a meeting in Erice, Sicily, at the Ettore Majorana Center for Scientific Culture. During dinner one evening, Professor Ugo Valdrè of the University of Bologna agreed with her that the science of cooking was an important and undervalued subject. He encouraged her to organise a workshop at the Erice centre. So she did.

That workshop's subject would be "Science and Gastronomy." Kurti was asked to head the event; Harold McGee was co-organiser and Hervé This made up the triumvirate. The focus was on traditional kitchen preparations, how they work and how they might be improved by an understanding of the basic physics and chemistry involved. The first workshop was held in 1991; in 1992 its title was changed to "Molecular and Physical Gastronomy," mainly because this sounded less 'frivolous', more academic. The foundations were laid.

CHEFS AND SCIENTISTS

But surprisingly few chefs came. Of those who were to exemplify the concepts espoused there, only Pierre Gagnaire and Heston Blumenthal ever actually attended the Erice workshop. Ferran Adrià was never even invited. Which further illustrates that the connection between scientist and chef was often coincidental. Blumenthal attended the two final workshops, in 2001 and 2004, and by then he was already following his own path of innovation. And Pierre Gagnaire, McGee writes, "was entertainingly ambivalent about the idea of technical innovations in *haute cuisine*."

He soon changed his mind, and ultimately it was in an association between Gagnaire and Hervé This that the world of the scientist and the world of *haute cuisine* would truly intersect. They would go on to collaborate regularly, to the point where there is a section of Gagnaire's website devoted to his work with This.

For example, in 2001 This completed a system which allowed him to classify tastes according to their chemical formula. In order to demonstrate its application, he generated a formula at random which described the physical microstructure of a previously nonexistent dish. He then asked Gagnaire to replace the chemicals with real ingredients. The result was concoction of scallops, bitter orange and smoked tea—by all accounts delicious—which Gagnaire served to his customers.

In another instance, This posted a letter on the website announcing he had just remembered that several years ago he had discovered a way to double all known tastes! He went on to explain that the molecules which give taste to any particular ingredient, be it carrot or cumin, are soluble in both oil and water in varying ratios. If one puts oil, water and a cinnamon stick in a jar and then shakes vigorously, those molecules of cinnamon which are more water-soluble will enter the water, while which are more soluble in oil will enter the oil. All you need to do then is separate the two solvents (oil and water); each will contain different molecules, and therefore they will have different tastes!

"What," he asks Gagnaire, "will you make of this myriad of new tastes?" You can almost see the grin on his face. Because even for scientists it's not really about molecules. It's about food.

Well, maybe not always. Sometimes it's about doing things just to see if they can be done. Like un-cooking an egg.

Above: Cloud of Carrot, a Ferran Adrià signature dish at elBulli and one of the representative dishes of alchemical cuisine.

Heston Blumenthal

THE SCIENTIST

"The door to his experimental kitchen now has a bell. On the wall are shelves holding old-fashioned glass sweet jars. A perfume house has been briefed to create the distinctive sweet-shop smell."

Probably best to get the snail porridge out of the way first. Because it's not as you expect. Things at the Fat Duck rarely are. You imagine it will be grey. It's not. It's green. A bright, almost emerald, green. It comes in a shallow bowl, and it tastes of parsley and garlic and snails and it is, frankly, delicious. That's the point. Heston Blumenthal makes food. And food needs to taste good. People sometimes forget this.

Blumenthal himself had cause to remember it, the time he tried to make foie gras ice cream. "You could taste the sliminess," he says. "The smell wasn't lovely either." Not like the famed egg and bacon ice cream, which *does* work—so well in fact that on first taste it can make one laugh out loud. It feels like ice cream! But it tastes like bacon and eggs! It's delightful, funny and, like the snail porridge, truly delicious.

Who would have thought?

CREAM

According to Harold McGee, it is for cream's *creaminess* that we value it most, its balance between 'solidity and fluidity, between persistence and evanescence.' The fact that it lingers in the mouth, yet offers no resistance to teeth or tongue. And there is its particular 'fatty' aroma, which comes from molecules—lactones—that may also be found in peach and coconut.

A substance that may feel like two things at once, and smell like a third. No wonder the breakdancing, kickboxing, former photocopier salesman with an interest in Neuro Linguistic Programming likes it so much.

There are other things Blumenthal likes. Liquid nitrogen, for example. He loves liquid nitrogen, because with it you can make ice cream instantly, from milk that is fresh from the cow. And he loves gadgets: he claims both the pH meter and the refractometer (for determing the chemical identity of unknown substances) to be crucial kitchen tools.

"Technology," he says, "is here to help. You'll use an oven, kettle, microwave, blender … so why not a lab-grade centrifuge to split amino acids?"

Why not, indeed?

WONKA

Not too long ago an elderly lady dined at the Fat Duck. She loved her meal, and afterwards spoke to the chef. "I'm so thrilled to meet the real-life Willy Wonka," the widow of Roald Dahl said.

Now Blumenthal has in his possession the original manuscript of Charlie and the Chocolate Factory, gifted to him by Dahl's widow. A man who had no training but taught himself to cook from books. Whose culinary destiny was changed by McGee's *On Food and Cooking*. And whose dream is "a massive factory in which to concoct lavish food experiments like a lunatic." It's almost frightening.

Heston Blumenthal. Even the name sounds like a character Dahl could have invented. But he is of avowedly middle-class stock, born to his father whose upward mobility meant that at 16, on a family holiday, they were dining at a two-star Provençal restaurant. The lobster sauce poured into soufflés, the gigot of lamb carved tableside—young Heston's destiny was set. "Gastronomy was for me."

It just took a while.

THE AMATEUR

Raymond Blanc took him on. He lasted precisely a week. Not being aware of the etiquette of the kitchen Blumenthal, on being upbraided by one of his seniors, threatened to "smack him one." Ironically enough it was Marco Pierre White, on his last stop before superstardom, who defused the situation. Still, Blumenthal did not last.

He earned his living as a trainee architect, a rostrum cameraman, a photocopier salesman, a debt collector. He got married. But he never lost his passion. His wife, Susanna, shared it with him, and they invested their money wisely, by

eating in as many three-star restaurants as they possibly could—even if that meant they had to sell their car to do so.

And if they weren't eating in French restaurants, Blumenthal was learning from French cookbooks, and practicing what he had learned. Yes, he was strictly an amateur. But he was a *determined* amateur. A *fascinated* amateur. And nothing fascinated him more than *On Food and Cooking*, Harold McGee's explanation on why food does what it does. Why heavy cream can be boiled with salty or acidic ingredients without curdling (because the fat globules attach to the casein, taking it out of circulation so that no casein curds can form) for example, or why whipped cream maintains its persistent structure.

It's amazing, the things you can learn from books.

THE FAT DUCK

For a while the locals thought it was a Chinese takeaway, but Blumenthal was serving classical French dishes in the centuries-old pub he had scraped up enough money to turn into a restaurant. (You realise the gumption he had, too, when you remember that Michel Roux's three-star Waterside Inn was just down the road.) It didn't even have inside toilets.

It did have duck legs that were cooked for up to 60 hours at very low temperatures, however, and chips that went through mulitiple processes to ensure they were both as crispy and as fluffy as they could be. The science was already in Blumenthal's blood, and there would be no getting it out.

No, the science would find its own way out.

Why do green beans have to be boiled in salted water, he wondered. "All the books said it was a must, but I couldn't figure out why." He had no one to ask. So he did what any curious person would, and called Nicholas Kurti, one of the pioneers of 'molecular gastronomy.' Only Kurti had died in 1998. So Blumenthal tried some of the participants in Kurti's annual food-science conference. "The answer is that green beans don't need salted water," one said.

Previous spread Heston Blumenthal in mad scientist mode for a publicity photograph.

Opposite: The Fat Duck, Heston Blumenthal's three-Michelin-starred restaurant in the village of Bray in Berkshire. In 2005 The Fat Duck was named 'best restaurant in the world' by *Restaurant* magazine.

Bacon & Egg Ice Cream

Roast 300 g of sliced streaky smoked bacon in an oven at
180° C (350° F) until slightly browned. Cool, then place in
1 litre of cold full fat milk and leave to marinate overnight.

Tip the milk and bacon into a casserole, and add 25 g of
skimmed milk powder.

Put 24 egg yolks, 50 g of liquid glucose and 175 g of
unrefined caster sugar in a mixing bowl and, using an electric
whisk, mix at high speed until white and increased in volume.

Heat the milk and bacon mix to simmering and, with the
whisk still going, pour a little on to the yolks. Tip this back
into the milk pan, and cook over a low heat until it hits
85° C (185° F). Hold at this temperature for 30 seconds,
then remove from the heat. Cool the mixture down by
stirring it over ice.

Put the mixture into a blender and liquidise until smooth.
Pass it through a fine sieve and churn in an ice cream maker.

The future

FOLLOWING THE LINE OF SUCCESSION

If, thirty years ago, one had asked Paul Bocuse whether it was possible for an untrained English chef to win three Michelin stars by serving snail 'porridge' he would probably have laughed in your face.

But things are different now. If a chef from Carême's staff had been somehow transported to Point's or even Bocuse's kitchen he would have found little there to bewilder him. But try to imagine that same chef materialising at elBulli; he would have trouble even recognising it as a kitchen. Where Point's old coal range was only exchanged for gas in 1977, and Bocuse always kept an open flame for grilling meat, at elBulli there is no flame, and scarcely even any heat—the cooktops are all induction, which uses an electromagnetic current to heat the pan directly, and the kitchen itself remains relatively cool. And should that same chef wander into the dining room at The Fat Duck, to see waiters dipping balls of green tea mousse into smoking containers of liquid nitrogen, and diners plugged into iPods, well … chances are he'd want very much to go home again. Or at least back to Point's kitchen.

Yet if our time-travelling chef *did* stick around, he would soon notice that things really are better now—particularly if he was in fact a she.

THE WOMEN

"Restaurant kitchens are a man's world. The work is physical and demanding. It is the men who rise to the top." So said Marco Pierre White. Yet it is telling that White no longer works in the kitchen; he may not have noticed that things have changed.

Maybe he should have spoken to his old protegée. Having once claimed that women couldn't "cook to save their lives," Gordon Ramsay has recently installed Clare Smyth as head chef at his flagship restaurant, making Smyth the first and only female British chef to be in charge of a three-starred restaurant.

And Ramsay's own protegée, Angela Hartnett, now serves as Executive Chef at two of his enterprises.

Perhaps most important of all, he should have paid attention to the 2007 Guide Michelin, where he would have seen that for the first time in 50 years France has a female three-star chef. He may even have recognised the name. Pic.

Anne-Sophie Pic. You can see a photo of her in *Great Chefs of France*, aged around eleven, lunching with her mother and father at the family dining table. Her father, Jacques, is one of the twelve three-star chefs featured in the book. His father, André, in his 80s at the time of the photograph, was a man whose name was mentioned in the same breath as Point. So in a way it is not surprising that she, too, now has three stars.

It is more surprising that Luisa Valazza has three stars. Twenty years ago she was the owner, with her husband, of a restaurant in the Alpine foothills north of Milan called Al Sorriso. It was popular even though it was well-hidden, and all was going well until one day the chef walked out. For Valazz, the decision was to hire a new one or "to do it all myself. I could hardly cook beyond our own dinner at home. Anyway, as there was no one in the kitchen, I decided I had to try for myself."

Valazza makes it sound simple. "I just went into the kitchen with a pile of recipes and books," she says, "all the Italian and French classics, and started to experiment, to see what happened." Eleven years later she became the first Italian woman to win three Michelin stars.

There are now three Italian woman with three stars; Valazza, Nadia Santini of Dal Pescatore in Canneto, and Annie Feolde of Florence's Enoteca Pinchiorri.

Feolde is also self-taught. "I started to cook because of my husband's wine collection," she says. Giorgio Pinchiorri's wine house, famous for its cellar of 150,000 bottles, was housed in a grand Florentine palazzo; Feolde, who is French, believed those who sampled the wine should also be offered something to eat. From canapés to accompany wine tastings, her offerings soon

became a buffet. Not long after that it was a full restaurant menu. "At the beginning I didn't mean to do anything important," Feolde says. "I liked exotic tastes. I did what I wanted."

She was, in 1992, the first female chef outside France to win three stars.

MAISON PIC

Anne-Sophie Pic did not have the luxury of being able to do what she wanted, at least not in the kitchen. Maison Pic had been a three-star restaurant under her grandfather. His health was poor, however, and by 1950 it had lost two of them. Then Jacques Pic stepped in, and managed to regain them, and in *Great Chefs of France* he speaks of his son, Alain, already working in the kitchen, following in his footsteps. "Our goal is always that Alain should be inspired," Suzanne, Pic's wife, said.

Instead it was their daughter. She had left in her late teens, to see the world, and returned five years later after management training proved to be not for her. She realised that cooking was in her blood, and came back to begin training with her father. And then three months later he died.

"The timing," she says, "was very bad."

She stuck with it. She learned. And then one day "I walked in and said, OK, that's it, I'm taking over." But Pic acknowledges it was not quite that easy. "I would see them speaking among themselves. See the eyes. Not only was I a woman but I was the daughter! Of the owner! And suddenly I am in the kitchen, in a French kitchen, full of men, telling them what to do ... *oomf*."

It is that *telling them what to do* that makes the difference. In Italy and Spain, women in kitchens telling men what to do seems slightly less problematic. "In Italy," says Nadia Santini "half the Michelin stars belong to women running small restaurants. This has always been a woman's kitchen: when I married [my husband Antonio], my mother-in-law and Antonio's grandmother worked here. That set-up is not that rare in Italy."

It would be easy to begin to generalise here, to make assumptions based on the idea that women are more comfortable running small, homely kitchens. Santini herself says "I think it is impossible for a woman to run a kitchen that serves 100 people. I can't give my heart to a dish if I am cooking for more than 30. And I think that may be true for most female chefs. Men want the 'wow' factor in the kitchen, but for us women it is more important to give something of ourselves."

This is not strictly true: there are as many personalities as there are chefs, male and female. Each has their own motivations, their own preferences and their own style. Some adhere to tradition, while others seek the cutting edge.

But even a scientist agrees that cooking is largely about giving. Hervé This claims that the next big idea he wants to investigate is the role that love—of the cook for the diners, the diners for the cook, and of everyone for each other—plays in determining tastes. "Cooking for someone is a way of telling them, 'I love you.' This has to be understood, of course."

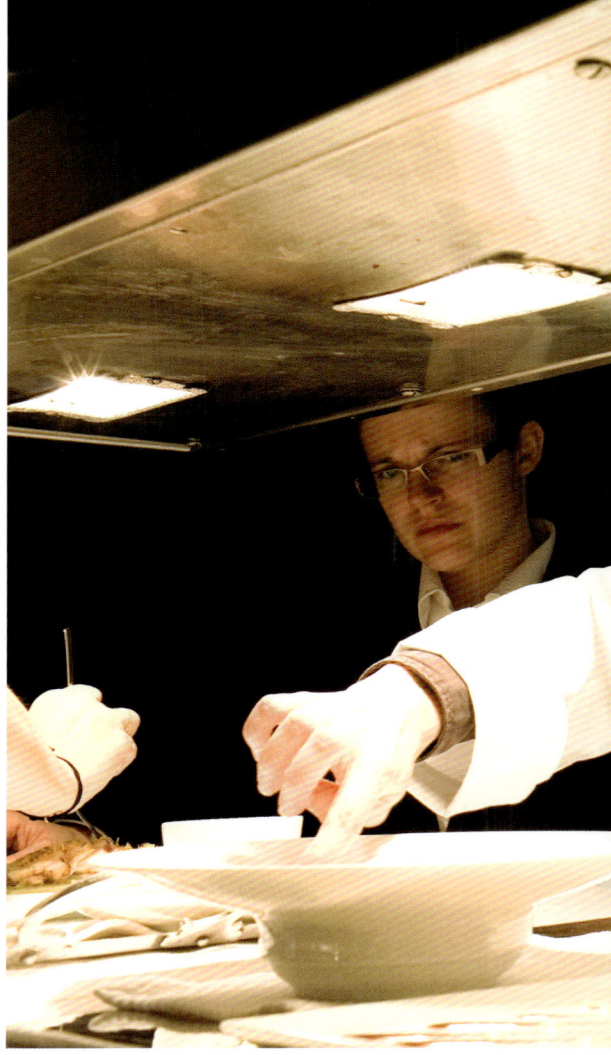

This is something that St. Pasquale, along with St. Laurence one of the two patron saints of cooking, well knew. Pasquale, a Franciscan monk, is acknowledged as the creator of sabayon (or zabaglione), which was employed as a tonic, giving endurance to new bridegrooms and restoring vigour in languid husbands, so that they might procreate more freely and thus create more believers.

Such is the power of food. And though cooking may be an incredibly demanding profession, it remains something that anyone can do, if they love it enough. As self-taught three-star chef Annie Feolde says, "Our job is to make people very happy and we have to love it ourselves to do that or it doesn't work. If you stop loving the business you have to stop immediately. That is the only way."

We are just lucky that more and more women are becoming believers.

Above: Anne-Sophie Pic working in the kitchen of her restaurant Maison Pic in Valence, a town on the river Rhone with a highway that runs from Paris to the South of France. In 200? when this picture was taken, she was only the sixth woman in the world to win three Michelin Stars and the first French woman for over ?0 years.

Below: Gordon Ramsay and his Chef Proteges, (from left to right) Marcus Wareing, Gordon Ramsay, Angela Hartnett, Mark Sargeant, Josh Emmett, Mark Askew and Stuart Gillies, photographed on July 16, 2003 at Claridge's, London.

Elena Arzak

THE DAUGHTER

"Nobody today would say, 'It's not Juan Mari in the kitchen tonight, only his daughter.' Everybody agrees that whether it's Juan Mari or Elena in the kitchen at Arzak, it's exactly the same thing."

Arzak

In 1897, the year Fernand Point was born, a young Basque couple—her great-grandparents—built an inn in the village of Alza, now a part of San Sebastian. Her great-grandmother's name was Escolástica. Her great-grandfather was José Maria Arzak Etxabe. They served wine, provided rooms. Around them, the village expanded.

When her grandparents, Juan Ramon Arzak and Francisca Arratibel, took over the inn they began to serve food along with the wine. They made delicious stew, and their renown as cooks grew. Then Juan Ramon died. But Francisca carried on. Her talents kept improving. Locals would schedule their weddings, christenings and communions according to whether Francisca was available to cater them.

Francisca's son was named Juan Mari, and in 2006, in a poll of 60 food writers from around the world, he was named the third most influential chef of the past decade, after Ferran Adrià and Alain Ducasse. He is her father.

Her name is Elena Arzak, and she just might be the future of cooking.

THE BASQUES

She would tell you that was nonsense, of course. Soft-spoken, humble almost to a fault, Elena Arzak considers herself as no more than a small part of a greater tradition. She will insist that anyone interviewing her speaks not only of her father (which is inevitable) but also the other Basque chefs—Pedro Subijana, Ricardo Idiaquez, Pedro Gomez, Martín Berasategui and others—who make up her community. She will even provide press cuttings.

Her father, at least, needs no introduction. Renowned as much for his outsized personality as his culinary genius, the name Juan Mari Arzak has long resonated beyond the confines of San Sebastian. It was this personality which made him the figurehead for *la nueva cocina vasca* (the new Basque cuisine) that made this small city of only 200,000 one of the culinary capitals of the world. But he did not do it alone. "We are a family," Elena says of her fellow chefs. "We exchange recipes and ideas, help each other with banquets."

And though she was only a child when her father was changing the face of Spanish cooking, she has now found herself the smiling face of this ongoing revolution.

ALL IN THE FAMILY

If Juan Mari did not … encourage her, exactly, he at least did not push his daughter away from the family profession. He might say that "Parents should discourage their kids from following the same path," yet Elena was permitted from a young age to spend as much time as she wanted in the kitchen, peeling oranges, or cleaning squid and shrimp.

It may be Juan Mari was too occupied in his quest to dismantle traditional Basque cooking and, in the style of *nouvelle cuisine*, reassemble in a whole new way. Either way, he let his daughter find her calling naturally, and did not prevent her from enrolling in a Swiss culinary school when she was 18. It's probable, too, that he may have helped her in finding a place in the kitchens of Paul Bocuse in Lyon, the Troisgros brothers in Rhone, Alain Senderens in Paris and the Roux brothers in London.

Nor did he discourage her from coming back to Restaurant Arzak when she had finished her training. Though she got no special treatment. "In my first years back I trained at each station, having little interaction with my father," says Elena. "I was learning, like the others."

Still, it is unlikely Juan Mari forgot how he had been trained in that same kitchen. "My mother was a patient and constant teacher. She was the one that step-by-step revealed all the secrets of gastronomy to me." And one suspects, in fact, that Juan Mari may have been pretty happy with the way things turned out. Elena too. "His greatest influence on me," she says, "was to leave me alone to develop my own vision."

BE PREPARED

He might also be thanked for sending her to do a stage at elBulli. "The entire time with Ferran, I thought I was hallucinating," she says.

"She is very well-prepared," Adriá says in return, "a very good chef."

She would need to be. In the kitchen at Restaurant Arzak both Juan Mari and Elena would soon be called 'chef.' In the masculine world of *haute cuisine*, it would never be an easy ride to command a three-star kitchen. Many even questioned that Juan Mari would permit it.

"My father is very broad-minded," Elena says. "He is, above all, a modern man."

"She's Basque," Juan Mari says simply. "We are a matriarchy. My mother ran this restaurant before I did. It is the most natural thing for Elena to take over." Not that he has given up just yet. "I'm going to keep working at her side until she kicks me out."

So for now the kitchen is both of theirs, as Ferran Adriá makes plain.

"Nobody today would say, 'It's not Juan Mari in the kitchen tonight, only his daughter.' Everybody agrees that whether it's Juan Mari or Elena in the kitchen at Arzak, it's exactly the same thing."

Because it all comes down to the food, and there it is obvious that Elena Arzak holds her own with any of her contemporaries. Certainly more than one critic has claimed to enjoy dining at Arzak more than elBulli. And though one can not yet separate Elena's food from Juan Mari's, their approaches are noticeably different. "He always wants to clutter the plate. I like clarity," Elena says.

Take her From the Egg to the Chicken. The dish features a poached egg that sits in a shallow pool of chicken *jus*. On top of that is a sprinkling of chicken crackling. The dish is covered in what looks like tissue paper, until you find that it is dehydrated egg yolk transformed into an edible sheet.

"What is important is that the eggs and the chicken are very fresh," Elena says. "We might experiment with the futuristic, but in the end what we want is to honor the traditional. For four generations, our restaurant has used fish caught that day, eggs laid that day. This is still very important to us."

In its transformations of the ordinary Elena's work has echoes of both Ferran Adriá and Heston Blumenthal, yet it is its own thing entirely. Much of its effect is based on revelation, how folded pleats made from crisp smoked potatoes will conceal sizzling prawns, or a lamb chop will wear another of those tissue-like veils, only this time tasting of coffee. A stream of warm broth is poured onto a dish of dense black which then melts away, revealing a cluster of bright orange discs—pumpkin ravioli veiled by squid ink—as if the sun has just come out.

NEW DAY RISING

It is for food such as this that Arzak has been called "the most exciting woman chef on the planet." The late restaurant critic R. W. Apple, who preferred her (and of course her father's) cooking to Ferran Adriá's, described her food as being "modern and entertaining … often witty, never overwrought."

Of all the three-star female chefs, Arzak is the one most closely allied with the great innovators like Adriá and Blumenthal. On the restaurant's website there is a page titled 'Investigation.' It carries a photograph of Elena and Juan Mari standing in front of a wall of perfectly ordered containers, hundreds of them, and in front of the pair there is a bank of waist high refrigeration units glowing with fluorescent light. The caption says 'This is one of the best kept secrets from Arzak.'

It is 'the spice room,' literally a flavour bank containing over a thousand products and ingredients, upstairs from the restaurant itself. Just as in the elBulli Taller, here Elena and Juan Mari lead "a group of alchemists" in search of the new, seeking to combine what they find there with the old, the trusted, and therefore "to find a perfect balance between the avant-garde and the roots of tradition."

Such investigation results in dishes like their Hake with White Clay. Juan Mari explains its genesis like this:

"The idea came to us because we were working with the land to make a sauce from the earth. After we started to do a type of compost of different types of earth, we collected the earth from parts where there is no deteriorating substances like that of the forest, and then we cooked this and what we ended up with was an extract that tastes of minerals and of truffles, and depending on what forest we take the earth from, the leaves that have fallen to the ground could be of cherries, could be of apples, and it gives the flavour a special touch."

Extracting flavour from the earth. After all, that is what vegetables do, so in a way it is little more than cutting out the middle-man. The idea manages to combine a feeling of tradition with a notion of bold, investigative daring, and goes to prove that of course women can be just as inventive, as radical, as men, and that they too will be leading cooking into the future.

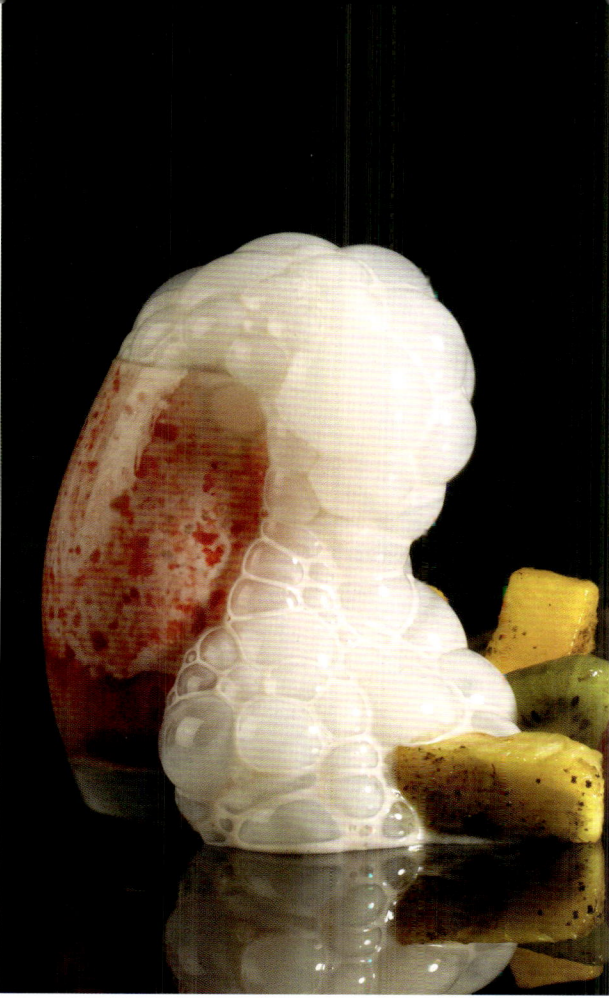

This page: A sample of dishes from Restaurant Arzak, including *pollo de aceite de oliva blanca y bogavante* or lobster with extra-white olive oil (far left); *pompas de fresa*, or strawberry foam (left); and *pato bien azulón*, or blue duck (below).

Overleaf: A view of San Sebastian Bay at night (above); a portrait of Elena Arzak and her father Juan Marie, in the kitchen of their family-run Arzak restaurant, in San Sebastian, Basque Country, Spain (below).

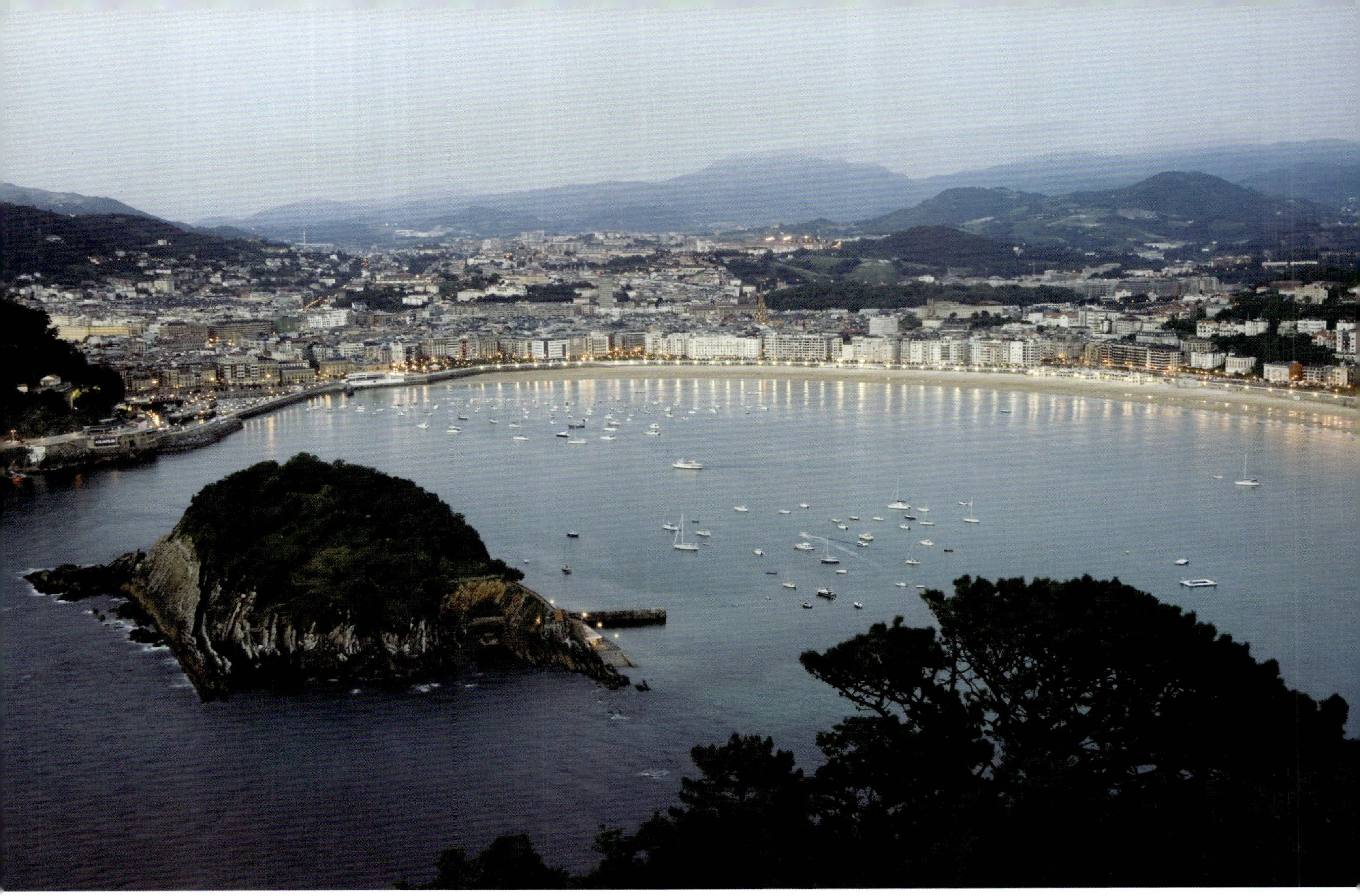

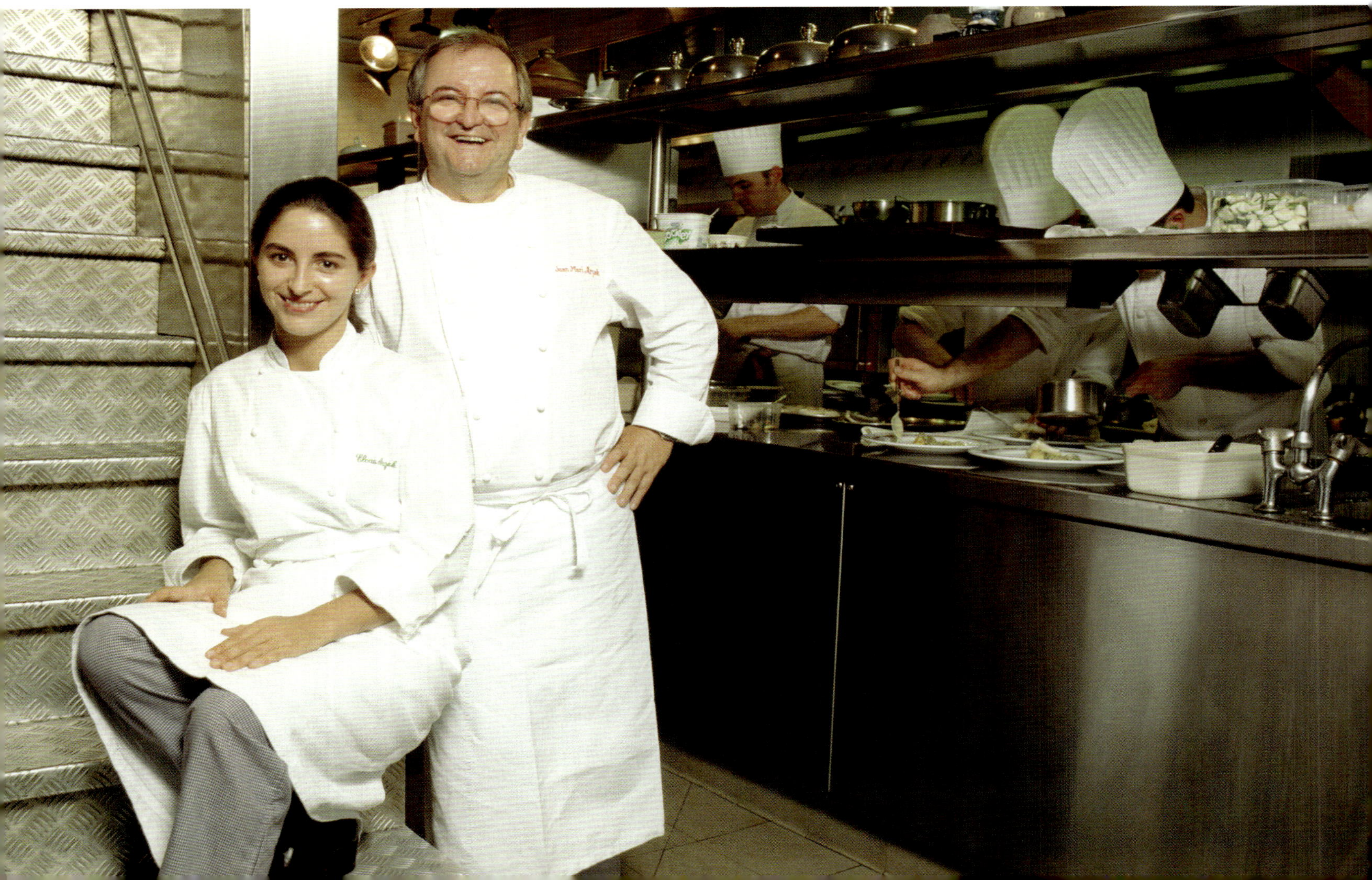

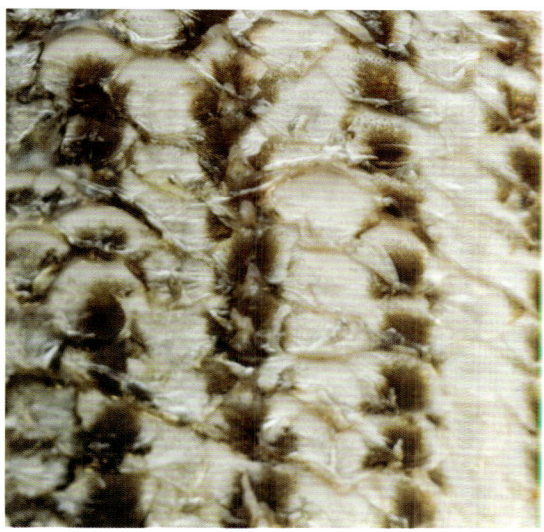

Sea Bass with Scallops & Leek Ash

Sweat some minced shallot with little oil until tender. Add 1 berry of rose hip, 2 raspberries, a pinch each of ground ginger and powdered liquorice, some clear millet, roasted almonds and a sp ash of sherry vinegar. Sauté for a few minutes and then leave to cool. When cold, add 40 ml of olive oil.

Wash the green part of 3 leeks and place them on a grill until completely burnt. Blend and whip in 100 ml of olive oil, then strain with a fine mesh.

Season 4 fillets of sea bass with salt and toss lightly with a little of the rose hip marinade. Cook the seasoned sea bass at 180° C (350° F) for 5–8 minutes, depending on thickness.

Mix the rest of the rose hip marinade with 20 g of minced pistachios and 6 blanched spincach leave and whisk until it emulsifies.

Sauté 8 scallops in a combination of sesame and olive oil, some crushed garlic, powdered hazelnut, sweet paprika, minced chive and lemon verbena, and a pinch of salt.

On a white plate, draw some black spots with the greased leek. Set two scallops on one side and on the other side the sea bass fillet, the skin side up. Ladle a line of the pistachio marinade along it.

A pinch of salt

BY FRITZ GUBLER

The ancient Greek poet Homer called it "a divine substance" and the philosopher Plato described it as "especially dear to the Gods". Without salt, no life can exist.

Chlorine and sodium atoms, the two major components of salt, are necessary for human survival. Chloride is essential for digestion and in respiration. Without sodium—which the human body cannot manufacture—our bodies could not transport nutrients or oxygen, transmit nerve impulses or move muscles, including the heart.

An adult human being contains about 250 grams of salt, which is continually lost through bodily functions. This lost salt must be constantly replenished.

Since human evolution began, salt has played a central role in humanity's development. Life depends on regular food consumption and early in human evolution it was discovered that salt enabled food to be preserved for a long period. Salt absorbs moisture from the cells of bacteria and mould through osmosis, killing the cells or leaving them unable to reproduce.

The ability to preserve food gave humans a huge advantage over other species, enabling them to survive long winters, droughts or bad harvests. Gathering, growing and hunting for food were necessary to maintain life, but before the nineteenth century, effective storage of food could be the difference between life and death.

SALT AND CIVILIZATION

The search for salt has always been a challenge. Even though it is richly available—it bubbles up from springs, it is in the water that fills our oceans, it forms crusts in lake beds and comprises part of the earth's surface rock formations—nevertheless, civilisations have risen and fallen over salt's availability. The ability to control salt's production and delivery has given communities, countries and empires powerful advantages.

Salt mines became part of the wealth of nations, alliances were built, empires secured, revolutions provoked and wars lost and won over salt. It was fundamental to many economies and acted as the basis of exchange between traders. Salt was even paid out to soldiers as a form of salary–the Latin phrase "salarium argentum" (salt money) referred to part of the payment made to every Roman soldier, and the word has been carried down the ages into the English word "salary".

Trade routes grew up to accommodate bulky and heavy salt shipments, Accessible transportation has always been the essential ingredient in salt trade; the first of the great Roman roads, the Via Salaria or Salt Road, was built to bring salt not only to Rome, but across the interior of the peninsula.

In Africa, where salt was located in the wadis and in the dry lake beds of the waterless Sahara, camels did the hard work of salt transportation. By the Middle Ages, caravans of up to 40,000 camels carried salt from Taoudenni, a remote city in northern Mali to Timbuktu, a 435–mile (700 kilometres) journey taking as long as one month. The trans-Saharan salt trade route brought great wealth to Timbuktu. By 1330 the city had advanced to become part of the powerful Mali Empire and a successful economic and cultural city equal in importance to acclaimed cities like Rome, Athens, Jerusalem and Mecca.

Salt was the engine of Genoese trade, which was in tough competition with Venice not only for salt, but for the other cargoes that were exchanged for salt, such as textiles and spices. By 1350, no salt could move on a ship in the Adriatic unless it was a Venetian ship bound to or from Venice.

This salt competition led to a war in 1378–80, known as the "War of Chioggia", in which Venice defeated Genoa, its only major competitor for commercial dominance of the Mediterranean. Numerous governments introduced a "salt tax" to raise funds to finance wars, infrastructure, royal households and voyages by explorers such as Columbus.

The notorious and unpopular salt tax *la gabelle* was fundamental to the income of France. To repeal "la gabelle" was a major aim of the revolution of 1789, but Napoleon restored it as soon as he became Emperor because he needed it to pay for his ambitious wars—it was such an easy and substantial income it was collected until 1945. The Habsburgs would regularly use the salt income to raise money in times of military emergency—they sold salt to the Swiss, then used the profits to pay for campaigns against the Swiss.

The Chinese government saw salt as a source of state revenue for centuries. Text has been found in China mentioning a salt tax in the 20th century BC, and salt revenues were used to build not only armies, but defensive structures including the Great Wall. At certain times the salt tax would contribute half of Chinese state revenue. As with other countries, China experienced many popular uprisings bitterly protesting the salt monopoly by the state; an angry mob took over the city of Xi'an in 880 in protest at the tax.

The highly organized salt trade of China was observed by Marco Polo, who recorded that the major item of trade on the Yangtze River was salt, shipped upstream from the coast to the interior cities.

HISTORICAL USES

In the Middle Ages, salt already had a wide variety of industrial applications apart from preserving food. It was used to cure leather, to clean chimneys, for soldering pipes, to glaze pottery, and as a medicine for a wide variety of complaints from toothaches to stomach upsets and even for "heaviness of mind".

The importance of salt is further underlined by its use in religious ceremonies, covenants and magic rituals, and is also often associated with fertility.

In the Pyrenees, bridal couples went to church with salt in their left pockets to guard against impotence. In some parts of France only the groom carried salt, in others only the bride. In Germany, the bride's shoes were sprinkled with salt, and in Egypt priests abstained from salt because it excited sexual desire.

On Friday nights, Jews dip the Sabbath bread in salt—in Judaism, bread symbolises food, which is a gift from God. Dipping the bread in salt preserves it and therefore keeps the agreement between God and his people.

In Christian tradition, salt is associated not only with longevity and permanence but, by extension, with truth and wisdom. The Catholic Church dispenses not only holy water but also holy salt – Sal Sapientiae, the salt of wisdom.

Salt mines were used as secret stores during World War Two. After the war, American troops passing through the German town of Merkers discovered a salt mine. Within the mine they found 100 tones of gold bullion, rows of sacks of gold coins and millions of US dollars. Also found were more than 1000 paintings, including Raphaels and Rembrandts. The total value of the treasures, preserved in the dry and stable environment of a salt mine, was estimated at US$3 billion in 1945.

Because of salt's properties as a sealant, some engineers think that dry salt mines are the safest places to bury industrial and even nuclear waste. The U.S. government has also stored an emergency reserve of petroleum in abandoned salt domes throughout the Gulf of Mexico.

SALT AND FOOD

Heat and salt are at the heart of food preparation and cooking. Originally salt was mainly used to preserve food rather than flavour it. Eating habits and regional, national and cultural diets were influenced by the availability of salt. At first, salting was a way to keep food through the winter, but by the Middle Ages foods preserved with salt were eaten year-round.

The origin of cheese is uncertain; it may be as old as the domestication of animals. Milk and salt are all that is needed to make cheese. The difference between fresh cheese and aged cheese is salt. Curds eaten fresh before they begin to turn sour, called 'ricotta' by the Italians, have not yet acquired an individual taste. Cured in

salt brine and aged, they become cheese with its distinctive flavours and variety of texture.

Fishermen learned that if they salted their catch, they could continue fishing for days rather than rushing to market before the fish began to rot. Salt made it possible to get the rich bounty of northern seas to the poor people of Europe. Salt cod by the bail, along with salted herring by the barrel, are credited with having prevented famine in many parts of Europe. Salted fish was at the heart of Mediterranean commerce, with ports were busy with ships unloading salt fish from Sicily, Sardinia and the Black Sea.

Salt was of strategic importance to the British, with salt cod and corned beef becoming the rations of the British navy. In fact, by the fourteenth century, for most of northern Europe, a standard procedure to prepare for war was to obtain a large quantity of salt and start salting fish and meat.

SALT, TASTE AND CUSTOM

For centuries, different types of salts were recognised by taste. The pleasant taste of salt from the Great Salt Lake indicated a high concentration of sodium chloride while salt from the Dead Sea had the bitter taste of magnesium chloride.

Placing salt on the table was a rich man's luxury, but all classes ate salted food. It was considered rude, sometimes even unlucky, to touch salt with the fingers. Salt was taken from the salt cellar on the tip of a knife and a small pile put on the diner's plate. Some medieval and Renaissance plates had a small depression for salt.

Most recipes that call for salt are referring to "table salt", which is refined salt with 99 per cent sodium chloride. In many countries additives like iodine and an anti-caking agent to prevent the salt from clumping in humid weather.

Salt is the most delicate and versatile flavour; too little and food is bland, just a bit too much and the food loses all other tastes. Used with skill, salt reduces bitterness and acidity and brings out other flavours in food.

Most master chefs give a lot of thought to

the salt they use in their kitchen. Which salt to use and how much to add is arguably the most delicate skill of any chef. It is often a key factor on which chefs and their food are judged by their critics.

TYPES OF SALT

Today's chefs have a wide variety of types of salt to choose from, each with their own nuances of flavour and texture, their own suitability for certain applications in either cooking or preserving food. *Exotic salts* include the expensive French and Hawaiian sea salts, the smoky, sulphuric Indian black salt or the intensely salty Korean bamboo salt. For a softer flavour, there is kosher salt for cooking and sea salt for table use.

Korean bamboo salt (jook yeom) is made by roasting sea salt in bamboo cylinders plugged with yellow mud. The salt absorbs minerals from the bamboo and mud, which in turn leach the salt of impurities.

Indian black salt is sold either ground or in lumps. It's more tan than black and has a very strong, sulfuric flavor.

French sea salt comes from sea water that is pooled into basins and then evaporated; it is hand-harvested from the Brittany coast and Camargue regions and contains minute amounts of magnesium, calcium and other minerals. This *fleur de sel* is the most sought after table salt. Gourmets are willing to pay a lot of money for it, claiming that it has a much softer and fresher flavor than ordinary table salt. It is generally acknowledged that the best *fleur de sel* comes from the small town of Guerande in Brittany. Known as *fleur de sel de Guerande*, the salt has been harvested here since the ninth century, using the same methods. Collected by hand using a special hand rake, it is gently raked from the fine upper crust of the salt pan and, once dried, has unique, delicate crystals of different shapes and sizes.

Hawaiian salt is unrefined sea salt. It gets its pinkish-brown colour from Hawaiian clay, called 'alaea', which is rich in iron oxide. The clay imparts a subtle flavor to the salt, which is hard to find and expensive to buy.

Italian sea salt, Sicilian sea salt, sale marino is a delicate salt which is good on salads and in sauces. This salt is harvested from the lower Mediterranean sea by hand using traditional methods of natural evaporation.

This page: An assortment of salt including including coarse salt, rock salt, fleur de sel, garlic salt, sel gris, kosher salt herb salt and sea salt.

Kosher salt is the preference of connoisseurs and master chefs. Developed for the preparation of kosher meats, it has coarser grains, giving each grain a larger surface area, and is free of iodine which can react adversely with certain foods. The large grains of kosher salt mean it isn't a good choice for baking, but ideal for salt crust meat or fish and for lining margarita glasses.

Fine table salt contains the flavourless additive potassium iodide to prevent goiter (an enlargement of the thyroid gland) and small amounts of calcium silicate, an anti-caking agent and dextrose, a stabiliser, but has most of its natural minerals removed. Because salt itself is a mineral, it can be stored indefinitely without going stale–and it won't taste any fresher if you grind it with a salt mill, which has become quite trendy in fashionable restaurants.

Non-iodised salt is sometimes called for in recipes, since iodine can impart a bitter taste and adversely react to certain foods. Another specialised salt is pickling salt, which is free of the additives that turn pickles dark and the liquids cloudy.

THE ART OF SALT

Mastering the art of salt is one of the most important skills a great chef can develop. The best chefs add a pinch of salt at every stage of preparation of a dish. This is called "layering", where each ingredient added to a pan or skillet is seasoned lightly to bring out its natural flavours. The end result of this process is retention of multiple layers of different flavours in the finished dish.

Salt has not always been used skilfully as a flavour by professional chefs. It is only in the last decade, with the availability of exotic salts from various corners of the globe, that salt has come into fashion. It is currently rising in popularity in the culinary world.

The taste is the most important aspect of salt—it should have the neutral, fresh, airy taste of a sea breeze to it, with no chemical harshness. Experienced chefs know that adding salt to water will raise the temperature at which it boils and lower the temperature at which it freezes.

Salt in bread dough controls the action of the yeast and improves the flavor. And chefs know that boiling eggs in salted water makes them easier to peel. Some advocate salting slices of eggplant to help draw out the bitter juices.

Sprinkling salt on citrus fruits, melons, tomatoes and even wine enhances the flavour. Experienced chefs know that adding a pinch of salt (preferably non-iodised) to cream or egg whites before they are whipped increases their volume and serves as stabiliser.

Whether to salt meat before or after broiling or grilling is a point still much debated: salting draws moisture from the centre, making it browner and crisper on the outside, but less juicy on the inside. Many delicatessen products are still preserved with salt and the amount and quality of the salt and the passion and skills of the producers determine the quality.

For health reasons, salt consumption is declining across the world. The average twentieth century European consumes half as much salt as the average nineteenth century European. But Europeans, in particular, still love salt cod, herring, hams, sausages, olives, pickles, duck and goose preserved in salt, while caviar, herrings and cheese are more popular then ever.

The anchovy is a fish that has remained more popular salted than fresh, but because salting is no longer a necessity for preservation, it has become considerably less salty.

Many chefs advocate a healthier cuisine with less salt, but are often cooking with more "noticeable" salt. It has become trendy to serve food on a bed of salt, cook it in a crust of salt or make it crunchy through the use of a lot of large crystals. This is not a new invention—more than 1.000 years ago, the Chinese were cooking in a salt crust. Chicken cooked in a crust of salt is an ancient recipe attributed to Cantonese cuisine.

THE FUTURE WILL BE SALTY

With many master chefs now using designer salts to complement their dishes, home cooks are eager for up-to-date information on using salt to best effect. For this reason, our next title will be a comprehensive guide for the home cook, featuring guidelines for the use of all types of salt, tips from top chefs, recipes, and guides to processes such as salt-crust baking, breadmaking, curing and pickling.

Opposite: Gravlex is salmon cured with salt, sugar and dill.

Left: Chicken cooked in a salt crust.

Index of Recipes

Opposite: Pierre Gagnaire adjudicates at the World Best Chefs Competition (Meilleurs Ouvriers de France) on March 15, 2007 in Thonon-Les-Bains, France. French chefs Paul Bocuse and Alain Ducasse gathered the elite of the world's cooks during the two-day competition where for the first time a woman, Andree Rosier, was awarded Best Chef.

"The duty of a good cuisinier is to transmit to the generations who will replace him everything he has learned and experienced."

FERNAND POINT